Lynne,

Your success is apparent thru the successes of all your divers & students. I am so proud of you... Are clearly a trendsetter in diving field! Much love to you and Shane. Thank you for all you do for so many unfortunate in the Atlanta area.

Love your sister

Chapter 21

TREND
SETTERS

Published by CelebrityPress™, Orlando, FL
A division of The Celebrity Branding Agency®

Celebrity Branding® is a registered trademark
Printed in the United States of America.

ISBN: 9780983340461
LCCN: 2011930493

This publication is designed to provide accurate and authoritative information with regard to the subject matter covered. It is sold with the understanding that the publisher is not engaged in rendering legal, accounting, or other professional advice. If legal advice or other expert assistance is required, the services of a competent professional should be sought. The opinions expressed by the authors in this book are not endorsed by CelebrityPress™ and are the sole responsibility of the author rendering the opinion.

Most CelebrityPress™ titles are available at special quantity discounts for bulk purchases for sales promotions, premiums, fundraising, and educational use. Special versions or book excerpts can also be created to fit specific needs.

For more information, please write:

CelebrityPress™,
520 N. Orlando Ave, #2
Winter Park, FL 32789

or call 1.877.261.4930

Visit us online at www.**CelebrityPressPublishing**.com

TREND SETTERS

The World's Leading Experts Reveal Top Trends
To Help You Achieve Health, Wealth and Success!

TABLE OF CONTENTS

CHAPTER I

THREE WAYS TO SYSTEMIZE YOUR SMALL BUSINESS:

CENTRALIZE, FOLLOW UP & AUTOMATE

BY CLATE MASK AND SCOTT MARTINEAU

I. CENTRALIZE

As an entrepreneur, you have an especially complicated situation. In many cases you are single-handedly trying to run a business. You're the sales team, the marketing manager, accountant, tech support and janitor all at the same time.

Small businesses are different. They're not just big businesses with a smaller staff. You have different fires to put out. Your own unique challenges. Less resources. And yes, they have hundreds, even thousands of people to do the same job that you're trying to accomplish on your own with a patchwork of part-timers, full-timers, contractors and the like. You have many systems doing many things. You have information, reports, customer records and financial statements everywhere. But the more a business grows, the more "systems" the small business owner adopts.

- As a business acquires more leads and more customers, they realize they can't possibly keep track of everyone's data, so they purchase a contact management system.

- Chaos is temporarily put on hold. A few weeks pass by, and the business owner realizes they'd like to use email to follow up with their contacts. So, they spend $50 or $100 a month to purchase an email marketing system.
- Of course, somewhere along the way the business owner has already picked up QuickBooks to speed up their accounting process. But realizing there is a big online market, this individual now wants to sell their products/services online. So, they spend a little bit more money and get a shopping cart added to their list of "solutions."

At Infusionsoft, we call this *multiple system chaos*. This chaos only increases as the business grows and you add more customers. This causes inefficiency across all areas of the business.

Technology has given us faster, better methods for managing all this information. However, in order to grow you've got to centralize all of that information into a single database. It's time to take everything you're doing and condense it into a workable system.

Let me illustrate for you how chaotic having multiple systems can be to a business.

When Infusionsoft first started about 10 years ago, when we were still a custom software and services company, we received a call from a man who was frustrated with his business. After speaking to this business owner, Reed Hoisington, for more than an hour, he commissioned us to build him a system to better manage his prospect and customer data. For Reed, it was something he'd been searching for desperately.

Reed was in pain because a "fire" had started in his business that cost him time, money and the trust of his customers and prospects. As a skilled entrepreneur, Reed was doing a pretty good job of building a customer and prospect list. One day he decided to run a half-off promotion for his prospects to see if he could win their business. So he pulled out all of his contact lists and went to work sending out emails.

In an unfortunate turn of events partly caused by Reed's lists not being centralized in one database, Reed ended up sending the promotion to his customers as well as his prospects.

Suddenly, customers who were previously content with their purchase were calling Reed on the phone, demanding he refund half their money.

Being a business owner yourself, you know how damaging this was to Reed's business.

Without a centralized system, you will always be putting out fires, losing critical information and making guesses (rather than educated decisions) about what you should be doing next in your business.

II. THE SCIENCE BEHIND EFFECTIVE FOLLOW-UP

We've spoken with thousands of small businesses who have confessed that if they could just figure out how to follow up more consistently with prospects and customers, they would have much more profitable and dependable businesses. Over 99 percent of small businesses don't properly follow up. Why? Because they don't have a centralized database, they don't have time, they don't realize how valuable it is, and the truth is, they don't know how to follow up.

There is a science behind effective follow up. First, you need to understand that a couple of random follow-up phone calls to each lead will help you close more deals, but it's not going to produce big numbers. Second, you need to realize that the purpose of your follow up is to endear you to your prospects and customers so that they trust you, like you, and want to do business with you.

(A) SEGMENTATION

Not every contact you have is exactly the same. Though many of them have similar characteristics, your contact lists cannot be lumped into one group. As the business owner, you need to make sure you're sending the right message to the right people at the right time. In other words, the messages you send to your customers and prospects should be targeted to their specific needs and wants.

(B) EDUCATION

Your follow-up needs to provide valuable information to your prospects and customers. If you're showing up with no value, you'll wear out your welcome fast. You need to communicate that you are an expert on their side and you deserve to be trusted. You'll accomplish this if you provide them with accurate, insightful information.

(C) REPETITION

It's a proven fact that human beings have to hear the same thing over and over before it sinks in. Follow-up is no different.

(D) VARIETY

This doesn't mean you vary your message! You need to consistently tell your message, but your follow-up delivery needs variety. To maximize your sales, *you must use multi-step follow-up sequences that incorporate and orchestrate direct mail, phone, email, fax, voice and other media.* Some prospects will respond to your phone call, others to your email or letters, and others to your fax or voice messages.

(E) AUTOMATION

The biggest challenge with follow-up is time. Reconnecting with your prospects and customers could take weeks. That's why no one does it. They're trying to do it on their own and failing miserably. Fortunately, follow-up doesn't have to be difficult or time consuming. All you need is the right software program to make follow-up an automated masterpiece.

Without follow-up systems in place, you don't have stability in your business. What you have is a never-ending search for the next hot prospect. Effectively following up will you grow your business without going crazy.

III. FROM MANUAL TO AUTOMATED

You don't see small businesses seeking out automation systems like they do QuickBooks. And that's a shame. The tools small business owners use are helping them effectively manage the front-end and back-end of the business, but nearly every business owner is trying to do the stuff in the middle manually. Processes like:

- Handling the sales cycle

- Following up with customers, prospects, vendors and partners
- Calculating their sales information
- Responding to emails, letters, phone calls and other inquiries
- Managing their employees
- Maintaining inventory
- Fulfilling on orders
- Creating marketing pieces
- Billing and collections

Automation is the key factor to saving you time, money and manual labor. But automation also tends to be the one principle that is missing from most small businesses.

Perhaps it's because automation isn't one of those things you just accidentally stumble upon and learn from experience. You meet another small business and they rave about how they are getting big business results on a small business budget using personalized, automated marketing (a.k.a. marketing automation). Automation is intentional and purposeful and it will propel you out of chaos into liberation.

Now let us show you why it is so critical for your success in conquering the chaos. If you were to show us the to-do list for your day, it would most probably look something like this.

- Follow up with your customers and prospects
- Create a new marketing campaign
- Generate more leads

If you are an exceptional small business, you might accomplish two of them. You'll likely talk to those unhappy customers, check and respond to your email, make a few sales calls and complete one other thing on the list. Why? Because that's all you have time for. You spend most of your efforts trying to close deals and bring in revenue. You're spending hours educating your prospects about your products or services over the phone and through email. Then, when you haven't got enough time to take care of your existing customers, you're forced to handle their needs *after* you've made a mistake and they're irritated.

This is not where you should be spending your time. You are the business owner. You have so much to take care of you can't possibly spend three quarters of your day on four tasks.

Besides, the reality is there are a million things you could be doing in your business. There are only a handful that will make you any money. Dealing with cranky customers, educating leads that aren't ready, and picking out tile aren't on the list. So why are you doing it? We'll tell you why. You're doing it because a business needs money to survive, angry customers will never go away, and sometimes it's more enjoyable to think about tile than to deal with chaos.

As our friend Michael Gerber says, "You should be working ON your business not IN it" (Gerber 1995, 97).

If you can relate to all the things we just shared, then you're too caught up in the chaos. It's time to pass the manual stuff on to someone else. So now you've got two options:

1. Hire someone to take over these responsibilities and live in the same mess you've been dealing with.
2. Get an automated system in place to manage it for you.

What you need is automated software to lighten your load. It's the only way you can keep up. As more demands are placed on your shoulders, you're getting more and more immersed in the chaos. The longer you wait to find an automated solution, the longer it's going to take to get the system working for you.

SO WHAT CAN YOU AUTOMATE?

Here's a thought: If automation is so effective and as critical to business growth as we say, then why aren't more small businesses adopting automation systems? Having worked with thousands of small business owners, we have a pretty good idea what keeps people from experiencing the beauty of automation in their businesses.

Automation has been around for a long time. But it doesn't mean small businesses are used to the concept. Automation has long been dominated by the corporate world. Only within the past few years have automated systems—that meet the specific needs of the small business owner—been available.

For those who don't work around other entrepreneurs, or are just getting started, they may not even know these systems exist. In fact, nearly a quarter of the conversations our sales representatives have with prospects lead to an exclamation like, "You can do that?" Yes, we can. Automation can. But unless you've been around it or heard someone discuss it, you may never have considered it for yourself.

Granted, there will be some things you'll never be able to automate; and you never should. But have a look at all the areas of your business that can easily benefit from the power of an automated system. When you don't even have the time to eat a meal, automatic follow-up software gives you the power to manage emails, voice broadcasts, faxes and direct mail to any and all of your contacts. It launches predetermined follow-up sequences based on the actions of your contacts so that you're sending targeted communications rather than "shotgun communications." You also can automate new lead follow-up, billings and collections.

Furthermore, as part of a powerful contact management system, automatic follow-up software instantly executes and records every follow-up effort you make. As long as you've invested the time in creating a valuable, educational, personal follow-up sequence, you're automatically doing the one thing you never thought you'd be capable of doing: You're leaving yourself time to close hot leads while your system is warming up a bunch of new leads for you. Even if you were a follow-up master, you could not do as thorough and complete a job as your automated follow-up system can. If there are multiple steps in your marketing campaign, you're bound to make mistakes at some point. How do you know which contact receives what and on which day? If you're only managing a handful of prospects, this can be done by a mere mortal. But once you have dozens, hundreds, even thousands of contacts to manage—you just can't do it anymore.

With automation, you get the benefits of follow-up without any of the pain or mistakes. Plus, you'll be building relationships that cannot be achieved any other way. With an automated system in place, you can:

- Follow up with leads captured on your website
- Automatically assign prospects to your sales reps
- Be notified as prospects move from one stage of the sales cycle to the next
- Enable sales reps to automatically respond to prospects' questions and concerns

- Instantly alert your employees when a sale is made (we love this one!)
- Billings and collections

Bottom line, with automation, you are making your business more scalable. Because things are set to run as needed, it really doesn't matter how many prospects and customers you add, the system can follow up with them all. Really, automation helps you can grow your business easily and effectively without growing your staff. It helps you get big business results on a small business budget.

ABOUT CLATE

CEO and Co-Founder

As Infusionsoft's CEO, Clate leads the company's vision, strategy and growth. His entrepreneurial spirit sparked early in his career and evolved into the software industry while he was at About.com. From there, Clate co-founded Infusionsoft with brothers Scott and Eric Martineau as a way to give small businesses a leg up with smart marketing automation tools designed just for them. His passion for helping small businesses grow is the driving force behind the company's success.

Clate has a B.A. in economics from Arizona State University, as well as an M.B.A. and a Juris Doctor from Brigham Young University.

ABOUT SCOTT

Co-Founder and Vice President, Customer Service

Scott's mission is to solve the challenges small businesses face in marketing their products and services. His vision guides the customer experience for Infusionsoft users, leading the support, services and training teams in their goal of revolutionizing the way small businesses grow. His own entrepreneurial experiences and his understanding of what small businesses need enable him to continually evolve the company's marketing automation software in innovative and successful ways.

Scott holds a Bachelor of Science in Computer Information Systems from Arizona State University.

CHAPTER 2

CONTINUITY:

TURNING YOUR PASSION INTO PROFITS

BY RYAN LEE

I don't know how into Greek mythology you are, but one of my favorite stories from that ancient civilization's myth-making is that of a dude named Sisyphus (and, by the way, that may be the first time "dude" and "Sisyphus" were ever used in the same sentence – I always like to make history any way that I can).

Sisyphus was a king that lied, cheated, stole and killed – and those less-than-admirable traits didn't just carry over to his subjects, but also to the gods themselves. Yes, he dared to mess with Zeus and his posse.

Now, that was a Clash of Titans he just couldn't win – and, as his punishment for his royally bad deeds, he was sentenced to roll a giant boulder up a steep hill each day. Sounds pretty bad, right?

Well, it was worse than you could imagine – because the whole set-up was rigged; the boulder would always roll back downhill before he could get it to the top. In other words, it was a whole lot of blood, sweat and tears to achieve exactly nothing – day after day, week after week, month after month, year after year.

Still, the gods enjoyed watching his pain. Apparently, it was their primitive idea of great reality TV.

So why does this story resonate with me? Well, when I think of Sisyph-us, I think of what yesterday's entrepreneur used to have to go through; it seems awfully similar to me. For example, if you sold widgets for a living, you might sell 100 one month, but still feel on edge. Because you knew, when the first day of the next month hit, you'd be starting all over again with a big fat zero.

In other words, the boulder's back at the bottom, Charlie. Time to push it back up – and, of course, watch it roll back down again. That's what one-off sales are all about. You make the deal and you start all over again.

Whose idea of a good time was that? Not mine. Which is why I resolved to *not* have to spend my entire adult life that way. And why I was always on the lookout for a new and better way.

And that's how I became a Trendsetter in Continuity. Accidentally, I might add.

GOING ONLINE

In 1999, there was no YouTube, Facebook or Hulu. There was barely a Google; the recommended search engines were AltaVista and Hotbot and the vast majority of users were connecting through dial-up rather than broadband. The online experience was far less commercial and far less professional.

But I saw a lot of potential.

Six years earlier, I had just gotten my first job out of college as a recreational therapist and trainer at a children's rehab hospital. While I really enjoyed working with the kids, I was determined to start my own venture on my own terms – so I began slowly building a training business on the side. Now, in 1999, I saw a way to promote that business – with a site that showcased who I was as well as my expertise. I published articles on training and began to attract my own little community.

Cut to two years later. I'm now a gym teacher at a school in the South Bronx. A notoriously dangerous area of New York, the South Bronx had a lot of kids looking for trouble roaming the streets. The school I was at handled the kids that couldn't hack it in the *regular* South Bronx schools. In other words, we had the worst of the worst – former gang members included.

I still enjoyed working with kids, but I also knew I had to keep focusing on another future – and I knew my training business was the way to go. But I still couldn't monetize it to the extent I needed to.

Then I looked at what a friend of mine was doing with his health and fitness site. Like my site, it featured a lot of exclusive content. The only difference was that he wasn't giving it away like me – he was actually charging people a monthly fee for access to what he (and *only* he) had to offer. This was a totally new idea, and it was totally working for him.

The light bulb went off. If this kind of membership site worked for Chad in his particular fitness area, there was no reason it wouldn't work for me in mine, which was training athletes. I knew it was cheap to start something like that on the internet (it's even cheaper now, by the way) and I knew it was an opportunity I couldn't pass up.

Most importantly, it brought the concept of Continuity to my consciousness. Having money come in automatically on a regular basis, with little or no effort, was actually a business model that was ironically pioneered *offline* in my field – with health clubs. By paying a monthly fee, members got to come in and use the facilities whenever they wanted. The health club didn't have to go out and round up all new members every thirty days or so – the same ones kept paying and coming back (and sometimes even when they were too lazy or too busy to come work out at all!).

With a membership site, the result would be the same. I would suddenly have recurring revenue – no more rolling the boulder up every single day. Instead, *my* boulder would defy gravity – and just stay on the side of the hill where I parked it the last time, until I began to push it further up towards the peak. Pretty good for a non-god.

(And, by the way, as a side note, I'm always willing to give something like this a shot – especially if that's new and makes sense. There's no reason not to. Many people think it will be too hard, it won't work or just plain procrastinate until it's too late. Others are perfectionists who never think anything is good enough to actually take out to the public – so they fuss with it endlessly or just talk about doing it endlessly. I've found that the most successful people I know always take action – and it's a trait I like to emulate.)

So I took the leap and transformed my formerly free site into a caged membership site. It wasn't easy. When I had a free period at my day job at the school, I couldn't work on the site there – the schools weren't set up for online access yet. Instead, I had to quickly walk down some of the South Bronx mean streets to the local public library and continue working on the site. You know what they say – no risk, no reward.

Well, I took plenty of risk and, fortunately, saw plenty of reward. At first, I set up an annual fee for access to my site and made about six grand right out of the box. Obviously, I was on the right track. But I had to not only sustain, but grow that membership list to fuel my new career.

BEYOND FITNESS

To get my boulder moving further uphill, I formed a relationship with a company in my industry that sells training equipment. They agreed to promote me and my site. I also set up a JV (joint venture) with a big fitness association. I helped set up web pages for them and they, in turn, promoted me to their members. Leveraging old school relationships like this to help promote new media ventures is a profitable combination that still works to this day.

My boulder kept lurching up the hill, without me having to break a sweat. 12 months after I started it, my site was making me six figures a year. Eventually, that became 6 figures a month and, at the moment, my companies are posting 7 figures a month. As you might have guessed, I was able to leave the South Bronx behind.

How did I achieve that level of success? Well, I spent the first couple of years using my membership site to teach fitness to athletes who wanted to know how to perform at their peak. Soon, other fitness trainers saw how well I was doing and asked if I could show them how to make money online with their particular niche. I soon got a reputation as the guy who helps trainers make money – and suddenly, I was now getting requests from people in totally different professions to help *them* set up similar membership sites.

And that was more found money. Because, when it came down to it, the principles were exactly the same no matter what the niche was. And even though my original expertise was in the fitness business, I had now also developed another strong expertise – in membership sites.

Result? I can now teach anyone with any expertise just how to turn their passion into profits. I know what works and what doesn't work – and I also know just how valuable Continuity can be to an entrepreneur's financial and mental well-being. When the money just comes in, month after month, you've created the perfect money trap. And your boulder starts rolling uphill all by itself.

MEMBERSHIP SITE SECRETS

Putting the power of Continuity into action separates the people who do just okay selling online from the people who are making hundreds of thousands of dollars – or even millions – online. I'd like to share in the rest of this chapter a few basic tips and tricks on how to achieve membership site success.

The first step is to figure out what your niche (the group you're going to sell to) is going to be. This can be easy or it can be difficult depending on what your expertise is. I went into my site with an established niche and an established following, thanks to two years of operating a free informational site.

You probably don't want to put in those two free years, so remember that the more targeted your niche is, the better your chances for success. Your niche should be specific enough where people think you're talking directly to them, and it also has to involve a market that's easy to reach and can also afford your programs.

Golfers are a great example of a market that works for this kind of site. Golfers love the sport, they're passionate about it and they're willing to spend money on it. The trick is to find the specific angle that will draw them in to your site. But other smaller niches work well too. Some of my clients have memberships based around clients that are into knitting, paper crafting and even concealed handguns, believe it or not.

One of the easiest niches to tap into is a profession. For example, my original broad-based niche, fitness, can be tailored and marketed specifically to accountants, attorneys, doctors and other affluent professions. Professions are good because they are easy to target and easy to reach through various trade associations and online groups.

Once you've determined a viable niche market, you need to determine what their biggest problem is – what keeps them awake at night. Within your exclusive membership area, you work at *solving* that problem for them – through articles, online videos, forums where members can answer each other's questions and where you can directly answer them as well. Then all you need to do is simply password-protect it, so that only members can access it.

You'll also need an easy-to-remember and impactful domain name (harder and harder to find with the overflow of websites these days, but you can search to your heart's content on any domain registration site such as GoDaddy.com).

How do you begin to attract members to your site? I recommend three different tactics:

1. Set up a blog and create new posts four to five times a week. In these blogs, you have to demonstrate your passion for your niche and provide good relatable content that gives away a little, but not a lot.
2. Utilize the incredible power of Facebook. Set up a Facebook fan page for your website, join Facebook groups that are in your market, comment on other posts in those groups and build relationships that will bring people back to your site.
3. Give potential members an irresistible offer to join – generally something like a trial membership. Tell them they can try out your site for fourteen days for just a dollar. The dollar is important only because it introduces the concept that your content must be paid for…even if it's only a buck for a starter look.

It's also important to realize that people tend to join a membership site for the content and stay for the community aspect. That means it's crucial to create and encourage that sense of community. Do whatever you have to in order to get people to interact and ask questions – create your own Facebook-like group within your site devoted to your niche content. Getting your members as involved with you and the rest of the members as much as possible makes it difficult for them to contemplate leaving.

When it comes to retention, however, the two most powerful words in your arsenal are "coming soon." By continually teasing and previewing what's coming next, you're keeping your group on the edge of their seat, much like the trailer for the latest Hollywood blockbuster aims to get people into a movie theatre.

You should also look at your membership numbers and see if there's any pattern or timing to when members don't re-up with your site. When those times come around, that's when you should offer them bonuses – a DVD, a webinar, anything that you haven't teased but might keep members around for a few more months (or, until the next bonus!).

The rule of thumb here is to *underpromise but overdeliver*. If people are getting more than you're advertising, they feel like they're getting real value – because it's extra stuff they don't think they're paying for. Don't pull any cons on them – be as transparent and authentic as possible, so you build up their trust. This is a long-term relationship, not a one-night stand – so act accordingly.

Finally, keep in mind that there is always a small percentage of your membership that will be willing to pay a premium price for premium value. That means, if you don't offer different levels of membership on your site, you're leaving a lot of money on the table. And a premium membership tier usually entails gaining *more access to you.*

As the site is built around you and your expertise, you become the "star" that's in demand. That means members will pay more for one-on-one coaching and other interaction that's solely between them and you. Imagine how much someone who's interested in marketing would pay to have lunch with Donald Trump. The irony is that Trump's head of marketing probably would be able to give the person a lot more useful, hard information – but Trump has the name, the brand and the value.

I'd like to leave you with this thought that I apply to my life – you should be doing something to grow your business every day. That certainly applies to your membership site. Yes, creating Continuity through a membership site allows you to park that boulder on the side of the hill – but, if you don't pay the proper attention to the care and feeding of your membership, you may see your pet rock start to stir…and threaten to roll back over your growing profits.

It's a whole lot more fun to keep moving it towards the top – because, once it's there, it's probably not going anywhere for a long time.

And that makes you the ultimate rock star.

ABOUT RYAN

Ryan Lee is an entrepreneur, best-selling author, speaker, success coach and the founder of ryanlee.com.

He started his first web site back in 1999 while still working full-time at a children's rehab hospital, and grew that one fitness site into multi-million dollar empire. Ryan has contributed to the NY Times Best-Selling Series "Worst Case Scenario Business Survival Guide" and has been featured in dozens of books including Moonlighting on the Internet, Attention! This Book will Make You Money, and The Phenomenon movie. He has also been featured on the front page of the Wall Street Journal, Millionaire Blueprints magazine and dozens of other major media outlets.

Ryan lives in New Canaan, CT with his wife Janet, and their 4 young children. You can usually find him taking his kids to endless birthday parties on the weekend.

CHAPTER 3

TRENDSETTERS: EATING AND EXERCISING

SOPHISTICATED AND GLORIOUSLY UNREFINED

BY ADAM MORDEN

've been involved in the fitness industry for a long time now, coming up on 16 years. I've seen fads come and go. I've seen people get great results from a variety of "systems," "programs," and "techniques." For a while I was puzzled. I wondered why X works for John, but not for Mary? How come Bob can eat anything he wants while Jack can't help growing bigger and bigger even as he starves himself? Then–epiphany! Everything I learned over all those years suddenly came together. The principles I'm about to divulge haven't always made me popular. I've had some major push back from clients who say, "You have no idea what I'm going through! You've always been fit; you've never been overweight." It's true, I've been fortunate. But as a highly effective coach who's trained Olympic athletes, everyday housewives, paraplegics, and professional fighters; I found their logic distressing. While I've never been in the Olympics, I still know how to take my athletes to the peak of their potential. So now I'm going to share a secret with you (don't tell my wife) that gave me insight into these individual battles and the solution to these problems.

When my wife turned vegan over a decade ago her dietary habits changed and she stopped eating protein. Her diet was mostly breads, pastas, rice, vegetables, and fruit. According to leading health authorities her diet was perfect; zero cholesterol, low in fats, and no red meat. She ate a lot of breads and processed foods, not the crazy ones that everyone knows are bad for you, but stuff from the health-food store labeled "Organic" and "Heart Healthy." She counted calories fastidiously keeping them below 1450 on average.

After a few months I started to notice odd behavior. When she got hungry, she got REALLY hungry, I mean scary hungry, I mean thank God she's a vegan otherwise she'd have eaten my arm hungry! What's more, when she got hungry, she would eat, feel stuffed, and then tell me she's hungry again a short time later. So we would eat some more. This cycle continued for years as her weight crept up. We organized our life around these hunger binges. It was distressing for me because her stomach was constantly upset, she was always tired, and her moods swung radically. We started referring to her hunger as "Going Carb Crazy" because it always occurred shortly after we ate a meal or snack that was primarily simple carbs. She'd feel full but shortly after would want more bread, more fruit, and more sugar. We both knew this had to stop. My wife had visited doctors and it didn't seem as though medical professionals could offer any help. We didn't know what to do. Fortunately, as an individual committed to continuing education for my clients, I stumbled upon a few simple laws of nutrition that flew in the face of conventional wisdom. I learned that there was a driving force behind her erratic behavior and hunger pain: her hormones, primarily insulin, were way out of whack.

In the decade and a half since, I've met thousands of people who've had similar experiences. I empathize with them and I have the solution to their problem. In order to control your cravings you have to change how you eat. Spiking your blood sugars (and hence your insulin) leads to the all too familiar sugar crash. You can observe this process best by watching children. Give them a candy bar and watch them buzz around like crazy for 10-20 minutes, then crash HARD. This is exactly the same thing that happens when we eat supposedly "nutritious" meals that revolve around simple carbohydrates. No amount of "willpower" will keep you from feeling hungry when you spike your insulin levels. Instead, you have to change your body to change your mind. The conventional wisdom, "Listen to your body," DOES NOT work. Listening to a body that's addicted to simple, refined carbohydrates will only result in an endless cycle of eating more simple, refined carbohydrates. Listening to a body that's addicted to simple, refined carbohydrates will only result in a bigger body, more health problems, and a less fulfilling life. If you want to know what the future of nutritional health is going to look like in the years to come, and if you get only one piece of information from this chapter, let it be this: use your mind to manipulate your body into a healthy, vibrant, and fantastic life.

In our house we cut out the simple refined carbs. We didn't cut out all carbs, for example, there are healthy carbohydrates in vegetables and grains. We just cut out "white" carbs. By avoiding foods that spike insulin in the first place, we would avoid the cravings and avoid going "carb crazy." This (almost) sounds easy, right? Well, sort of. My wife was very skeptical and even angry at this new knowledge. As a vegan who was already so limited in her choices, limiting tantalizing food items like pasta and sandwiches was not appealing. But living day to day at the mercy of mercurial insulin spikes was even less tempting. I convinced her that it was worth a try and asked her to give me two weeks. The first few days were challenging as one expects when making any major change. We had to learn new ways to prepare food, new recipes, and more than anything we needed to change what we thought a meal should look like. The good news is that feeling better happens really fast! Within two weeks we knew that we would never go back to eating the way that we did before.

How to use your mind to manipulate your body to get the life you want:

7 NUTRITION PRINCIPLES & 2 LAWS OF EXERCISE

1. REPLACE SIMPLE CARBOHYDRATES WITH HEALTHY FATS AND COMPLEX CARBS.

That's right, no simple carbs and sugars. Simple carbohydrates essentially act as poisons in our bodies, upsetting our hormonal balance and leading to unnatural cravings. Let me say it again: simple carbs have a TOXIC effect on our bodies. It is because of their toxic effects on our bodies that they have also enslaved our minds to think that we need them, much like cigarettes. Getting off the "crack" of simple carbs is a lot like quitting smoking. In fact, simple carbohydrates have been found to be more physiologically addictive than heroin or even crack cocaine! Science has shown that if we just THINK about a simple carb we get an insulin spike that triggers a need to eat in order to regain equilibrium in our bodies and feel normal. If we SEE an insulin-spiking carb the same thing happens. So if you've ever felt, "I just need to look at food to gain weight," you could very well be right! Strangely, when someone is quitting smoking they are told to tough it out through the withdrawal symptoms such as intense cravings, headaches, nausea, low energy, and even depression. However, when someone is quitting simple carbs the same doctors will tell them to change their diet back to eating simple carbs! What?! Ridding your life of these killers is the first step to creating a healthy and powerful new you!

I understand that this might be scary. Simple carbs are celebrated, revered, and NORMAL in our society. But just because something is common doesn't mean it's healthy or desirable. Normal is NOT normal when it comes to what we eat in modern day America. The sad fact of the matter is that these "FOODS" are killing us and setting our children on a downward spiral that they will struggle with for the rest of their lives. Smoking was considered cool for a long time too!

Here are the main simple carbohydrates that you should avoid: WHITE FLOUR, BREAD (all breads especially white processed breads), PASTA (in all its variations), and BOXED CEREALS (even "healthy" or "organic" ones). Why? Because they are all heavily processed, extremely insulin spiking, and nutritionally suspect. Shedding the use of these foods in our diet will be like a caterpillar turning into a butterfly. It will allow our lives to take flight.

2. ADOPT A PLANT BASED, REAL FOOD DIET.

A massive body of evidence points to the long term health and disease preventative effects of a plant based diet. Equally important to the "plant based" diet is the "real food" component. Eating real foods, in as natural a form as possible, prepared as freshly as possible, is a powerful way to increase vibrancy. Cut your own veggies, soak and cook your own beans, and choose whole grains not processed imitations. Once you get into the habit of eating real food you'll find it is far easier than you think and you'll feel far better than you ever thought possible.

3. AVOID THE SUPERMARKET, EAT WITH YOUR FAMILY, AND USE CSA FARMERS MARKETS (LOCAL PRODUCERS).

Our bodies respond to the sight of food, specifically simple carbohydrates, by releasing insulin. You know the feeling; your mouth starts watering, your stomach starts growling, and you just finished dinner! Supermarkets know this and they are designed around exploiting these psychological facts to get you to buy more. Avoiding the supermarket, or at least the aisles that store your favorite simple carbs, is one of the best ways to manipulate your body to invigorate your life.

4. MONITOR PORTION SIZES.

Did you know that the average American plate has more than doubled in size in the last 25 years? It has gone from an 8 inch plate to a 14 inch plate. Food that would have overflowed a plate from the 80's would barely cover the middle of the modern plate. Scientific research has proved that eating off a bigger plate causes you to feel hungrier and eat more versus eating the same portion off of a smaller plate.

5. DRINK WATER.

To really ensure your success when it comes to nutrition, one of the easiest, most often ignored, steps that you can take is to stop drinking calories. Drink water, and lots of it. Cut out juice, soda (including diet), and energy/sports drinks. The human body is not designed to need any other form of drink other than water. Juices and sodas are very high in the simple carbohydrates that will wreak havoc on your hormonal balance and lead to more cravings. Diet soda has nearly the same effect with the additional disadvantage of the potential toxicity of several ingredients. The sweet taste of artificial sweeteners tricks your body through your taste buds. Your confused taste buds think sugar is coming and signal your body to produce more insulin. When you don't actually ingest any simple carbs your body sends signals back to your brain saying, "Hey!

We've got too much insulin floating around here, send us some more sugars!" Bam! The cravings start again. So while a person going for a 30 minute walk MIGHT burn 100 calories, drinking a sugary sports drink worth well over 250 calories negates the walk and instigates cravings for more calories.

6. AVOID TV COMMERCIALS.

TV commercials are brutal. They will make you hungry even when you are eating. You know when you think just looking at food makes you gain weight? Research has shown that your brain releases insulin in response to seeing food on TV. As soon as you release insulin you get hungry and your body is primed to store fat. So even if you just ate a great, healthy meal; you can find yourself craving food that you don't need or want. What's worse is that because of the insulin spike you can go from watching these commercials (or smelling the bakery, or spotting the conveniently located chocolate bar stand at the gas station) to craving the worst thing for you–simple carbohydrates.

7. JUST DO IT: DOING THINGS KEEPS YOU OCCUPIED, PRODUCTIVE, HAPPIER, AND NOT THINKING ABOUT FOOD.

What are you passionate about? Hiking? Painting? Gardening? Whatever you're passionate about, just do it, and do it often. Keeping yourself active and occupied with things you enjoy not only increases your happiness, but it has actual physiological effects on your body and your health. First off, you won't be spending as much time in front of the TV, and as you read above, that's important. Next, doing things you love significantly reduces blood cortisol, a hormone produced by the body when it's under stress. Elevated cortisol leads to inflammation, joint pain, weight gain, and disrupted sleep which further elevates cortisol and disrupts your hormonal balance.

TWO LAWS OF EXERCISE: INTENSITY TRUMPS DURATION & LIFT REAL WEIGHTS

Walking is fantastic, I walk every day and I highly recommend it, but for most people I don't recommend it as exercise. As exercise, a 30 minute walk 3 times a week isn't going to cut it. A session with the little pink dumbbells won't cut it either. In order to get the health and fitness results we all want, our exercise must support our nutrition–not the other way around. Traditional "cardio" or Long Slow Distance (LSD) training will sabotage weight loss goals by actually making you hungrier.

Aerobic only exercise and the mythical "fat burning zone" (FBZ) are two of the worst things to ever happen to fitness. Misunderstood, or deliberately misled by clever marketers, the FBZ is nonsense to anyone who understands how the body works and how to lose excess body fat. It is true that in the FBZ you will burn more fat *as a percentage* of calories burned, but the total amount of calories burned will be far lower for two reasons. One, you'll burn fewer calories during the actual activity. This is intuitive. If you work harder you will burn more calories. So working at, say, 60% of your capacity is obviously less tiring and uses less energy (calories) than working at 90% of your capacity. Two, you will also stop burning calories shortly after you stop exercising. On the other hand, when you perform anaerobic workouts you will elevate your metabolic rate for up to 24 hours afterwards.

Combine the short, intense intervals I described above with some serious resistance training and you will see your body literally change before your eyes. When you increase muscle mass you also increase your base metabolism and burn more fat every moment you breathe, even when you're sleeping. If you don't want to get bulky stay away from the moderate weights for medium to high reps which is the recipe for gaining size, ask any bodybuilder. Instead superset your intervals with moving large loads great distances, just a few times (5 or fewer reps in a set). Stick with the classic barbell exercises: the Squat (king of all the lifts), the Dead-lift, the Press (standing and pressing a weight directly over your head), the Bench Press, and the Bent-Over Row. If you have access to the appropriate facilities also train with the Olympic lifts, my personal favorites. A truly healthy body is a strong body.

CONCLUSION

I've learned a lot about nutrition and exercise over years of working with my clients. I have seen (and experienced) firsthand the beneficial effects of the steps I outlined above. The results are completely transformative. You will have more energy, you will feel amazing, excess weight will drop off your body, and you'll feel stronger and more vibrant than ever!

ABOUT ADAM

Adam Morden can't say he's done it all, but he has certainly done a lot. As a man who studied the art of boxing and ballroom dancing at the same time, he is a study in contrasts. Known as a rebel in his teenage years, he has owned the titles of stuntman, commercial diver, bartender, and youth leader all the while biking down mountains and climbing steep rock faces. He loves a challenge and pursues any interest with an obsessive, overriding passion. He is a firm believer that a life without experience is a life without living. A desire to share the secrets of a vibrant life full of exhilarating experiences inspired him to carve a career in fitness and health.

At a time when North America was grasped in the clutches of severe recession, Adam opened a successful training boutique in Hamilton, Ontario. His charisma, knowledge, and care for his clients quickly translated into making him a community leader. The tag line for Adam Morden's gym is "building your extraordinary." This phrase speaks to the level of commitment Adam instills in his clients furthering his goal of building lively lives. Olympic competitors and reformed couch potatoes alike receive unwavering encouragement paired with sound scientific knowledge that demands results. His small gym has received numerous accolades including best co-ed facility and best personal trainer, beating out giants that have been around much longer. Adam is often sought out to share his knowledge in fitness and nutrition as a contributor to national newspapers and as a lecturer to medical professionals at McMaster University. With his building success Adam feels a duty to share his knowledge to a wider audience by managing a popular blog and contributing information online.

Adam has learned, through the thousands of athletes he's had the pleasure to coach, that conventional methods need serious revision. It's time for a health revolution. Traditional schools of thought that haven't accepted current science and evidence are not only holding people back from reaching their potential; they are literally causing a health crisis. Adam isn't satisfied to simply critique the old ways, he also has a guaranteed, proven solution. Adam's goal for sharing the secrets in this chapter are simple and resonate with his life mission and message: it's time to start living, it's time to be vibrant.

Highly accredited, Adam Morden (NSCA-CPT, CSCS, Cross-Fit Level 2, NCCP Boxing and Weightlifting Coach, etc), is the founder of Vegetarian Power TV. This organization is dedicated to showing how a plant based diet is the path to a strong, healthy body and a powerful, passionate life. He is committed to building your extraordinary.

You can reach Adam via his website at http://www.vegetarianpower.tv where you can sign up for his e-newsletter, and receive free guides and articles on living an extraordinary life through good health and nutrition. You can also connect on Facebook: http://www.facebook.com/vegetarianpowertv.

CHAPTER 4

THE TIME HONORED TRENDSETTERS ARE LEADERSHIP AND CULTURE

BY PETER A. HOWLEY

I have been involved with some of the fastest-growing, most innovative and exciting "hot" companies in America. The secrets, if we choose to call them that, that I have learned are just as applicable today, in fact even more so, than they were in the recent and sometimes distant past when I first learned and applied them. One of these companies not only changed the face of telecommunications within the United States, but throughout the world, affecting even the amazing growth and power of the Internet today. Another was the fastest growing service company in the United States; it was a Harvard Business School study and went on ultimately to be acquired for close to a quarter of a billion dollars. A third company was one of the fastest growing Internet hosting service companies of its time. A fourth is today establishing the technology standard for powerful, high speed mobile broadband communications.

In this chapter, I am going to show you what contributed to and caused these great successes. These are techniques that you, as a business person and as an entrepreneur, can apply. They are absolutely critical in this era of tech smart consumers, instant mass communications, powerful social networking, Twitter, and the ubiquity of mobile communications.

I divide these techniques into two categories. First is what I call the "Science" which basically involves doing everything in your and your team's power to base decisions on facts; hard cold facts. These facts are vitally important not only initially when analyzing the practicality of your business, but also later as you need to make strategic and tactical adjustments. Get the facts and then make your decisions. Be careful of believing in your own hype.

The second category is the "Art" or culture within the business, focused on customer satisfaction and retention. Culture is extremely dependent on both leadership, *your leadership*, and the attitude and spirit *you create* within the organization. Great success is almost always dependent on great employees and that comes back to culture. Creating that powerful effective culture is the focus in this chapter.

Twenty years ago, I was giving a talk to a business group explaining the steps that I had taken as CEO of an extremely successful company. Afterwards, an individual came up to me and said that he was impressed with the company, but certainly would not want to work for it. The implication was that I was a ruthless tough leader. Very recently, Henry, a former employee of that same company, told me that company was his first job after college, and was the most fun, exciting, dynamic job that he has ever had; in short, a phenomenal work experience. He even had a story. I was preaching to his sales group saying I'd give the shirt off my back if that would help them. Henry blurted out, "How about your tie?" a beautiful expensive Ferragamo. I tore it off and gave it to him! Twenty years later he still remembers that gesture! He loved working for us.

Is there a disconnect between the ruthless boss above and the "Here, take my tie" fellow? No! They are part of the same success-generating style. I'll explain.

Two key qualities apply to creating this powerfully effective style. The first is *toughness*. Building a successful business is tough with little room for errors and every chance of running out of money, attacking the wrong market with the wrong product or pricing, being copied and outperformed, being sabotaged, or worse after having some success, being eaten alive by the big guys. So a company and its leadership have to be tough, driven, *obsessed with the desire to succeed*, ruthless in some ways and willing to do whatever it takes to legally and honestly succeed. Roughly 90% of start-ups fail! Even more than half of the companies that have received venture capital backing ultimately fail.

The second key quality, a strong sense of *ownership,* is even more critical and needs to be firmly and deeply cultivated with the employees. This is their company. You want them to take great pride in what the company is doing and in the importance of their jobs. Step by step, you want to build a highly focused, enthusiastic, energized team, happily and aggressively working together, and working with a tremendous emphasis on the customer and customer satisfaction. That's a tough assignment. It can also provide deep long lasting satisfaction for everyone, be financially rewarding – sometimes beyond imagination – and even be FUN. Yes, fun!

Years ago I joined a Silicon Valley startup. It was the first venture capital deal for a young hard charging new venture capitalist. He was all of 26 and was still working on his MBA. I had over 20 years of very successful management experience and an MBA in Marketing. Yet, I also had a very healthy fear of failure (a real motivator), as I took over this unprofitable embryonic company. One of my first dilemmas was what to do with this bright, inexperienced venture capitalist. As the new CEO, I did not want any interference or confusion about "who's-in- charge". I could easily restrict his access to the company and employees or, perhaps I thought, I could have him really help us.

Being ruthlessly honest and non-political, by the way, are great traits for entrepreneurs. There is no room for games and personal agendas. As I thought about it, I realized that his goal was identical to my goal: *Make this company a great success.* So I encouraged him to stay very involved and gave him permission to talk to anybody in or outside the company, but I had two requests. First, do not criticize management or tell employees what to do. Rather, take notes. Second, meet with me weekly, which we did each Tuesday night for the next year, to review his findings. At every meeting, I listened carefully to his concerns and suggestions, usually eight or ten items, and later would decide what was critical and needed my immediate attention; what was important, but would have to wait; and what could be put off or ignored.

This same young fellow had an idea that, if implemented correctly, would give the company a very unique clear focus and targeted market. I immediately saw its value and implemented it. Concurrently, I discovered a new term which perfectly described what we were now doing and even incorporated it into the company name. This new concept was immensely successful and ultimately fostered a slew of new industries.

At that time, this company also needed a strong, experienced sales executive to truly take it to the next level of aggressive nationwide expansion. One candidate stood out above the others, but despite a number of interviews, I hesitated, not wanting to make a mistake. Again, this young fellow spoke up. "Hire her, Pete. If she doesn't work out, fire her!" I followed his advice. She turned out to be absolutely superb, a tough, strong sales executive and leader, who contributed hugely to our subsequent sales and corporate success.

That company quickly became the fastest growing service company in America, according to Inc. Magazine. Then a month after we completed our initial IPO, the economy stalled badly, but our company continued to grow rapidly. Equity magazine wrote that we were one of the few companies on any exchange in America to successfully grow revenue and earnings in both good and bad times. The WSJ called us the "darling of Wall Street". None of this would have been possible without solid focus, super sales, and my listening to a young mentor.

I do want to emphasize the value of properly using mentors. I use the term mentors, but could just as easily call them advisors, consultants, experts, or coaches. To me, mentors are pretty much anyone who can add to the successful running and growth of your business. As one experienced gentleman advised, "Put your ego in your back pocket, Pete, and you'll learn a lot."

With our new direction, I quickly came up with *a clear concise mission statement.* I then set very high, but attainable goals for every aspect of our business: finances, sales, pipelines and back orders, retention, collections, complaints, service response, and other key indicators. These were summed up on a monthly report that displayed current results, twelve months of history (great for quickly identifying trends), and annual goals.

Creating the proper culture is mandatory for scalable success. I firmly believe that *every employee is in sales,* even the Accounts Receivables

Department. Every contact with a customer should make that customer feel that this is an exceptional company always treating its customers beyond expectations. And a process needs to be implemented for following up on problems that have been "fixed" to determine if, in fact, they were fixed and fixed satisfactorily. As another mentor told me, "Inspect, don't expect".

You cannot create great customer service and true business success without highly motivated employees. Employees are key. One of the first things that we did was to not call them employees, but Associates, and our sales and service people became Membership and Service Directors. Then we empowered these Associates at all levels with the responsibility and authority to make decisions. But making timely decisions at the point of occurrence does mean occasionally making mistakes. The worst thing that a company can do is hide these, perhaps allowing them to grow and become toxic. The culture must insist that mistakes and problems be immediately brought to light, with suggestions for effectively fixing them without punishing the good employees who occasionally err. Find the problem, fix it and move on!

The best companies are inevitably ones where the employees operate as if they are owners. Better yet, actually make them owners with stock or options, perhaps with a 6 month cliff and 4 year vesting. Hold regular "investor" sessions, so they understand their company's goals, accomplishments, challenges, and opportunities, and their critical role in meeting these. And no "rank has its privileges". We're all in this tough exciting venture together and if I, as CEO, have to sweep the floors, take out the trash, or give you my tie, it's DONE!

I also believe that proper recognition and incentives are critical, and should be as broadly based across the company as possible. Employees then know that if they perform well, they'll be appreciated, acknowledged, and well rewarded. An example was having all employees eligible to earn The Presidents Circle. As the company grew this award included exciting five day all expense paid trips to Cancun, Hawaii and even Caribbean cruises. Outside of sales, these were based on contributions to the company, to teamwork and for exceptional service. The effect of this "equality" was extraordinary on individual morale, motivation, performance and the development of companywide teamwork.

Teamwork is essential. To create genuine teamwork, it's critical that those who do not perform to expectations are quickly identified, corrected or terminated. One or two "bad apples" can do immeasurable damage. A well-run company is also extremely cost conscious. This requires working smartly as a team with no duplicate or wasted efforts. Cost control, I preach, is also a customer service. Who pays for excess costs: obviously, the customers and investors or owners.

Hiring the right people to fit this demanding culture is important. Initially, a clear specific job description clarifying exactly what an ideal candidate must have, should have, and would be helpful to have is truly necessary. Then a thorough interview process should be conducted including sessions with potential peers, along with research on the candidate before and afterwards. In one interview for a critical service leadership position, my meeting with the candidate, in an oppressively hot muggy office, lasted over eight hours. It was the toughest interview he'd ever had. But as I dug deeply into his work history and background, I came to fully appreciate this unusual candidate. I hired him. He turned out to be the best Chief Operating Officer I have ever worked with. An interview doesn't have to last only an hour or two!

The officers must set the example, whether it is long hours, lost weekends, making sales calls, or handling trouble calls. I once had an angry customer call me because his service was interrupted in the middle of his annual sales campaign. Worse, he had called for help earlier and his problem wasn't corrected. Our receptionist immediately forwarded his call to me, the CEO, (standard company procedure), which unfortunately forced him into my voicemail. He started to leave a rational message when he exploded, screaming away at the top of his voice with, I must say, more than a few expletives. I quickly contacted him to apologize and resolve the issue. Then I listened to that message a second time and decided to forward it to every employee in the company, some 600 people in 22 locations. Wow, did that get the customer service message across.

I also required each officer in the company to spend one half day monthly handling service trouble calls and making sales and customer calls. I have always believed that talking to five or ten customers was more informative than doing a survey of a thousand. Of course, both have their roles. Understanding customers, recognizing problems and potential problems early and identifying customers' changing needs is important, no less so now than in the past. There are many excellent analytical and social media tools available for addressing these today, but it is still hard to beat an actual conversation!

So in brief summary, there are two powerful considerations that must be thoroughly analyzed and then appropriately and aggressively implemented for success, particularly in a new disruptive upstart business. They are the Science, cold hard honest facts essential to understanding the business and its customers and industry. But, far more important to true business success, phenomenal growth and industry disruption and revolution is the Art. Art starts with tough honest *leadership* and a strong enthusiastic customer-oriented *culture*, and ends with delighted *customers*.

Below is an express checklist of *"My Secrets"* to help guide you as you go forward in this exciting world of opportunity and adventure.

<u>Leadership</u>

- Aim high, be tough
- Create and incentivize an ownership culture
- Lead by example and be available
- Ask, listen, learn, and use mentors

<u>Culture and Customers</u>

- Focus 150% on the customer
- Everyone is in sales
- Exceed expectations
- Inspect, don't expect
- Action over analysis
- And, don't forget, have fun!

ABOUT PETER

Peter A. Howley is a serial entrepreneur with unprecedented successful experience in building high growth disruptive technology and service companies in a broad array of industries including telecom, mobile, healthcare, social media and various internet sectors. As Chairman of The Howley Management Group he works closely with Entrepreneurs, CEO's and Boards to turn good ideas into great fast growing sustainable businesses.

"It would be hard to find an advisor with a broader depth of experience, and more integrity, than Peter Howley. When I needed no-nonsense straight shooting advice, I always thought to call him first." Steve O'Neil, Founder of ITC ThinkLink

Peter Howley has the unusual reputation, even in Silicon Valley, for making good things happen fast. He has the distinction of accelerating a disruptive Silicon Valley venture-backed company, quickly leading it through an IPO and later acquisition, into the pages of American business history as CEO. Centex Telemanagement was recognized as one of the fastest growing, best managed, most profitable companies in both good and bad economies in America. Howley initiated an innovative and successful business culture that retains a magical cult status within customer service focused companies such as Zappos.

Mr. Howley joined the founders of Exodus Communications at its inception. He advised and served on the Board through IPO until June 2000. Exodus still holds a NASDAQ record for 13 consecutive quarters of greater than 40% revenue growth.

"Great guy and huge reason why Exodus succeeded."
Craig Buda, Senior Sales Executive

Later as the Co-founder and CEO of IPWireless, Inc., Howley raised more than $120 million in venture capital. His leadership was instrumental in the company's successful growth and acquisition by Nextwave.

"Pete has the rare ability to provide broad strategic advice matched with keen insight on the operational details that keep new ventures afloat and all stakeholders engaged and encouraged. This was crucial to my early success at SOS Wireless. Pete comes by these talents the old fashioned way; through a great education, tremendous experience, brainpower, and a hefty dose of practicality." Gene Russell, President and CEO, SOS Wireless, Inc.

Mr. Howley frequently speaks to business and students groups. He recently co-authored the best seller "TrendSetters: The World's Leading Experts Reveal Top Trends to Help You Achieve Greater Health, Wealth & Success." The National Academy of Best Selling Authors honored him with the Golden Quill Award. He also appeared on America's Premier Experts television show.

CHAPTER 5

TRENDSETTING SHAPED BY EXPERIENCE

BY CHRISTINE RAE

A s a working woman in the 80's, I think I was 42 before it dawned on me I didn't need my mother's approval to do something, and that I didn't have to do things just to please her anymore. Let me explain: It was a Friday night; she had called to see who I was going out with that weekend. I wasn't going out with anyone (I believe she was hoping for a rich lawyer and I felt guilty, that somehow I was letting her down). Truth was, I was tired, I had finished a stressful week and I was really looking forward to relaxing, watching "Dallas" and indulging in a glass of wine! When I told her what I planned, she said "That sounds nice!"

Now that might seem innocuous to many women today, but as a women of that era, it was a tough nut to crack. Especially as my upbringing had been a straight-laced, British girl school, don't "cheek" your elder's, background. We didn't have the benefit of Oprah, Dr Phil, or the self-help books/magazines of today. We were seen but not heard; women were still fighting the equality battle, and if you were a successful woman then Lord knows, you must have slept with someone! If you were single there must be something wrong with you (because isn't it every girl's dream to want to be married?) It was a struggle to maintain independence, earn more than "enough", be respected for what you did in business and create a work-life balance you could live with. The "Super Woman Syndrome" was just as prevalent in the 90's but life did get easier from an acceptance perspective – but then women hated you if you were good looking, successful AND independent!

Oprah says "everyone has a story." When I teach, people are always interested to know how I got started in this business of real estate staging; what is my story? In his book "Self Matters," Dr. Phil says you can trace who you've become in this life to three types of external factors: 10 defining moments, seven critical choices, and five pivotal people. Well, that conversation with my mother was one of my defining moments. I never quite know where to start my story because so much of what has happened has contributed to who I am today, but as the King said to the White Rabbit in Alice's Adventures in Wonderland, "**Begin at the beginning and go on till you come to the end: then stop.**"

I was born and raised in Yorkshire, England. I went to an all-girls school all my life, wore a school uniform(which I liked). I did ok at school, did not excel in much (although I did like Domestic Science). I was good at field hockey, running and the high jump. In school I really didn't have any aspirations for doing amazing things; no one in our family had gone to university and many girls really only thought about leaving school, getting a job, getting married and having babies. I wasn't one of those girls – I wanted to see the world. Travel was my dream. I had been fortunate to have travelled extensively as a family to France and Spain from about 5 years old – it left such an impression on me.

When I was about 10, my uncle went to Australia as part of the colonisation program. It was the other side of the world and we all cried because we would never see him again. I remember receiving postcards of his journey. A Pan Am flight to New York City, on to San Francisco, Hawaii, Fiji and Sydney; such exotic destinations – I so wanted to see them! If I thought of anything in school, it would be what job I could do in order to travel. Now that I travel great distances for the work I do, I realise that unless you have time and money, it isn't pleasant. One thought I had was to be an air stewardess (if you have seen the "Catch Me If You Can" movie, you know it was a glamorous job back then). My headmistress said "No girl of mine will do that," so my next choice was the British Army. I didn't want to be a foot soldier of course. Honestly, I probably thought it was more like Goldie Hawn's version of the army, but I had it all planned out. I would be able to travel safely around the world, wear a uniform, be a physical training instructor and retire with a full pension before I was 50! My mother said "No way"; I always listened to my mother, so I thought, "Ok, I will teach Home Economics."

None of those things came to be. Years later, when I was bemoaning the fact that my mother had stopped me going into the Army, at first she couldn't even remember the event (OMG, it changed the course of my life), and then she said you can't have wanted it badly enough because nothing should stop you from getting to your dream! (Light bulb moment! … as Oprah says). Although many thought I was crazy, and should just get a job and get married, I did go on to college. I majored in English Literature and Political History, but truly it was a difficult transition from an all-girls school. I felt out of my depth and exhilarated at the same time. I also had a niggling thought that I wasn't good enough to make the grade, so I was easily influenced to leave after a year, take a job and get married at 18 no less! It is interesting to me, that in all the situations where I made life-changing decisions, I always felt like an observer of my life. My inner knowing knew I could just as easily make other decisions which would be more difficult, but which would take me on different paths. As my personal confidence and self-esteem had not developed or matured, I usually chose the path of least resistance. Then, as always, a pervasive nagging feeling ...I had let myself down.

I did marry. I wanted us to do something exciting like go to Australia, hitch hike to Greece, pick oranges in Spain – my husband was too practical for that, so we bought a house and "settled down." I had a series of uninteresting jobs, went back to college and just before graduation we took a chance and emigrated to Canada (easier than final exams). My sister and her husband were living there so we moved to the same town and started our new life, in a new country. That was when I realised it doesn't matter where you live – there you always are. You are the same person with the same hang-ups and the grass isn't always greener, and now I was 4000 miles away from all which I held safe. The retrospective learning from that experience was that in order to reach a new destination, you have to be willing to leave the shore.

We found work within a few weeks, found an apartment, explored the area, built a life and, at 25, discovered I was pregnant. We were happy. We bought a house, appliances, air conditioning, cars. I settled in to being a stay-at-home mother, and for about three years, life was good. It was years later when I started working full time, I learned, that when we came to Canada there was a recession! We didn't know about it so we got jobs, spent money and got on with our lives. The learning lesson for this was easily that you can think and behave negatively or positively. In class I always say "What would you be doing if you knew you couldn't fail?"

I loved being a mum, the wonder of watching a child grow, the privilege of teaching that little person. Around this time I started working part time for a party planning company with decorative items. It got me out of the house and I discovered I had a talent for sales and décor. I won trips, household items, and the use of a car. I distinctly remember receiving my first $1000 cheque for one week's work when most people my age were making about $100. I did that for three years. The distance between myself and my husband grew, so we parted and I decided I had to get a "real job" 9-5, as my son was in school and I needed to be home in the evening. Although there were some ups and downs, eventually I took a salaried job as a sales rep for an employment service. I stayed with that company for 22 years and was a single parent for 17 years. I know how difficult managing a child, household, work and a life can be.

Working in the corporate world in the mid 80's and early 90's was a challenge. I had heard of Gloria Steinem, the American <u>feminist</u>, <u>journalist</u>, and social and political <u>activist</u> who became nationally recognized as a leader of, and media spokesperson for the national women's liberation movement in the late 1960s and 1970s. I wasn't conversant with her beliefs. I didn't see myself in a repressed position as I worked my way through the "glass ceiling," but remembered the shock she created when women burned their bras! In the 90's she wrote a book which many of my friends read called *Revolution from Within: A Book of Self-Esteem.* My boss bought me the book. I didn't read it; I didn't think I had a problem. There was another popular book at the time, *Women Who Run with Wolves.* I did get the book, I read the introduction, and it spoke to me of a woman who is really living her life (as opposed to simply existing in it). People said it was a great book; a book for any woman who "longs in her secret self for something more, who knows that her mind works better than her heart, who feels as if she's stretched too thin, who has forgotten how to create, have fun, get dirty, laugh, cry or growl."

That was me alright, but it sounded dangerous and I wasn't in a position to lift the lid on Pandora's Box. I would be like Scarlett O'Hara and "think about it tomorrow." I was perceived as a strong, independent woman. I ran my own life, had savings, went on holidays, provided a good life for my son, had friends, went to the theatre, and worked hard …I worked really hard. I was promoted to management, regional and then general manager, heading up a $10 million operation for a franchise owner, 8 offices, 50 people – and I hadn't slept with a soul to do it!

During all those years, I was a prolific reader, mainly fiction because I needed to escape and be entertained when I wasn't working. While I was doing all this, I also went to night school for four years to get the piece of paper which said "I am smart." I also started reading more nonfiction, biography and history. Three books which really changed my thinking were: Faith Popcorn's *Popcorn Report*, Donald Trump's *Art of a Deal* and Norman Schwarzkopf's *It Doesn't Take a Hero*.

From these books I learned to be brave in business, trust my instincts, take risks, think big, not let anyone trample on you, have a strategy, think 'outside the box', be a 'big picture' thinker, don't worry too much about what the 'experts' say, but use your own knowledge and maximise your options. My favourite quotes from Schwarzkopf which moulded me into a good leader are, "Do what is right, not what you think the high headquarters wants or what you think will make you look good," "Leadership is a potent combination of strategy and character. But if you must be without one, be without the strategy," and "True courage is being afraid, and going ahead and doing your job." This was an army I was in!

I learned to have the courage of my convictions, as Trump said, *"As long as you are going to be thinking anyway, you might as well think big."* I honed my entrepreneurial abilities to improve the bottom line of the company I worked in, and I worked as if it was my own …and created innovative ways to have multiple streams of income for the company and learned too late that it wasn't my own business. I learned you cannot have blind trust, you must protect your flank AND your back and always have an exit strategy. After 22 years of pouring my heart and soul into this company, I was the last person to know the business was to be sold and I was no longer needed. I was cast off like an old shoe and felt it! – no pension and no recourse. It reminded me of an aphorism I learned, "Whenever your ego is in bloom, put your arm into a bucket of water. When you remove it – the hole that is left is how much you will be missed." I had always been so careful to not exalt my position, my status, or talk about the money I earned. I had kept corporate secrets and turned down other lucrative offers of employment because I was a loyal, dedicated and trusting employee who believed good work would be the protection I needed for a secure future. The lesson? *It's not what happens to you, but what you do with what happens that counts!*

Another interesting observation of that time was to be careful of what you say; a friend of mine brought me a book as soon as she heard I had lost my job. Neil Donald Walsh *Conversations With God* – Book 1 and some audio tapes of Dr. Wayne Dwyer. From these I learned that we create our own world. The power of the spoken word – what you say and believe with your heart will come to pass. I also acknowledged to myself, that I had had a hand in these things which had happened to me. I had been a contributing architect of this demise. Occasionally, I had mentioned to friends, that I actually hated the work I did, that I wouldn't be there much past 50. Two days after my 50th birthday I was without work! Talk about self-fulfilling prophesies!

I stayed home for a while; believing I had retired from work. I enjoyed my house and my new normal. My husband, however, had other plans. While encouraging me to "find out" what I wanted to do, he very definitely wanted me back at work. We had a mortgage, bills and no pension. Every time I went for an interview, I could literally make myself sick at the thought of working in a corporate setting again. So I started exploring options for having my own business.

I told my husband my idea; he was very supportive, assuming I was going to do what I had been doing in the corporate world. When I told him I wanted to open a decorator store – I think you could have knocked him over with a feather! If I had said 'brain surgeon' I don't think he would have been more surprised. After much discussion (mainly around what qualifications were required and whether it meant I was going to school for four more years), I finally told him, "When I was in my mid-30s, I had an opportunity to be one of 12 people to take a risk by investing $1000 (of the $1500 I had saved) as seed money for a new board game. I was a single mum earning $250 a week – I couldn't risk the loss – besides adults played cards, not games. That board game was Trivial Pursuit! I could now be a wealthy woman. If I don't take this risk now I will never know what I can achieve. If I do this and fail – it's ok, but if I don't do this, I know I will harbor resentment for a long time, because all my life, I have allowed other people's opinions to sway me from what I really wanted to do. Another defining moment changed my life.

Long story short, we agreed I would have the time to TRY to make this work. Secretly I was thinking, Yoda said "there is no try – only do." The problem was of course I didn't have any qualifications. I was good at décor for my house, I was the "go-to" person in our family whenever anyone had a décor dilemma, but I really didn't want to go to decorating school for four years. I was researching online and "stumbled" (there are no coincidences) upon someone who had pioneered an industry in the USA called ReDesign- no one was doing it in Canada – I would be first to provide a unique service. The class was in September in New York City (it was now May), and it was a lot of money ($8000 with flight and hotel), BUT I would have credentials, I would have knowledge, and darn it, I was worth it.

September 11th 2001 will go down in infamy, and thankfully I was not there at that time. The class was scheduled for one week later; I can't tell you how many people called to plead for me not to go. I was amazed – not go? It cost $8000; not go? And not move this dream forward – no way! A disaster of that magnitude doesn't get planned overnight – It wasn't going to happen again. I went and there met an amazing woman who became my friend and, even though the training was not as good as I thought it should be, I decided I could go away feeling cheated, or I could make the most of it. I resolved to focus on the good. I told myself what I have learned the most from this week is to trust myself more, give myself credit for more and to keep moving forward.

I started my business, realizing soon after that I needed multiple streams of income if I was to earn at least the same base salary I had in the corporate world. I determined my fee for service. All I had to do was find ways to bill hours of work at that rate or find other ways to make money related to the business I was in. I have the ability of being able to think on my feet. I thought I could figure out the details as I went along. One of my favorite TV shows at that time was Star Trek – The Next Generation. I love when Picard said "make it so, number 1." I used it often in business; in the corporate world I had a secretary, people to answer phones, file, research, etc. ...Now I was finding out how difficult it is to be everything for yourself within your company.

Another challenge I had at that time was adjusting to being "no one" in a big pond after being "someone" in small pond. Customers wanted credibility AND talent! Go figure! Remember this was ten years ago. I had a website (perception of people at that time was if you had a website you MUST be legitimate). I had a cell phone (which meant you must be a "fly by night" if you didn't have a real phone). Time flew; I found I could be busy all day and get nowhere near the billed hours I needed. Hmmm, what if I hired someone? By coincidence, my secretary from my corporate world had just been laid off. As there was no real cash flow in the business, selling my husband on the concept was tough but heck – what about ten hours a month at $10 hr? It would mean I HAD to earn at least $100 to pay her. Well that turned out to be a great decision; my office became organized, the phone was answered and I felt legitimate. I had to find work to pay her so I advertised, got an 800 number and put my business into the Yellow Pages (even though there was no section for it), and I was on my way.

Late 2001, I was speaking with a real estate agent at a networking meeting; I talked peripherally about staging. He was intrigued (as was the plan) then he dropped a bomb, "Would you speak at my office on the subject?" Of course, I said yes, and literally drove home at breakneck speeds to learn what I could about a subject I had no knowledge in! The result of that research had me on a plane going to North Carolina for a session being provided by a real estate agent the next week. Again I was disappointed in the scope of information and material, but I had an AH-HA moment. Obviously no one was doing this in Canada and I wanted to be the pioneer. I contacted a woman in Seattle, arranged to spend a week with her and ended up with licensing and territory rights for her program, in Canada, the NE United States and the UK.

I worked to improve the program for four months before I gave my first class; I chose Boston because it was far enough away from where I live not to ruin my reputation should I be unsuccessful. The rest is history as they say. I discovered I actually loved teaching. As I spoke, I discovered I had more knowledge than I had written into the program and I also felt there was room for improvement. In my opinion, you cannot teach well what you are not master of. I launched a staging component to my business back home and brought the lessons from the field to the classroom. I worked hard, learned much and built my staging training business so much that I was acknowledged as the premier trainer for the company where I worked.

Then in 2005, four and a half years into the career I loved – everything changed overnight – again. There were four contract trainers in the company at this time – all of our contracts were not renewed. Obviously there were untold discussions, but the end result was that I needed a replacement income solution again fast!. Over the preceding four years, I had gained much knowledge, grown in confidence and so "how to make lemonade again" filtered through my brain. I would build/ develop grow a staging training company which would be superior in every way to anything in North America – no, indeed the world. I set to work writing a workshop manual, PowerPoint and business plan. I worked night and day. One month later I held the first Canadian Staging Professional workshop for 17 brave souls who trusted me with their business and life dreams. After the champagne bubbles had fizzled, I realised what a huge undertaking and responsibility I had taken on. In an industry where no one was watching, where there were no rules, I laid out the foundation for integrity, professionalism, certification, examination and knowledge. Within a year we had graduates from coast to coast, expanded to the United States and secured five very senior staging instructors whose business philosophies mirrored those of CSP International™. I had secured a well-known TV personality and original TV stager known as the "House Doctor" to endorse the CSP program as the best source of education for building a staging business.

In 2007, we launched the first-ever continuing education program which truthfully was not embraced at that time because the industry was growing in an *ad ho*c way. More people were beginning to offer training, but no one was operating as a catalyst for change the way I was, so no one saw the need. It did not deter me; it actually positioned me as the leader, when the industry started to catch up. Later when the trade association RESA opened its doors, CSP International became a strong advocate for its existence. When they needed a continuing education program, they came to us. Today the biggest challenge we face in this industry is the influx of people who think all they need for credibility is membership in the trade association. As that association influence grows, the real estate community will require more stringent guidelines. With that knowledge and an eye on tomorrow, CSP International launched the "International Masters" certification in staging, and re-engineered the continuing education program to enable the CSP International Academy to support the staging community as a whole.

My decision to be the best in everything we do positioned me as a leader and forerunner. The responsibility of leadership for the thousands of people who entrust their tuition dollars and dreams to CSP required me to become an advocate for change in the industry – because otherwise, in my opinion, it wouldn't survive for long. It wouldn't survive because the majority of people who want to do this work are decorators at heart; they love the work, the adrenaline rush of pulling a project together, the blush of pride when the compliments come. As a whole their weakness is that they are not business oriented. This doesn't mean they can't become that, but when they realise how much business, sales, marketing, invoicing, administration, organization, etc., is involved in an entrepreneurial venture, they often become overwhelmed and quit. I know this because of the work I did before CSP. It was one of the motivating factors behind the business content in the CSP program. I initiated, and to date, have the only operational apprenticeship program where real estate staging graduates have the chance of job shadowing with approved CSP Mentors. My philosophy is built around "pay it forward."

Mentors are graduates who have built successful businesses and are at a point in their work/life where they want to help the industry grow strong. I developed expertise by learning to keep an eye on the future, being an observer of global trends, and interpreting how they affect the work we do and those we teach/lead. Over the past five years, I have always held myself accountable and practiced what I preached.

I believe there are no coincidences. We are all co-creators or architects of our life. In 2007 when a simple rain barrel purchase opened my eyes to the global water crisis, I prayed someone else was taking care of finding a solution. In the middle of the night an awakening moment was that I could do something about it! The CSP community is perfectly positioned to bring the message to sellers and agents if I could only find a marketing differential to leverage. Making property marketable is the goal; uncovering energy efficiencies would help!

The EcoStaging® program was developed from there. In 2009, when the world economies were falling apart, we moved boldly forward into a 4,000 sf facility which is as sustainable as I could make a leased facility. We began my quest to educate the people we come in contact with about the plight of the planet and how it affects everyone's business. I sometimes feel like a disciple, but it is a passion for me and has led me into interesting directions. This venture caused me to meet Peter Lytle who founded the LiveGreen, LiveSmart Institute and with whom CSP International partnered to be their global education arm for the Certified EcoProfessional™ program.

INTERESTING DEFINING MOMENT

I started the business as a solution to a financial need in my family. I realise it has never been about the money. It is about providing a place where people can get all they need in terms of education, training, tools and support to help them achieve their own dreams. In doing that, we are helping create a better world. Difference is our direction. We confront challenges with courage and strive to serve others so they can be better at what they do for their customers.

Looking forward to how I could I fix the problem of building better business people led me to Michael E. Gerber's books, *Awakening the Entrepreneur Within* and *The Most Successful Business in the World* ...hmmm, this could be a solution. His dream is to help good businesses become exceptional ones. I contacted the Gerber organization. After a few discussions, I entered his training program and became certified and licensed to conduct "Dreaming Rooms, to awaken the entrepreneur within." May 2011 saw the inception of my new venture; I have no doubt in Mr. Gerber's mission or my abilities to help small businesses become exceptional. When I conclude a CSP workshop I always say, "Go forth and prosper."

What I know for sure is: *Every day is a blessing, we create our own reality, we need to get out of our own way, and believe that whatever we want – will be.*

We just have to "make it so."

ABOUT CHRISTINE

Christine Rae is known as the leading expert and trend setter of the Real Estate Staging Industry. In her role as President and CEO for CSP International, she steered the company to the top of the excellence chart for her industry. The CSP International Academy is known as a successful incubator for 'would be' entrepreneurs with a decorating flair who want control over their own destiny, while building successful, profitable businesses of their own. CSP International provides a safe haven for learning, support, knowledge, best practices and leading market trends. Graduates from the Academy benefit from a reputation of excellence, helping them gain credibility and recognition as they market and develop their own business.

Christine is recognised as the world's leading authority on staging from her global experience as well as through her work in developing standards, examinations, professionalism and trend forecasting. She is the author of Home Staging for Dummies® (Wiley press), editor of the world's only Staging Industry Magazine, and is co-authoring two new books in the works for release this fall, Trendsetters and Sold.

Christine developed and trademarked EcoStaging®. She is an Industry Expert Blogger for REALTOR® magazine, a regular contributor to Real Estate Magazine and is the Green Staging Expert for HomeGain®. She has been a featured speaker and keynote for many industry events including six Stagers Expo's, Real Estate Staging Association, Sydney, Australia Real Estate event, Key Note for a European convention of stagers in the Netherlands and expert speaker at the California Association of Realtors convention. Christine and her unique, signature CSP® Real Estate Staging Business Program has received awards, accolades and recognition – including accreditation by RESA. Currently five US colleges across the country endorse the program. Her book, Home Staging for Dummies ®, has also been selected as the textbook on staging at several colleges in Canada.

Christine's success stems from her work ethic, desire for excellence, integrity and integral goodness. In a very competitive industry, what sets CSP apart are the differentiators and the driving force to be of service and value to the student. From the outset, CSP International core values, mission, "pay it forward" philosophy and their apprenticeship program have been the catalyst to the myriad of differentiators which set CSP apart. Christine has worked with TV House Doctor Ann Maurice. Many of Christine's graduates have appeared on popular HGTV real estate shows, she was recently certified to facilitate Michael E Gerber's "Dreaming Room" event, was interviewed by Michael, and had a guest appearance on The Michael E Gerber Show. She also has appeared on ABC, NBC, CBS and FOX television affiliates speaking about staging.

CHAPTER 6

UNLEASH YOUR MAVERICK MOJO AND BE WHO YOU ARE

BY CORINNE RITA

Life is either a daring adventure, or nothing.
~ Helen Keller

When do you feel radiantly alive?

Are you there now?

If you think it's about your business, it is.

And it isn't.

It's about your life.

YOUR BUSINESS REFLECTS WHO YOU ARE <u>BEING</u>

Feeling everything – passion, joy, excitement, uncertainty, doubt, shame, craziness and fear, and being willing to boldly remain myself has brought me an extraordinary life. I've done whatever I made the decision to do. I've reinvented my work across industries and professions. If I told you my story you'd think I made it up. The reality of it is that I did! And I continue to do so. You can too. We create our reality in business and life.

Life is a process. Who you were may not be who you are becoming. Your values could shift in importance and call out different strengths. What matters is remaining true to the unique unfolding of your life. Be who you are.

Every moment you breathe is your time alive. If you are not doing what you love you, you have a choice to create what you do love. Your responsibility is to take nothing for granted and to live your gifts. *Why would you ever choose to be less than who you are?*

WHEN DO YOU FEEL RADIANTLY ALIVE?

Call to mind a peak experience in your life. Right now! Feel yourself shiver with anticipation. Let your heart pound with excitement. Make this moment matter. Make it feel like the blazing intensity of fire and the absolute stillness of an icy pond all at once. *Do you have it? Where are you? What are you doing? Are you with anyone? What are you feeling? Are the colors vivid? What can you taste and smell? What's happening for you?*

Be in it. Write it out in detail. Read it. Now close your eyes and be in it. Be in it. Be radiantly alive.

BECOME AWARE

Breathing into that experience, ask: *What shifted? What's different for me? What's significant about reliving who I was at one of the best times of my life? Where am I now? What am I now aware of about myself? What did I rediscover?*

Write it down.

DID YOU DO THE EXERCISE?

Here's my memory. So there I was in Tokyo. Eyes wide open, heart in my throat, jet lagged and confused in a taxi staring up at buildings that made NYC the size of a gecko. Was I really here? And with my Mom? K-san was gesturing to the white-gloved driver to stop at a sushi-ya. The initial shock of being greeted by two men bowing deeply while yelping Miss Corinne through fits of giggles gave way to wonder. We were really in Japan.

I'd been invited to do a national speaking tour. My products were sold throughout Japan in multiple channels. Department stores, luxury goods boutiques, garden shops, home furnishings, clothing stores, really every conceivable place I could think of marketing a unique design. I'd no idea what I was going to speak about or how I was advertised until the week before we left. They just wanted me in Japan. Sales skyrocket when a company founder, the literal life and soul of the brand, directly interacts with consumers.

LISTEN FULLY THIS VERY MOMENT

Remember that. Your job is to create a following from the strength of who you are. Our following came naturally from sharing authentically our vision, our story and ultimately ourselves. Although I was "the brand" in Japan, my Mom was integral to my success. Taking my Mom on this adventure was my only stipulation because you only live once.

Never mind that I was terrified of flying, I had to go. When I write terrified, I mean serious panic attacks on the scale of OMG, …am I dying? …What is wrong with me? …I must be insane, help me now, get me out of here terror. I couldn't drive down the highway at one point in my early 20's it was so bad. But that's a different story.

So there we were. The shorter man understood and spoke a little English. The tall man laughed a lot. No English. I spoke passable Japanese. I learned they had no idea who we were. In fact, they were chemical engineers! Their division of the trading company had nothing to do with our products, but as good 'salarymen', their job was to treat us like American Royalty.

ANYTHING IS POSSIBLE

Speaking of icons, did I mention I'd been billed as "an Urban Martha Stewart" throughout Japan? Yes, you read that right. Maybe it was a lost in translation moment. She'd been our customer. But I am not her. I'm me. The tour was advertised and it was up to me with a week's notice to summon my inner Martha. No small feat. Take her qualities and make them Urban, and all about me? Ok. I'm an artist. I can do this! Showcase your American Style Design. Easy. And do demonstrations like Martha with your garden pots and vases. Oh my. Wondering what'd come next, I scrunched over in the tiny round portal bathroom looking out the tiny round window of our skyscraper hotel – feeling like I'd climbed 'through the Looking Glass' and 'on board the Yellow Submarine.'

CONNECT TO THE BEING BEHIND THE DOING AND HAVING

Can you feel my memory and know who I am through it? We haven't met, but I'll bet you have an idea of what moves me. How about you? What did it feel like for you to be in that place where anything is possible? Your peak experience probably had an element of what felt like magic. Is your heart racing with knowing your own potential again? What did you rediscover about yourself?

PRACTICE SELF – DISCOVERY

In doing this exercise, I re-learned that if I defined myself by potential problems, I'd never have had the courage to throw all that I am into business. I developed what was initially an experiment to see what might be possible into international wholesale, retail and private design divisions. I did not do it alone. My family provided the opportunity with their belief in me. That's why Mom came with me to Japan. I wish my Dad could have been with us. He's always believed in me. I remembered how much I love the people who matter most in my life. I felt again how being in business was about being in the dream of what we could create together.

I re-experienced my audacity and determination. I felt that rush of pushing myself to places far beyond any comfort zone. I rediscovered how I define myself by my strengths. It was ultimately my belief in myself that exploded our work into an international phenomenon. The best way to do anything is to lean fully into the thing that scares you most and embrace it. It's trying to tell you something about who you are. Panic was a sign that I needed to live larger. I felt again how I chose to experience anxiety as excitement. I trust my desires. I got to live again in the magic of seeing a sea of Japanese brides waiting for me to take the stage. Me!

KNOW WHO YOU ARE

Most importantly I recalled what's possible and what it was like to be who I am. I remembered what it felt like living from what I want – my desires, values and purpose.

WHO ARE YOU?

This was an exercise to experience immediate fulfillment. In a few minutes you pulled the self that you were at a time of sheer aliveness from the past into the present.

YOU CREATE IT ALL

The reality is that you make it all up. Every moment of your life you make it all up. You are powerful beyond description.

YOU ARE A LEADER – UNLEASH YOURSELF

Unleashing your maverick mojo is living your strengths and being who you are. When you choose the path of freedom, self-expression and daring to live your passions, you elevate the lives of everyone around you and inspire joy in their journey.

WHAT'S YOUR MOJO?

You can feel it. You can't fake it. Your mojo is magic. It's what makes you authentically you! Fully present in the moment, outrageously joyful, living your truth. Mojo is the essence of who you are. It's your hidden superpower that shines through magnetic self-confidence when you are yourself. And who doesn't want to be a superhero?

YOUR MOJO REVEALS YOUR STRENGTHS

Radiance is mojo. Think of the emotional force of your strengths as synonymous with mojo. Mojo is magnetic attraction. This pulls us toward action that illuminates our values – our core beliefs. When you are radiantly alive, your strengths are pulled through your being into self-expression. Strengths synthesize your unique knowledge (life experience, education and skills) with inherent talent. Understand your strengths by examining moments of fulfillment. Our earlier exercise was really a call to action for your superheroic self to emerge. *Who were you be-ing? What was present?*

CREATE YOUR OWN DEMAND

When I was asked to contribute to this book, I focused on what it means to be a *trendsetter*. Being thought of as a branding authority, design innovator, and motivational expert has really meant seeing the potential before it emerges. It's already there and you've got the ability to call it forth at some level. I think this is about personal leadership. When you're immersed in your creative genius, your awareness shifts and intuition flows. You create your own demand from the power of who you're being.

In my experience, in states of peak awareness or hyperfocus on a person, product, whatever, what I'm really doing is noticing what's already present. I'm paying attention to the hidden gift and unveiling it. With coaching clients it's an experience of absolute recognition – who the person is at a level they've been afraid to go. "Work" is love made visible – through connection. Work becomes play. Make sense? Notice when you're championing a person's strengths, they move toward greatness. You might hear their brand or see their product because of your commitment and belief in what's possible for them. It really feels like magic.

When you do it for yourself, in an instant you become fearless. So, trendsetting is initiating the general direction in which something tends to move. It's being a catalyst, leader and a role model for the movement you generate. Think about that. When you focus on your unique abilities you have the power to create a movement. I did it and I know it to be true.

YOUR STRENGTHS CAN START A MOVEMENT

My original brand pioneered the green movement in home furnishings. I had no idea what we were unleashing. All I knew at the time was that I was taking a stand for my core values. Integrity, freedom, creativity, responsibility, and self-expression are 'being me' at the level of conviction. What I wanted was to leave a lasting impact on the world. My products were symbolic of a deeper psychological drive. I was convinced of it and that passion resonated.

Your customers buy that compelling experience symbolized by your offering. I wanted to inspire people to be conscious of their choices in how they live. Your life is a celebration. Choose your environments wisely. Surround yourself with what you love. That drove me to take risks. The higher value was improving the quality of life for everyone I could. Leaping into the unknown was what made me tick because it was for a greater good. Sounds over the top, but when you're in the thrill of your business, it has to be for a greater good. We all want to create significance and have meaning. For me, at the time, it was designing products with a purpose and sharing the story of our vision. Dreaming the story to life, I was living completely in my strengths. The business was effortless and our success was unprecedented.

BECOME UNSTOPPABLE

My mojo is fearless passion. When I'm there, I am unstoppable. I had a vision of where I wanted to be and made the decision to go there. I had absolutely no business education whatsoever. Zero. I'd co-authored a textbook in psychiatric sociology and wanted to be a shrink! That took all of me. I thought I'd change the world by being a pioneer researcher in mental illness. What I realized is that when you fully engaged your strengths, they're powerful wherever you choose to focus. With a roar, I'd felt the calling to push my boundaries in another direction. Had no idea it would be in product creation. It represented a new challenge. Entrepreneurs thrive at the edge. It's that place where you meet resistance and lean into it, knowing you are powerful. I knew when I leapt that I was my own safety net. *Is that where you are now? If not, **leap***. I'm calling out your inner maverick.

BE UNDENIABLE

As an entrepreneur, the only real security you have is your own ability. You chose to invent, create and assume the risks of business. Consider the commitment. *What does it say about you?* You are a maverick by nature.

Mavericks are unabashedly independent in thought and action with the determination to live by their own values. *Is that an accurate description of you? List the values that are present in what you do. Can you?*

BLAZE YOUR BRILLIANCE

Most entrepreneurs are driven by the need for self-actualization. It's who they're being when they're living from their powerful center. It's brilliance in action. The path to finding your essential self differs for everyone. That's what makes your mojo uniquely yours. The path and the process together reveal it. You've got to find it before you unleash it. Your business as the work of your life is the external expression of it. If you've been in business, it might be time to re-evaluate it. You'll know it if you no longer love what you do.

I think of the process of uncovering your values and strengths as blazing your brilliance. When your brilliance is present, it gives your life immediacy and business succeeds with effortless effort. You are the most unique asset in your own business. The best strategy is to develop your own strengths. Plan your business around you. *Is that how you've strategically designed your business?*

FOCUS ON WHAT YOU WANT

Moment by moment, decision by decision, you create it all. You just experienced that reality. You can dramatically change the quality of your life in any given moment by your choices.

WHAT DO YOU WANT?

Let's consider how you made up your business. It's a construct you've created and its reality exists because you designed it. Do you live in the passion of the inventor working on the invention? Or have you become stuck in your own self-created construct? Has your business become a job?

Take the time now and ask:

What was my reason for being in this business? Write it down! Given that answer, now ask:

What was important about that? Look at both answers and write:

What did having those do for me and am I there now? Is it still important?

KNOW YOUR VALUES

Am I living my values expressed through my strengths? Your values are the fundamental commitments that influence and guide your choices. Can you list them?

I value being……..I value being………...I value being……….

Are they present in what you do? Are they reflected in who you are being? We led with the exercise in reliving that time when you felt radiantly alive. It's your right to live that way every day in all that you do. I'm your coach right now. What I care about is you. I want you to live a remarkable life and do work that leads to fulfillment. Fulfillment is getting your wants met. Remember, a want is emotional. A need might represent a rational choice. Let your business be driven by what you want. It's the voice of your true self being known. Listen carefully to the answer when you ask yourself what do I want?

YOU ARE A CREATIVE GENIUS

Ask yourself if you've created a position that reflects a comfortable existence. *Is that enough? Do you feel engaged in the creative process?* This is what matters most. What if your return on investment were measured in terms of sheer aliveness? The monetary ROI is linked to your state of fulfillment. Please do not forget that your business exists for creating quality of life. Profits are money functioning as a transformative tool that creates opportunity. Do you have an audacious existence and does your business have meaningful impact? Be honest.

TAKE RESPONSIBILITY

If you are going to do it, why would you do it for less than all that you are? Give yourself fully to your invention. Ask yourself right now, *do I feel fully alive?* Right now does the path you've chosen for your business lead you (and everyone involved) to fulfillment and happiness?

BE TRUTHFUL – BE TRUE TO YOURSELF IN BUSINESS & IN LIFE

If your answer is **No**, decide to ask yourself **Why not?** and **What if it did?** The first step on your path is refusing to accept anything less than your best life. It may mean leaving your business as you know it completely. It may mean reinventing the work you currently do in service to your greatest vision.

It's like in life when we forget that what we believe is what we create. Our life gets led by early beliefs that haven't been re-examined for their fit with the life where we currently exist. This shows up as dissatisfaction and a feeling that things are not right. Remember that none of the domains of your life are an absolute reality. They are "a" reality with dynamic and changeable characteristics – based on your decisions. So you have the power to build a remarkable business and life. In any moment, you have the option to deconstruct what isn't working and build what you want.

BECOME A MASTER MAPMAKER

Mavericks blaze their own paths. They make the maps that create their life and work. What we've doing is MAP making. Think of the process like the acronym **MAP**. **Meaning, Awareness and Purpose.** Make **MAPS! S is for Strengths**. If you've built a business but forgot your own true nature, you no longer have a compass, let alone maps, guiding directed growth. The time is now to wake up. <u>You are not your business. But your business is you.</u> Its success depends on who you are being. Your choices come from that space of aliveness and self-awareness. It's critical for your success to identify and fully live out your best self. The relationship to your work is when you've unleashed your maverick mojo you are being in your creative genius. Anything is possible. It's not about the doing or having – it's the being state. Who you were being in the exercise is always available to you. Has it been hidden? Call it out now.

Your life is a celebration. Know who you are. Be who you are. Love who you are. Be inspired by your actions. Inspire and empower others.

ABOUT CORINNE

Corinne Rita has worked with thousands of people on transforming stress into strength, and fear into focused action. She lives her core philosophy that business and life mastery begins with personal transformation and the confident belief that anything is possible.

A true maverick, Corinne is a published author, professional chef, international product designer, private brand and business catalyst, personal coach, motivational speaker and mind/body expert. She is a Phi Beta Kappa scholar with degrees in Psychology and Japanese. From teaching power yoga in Bangkok, to leading private retreat days with global CEOs, Corinne demonstrates you can be, do and have what you want in life.

Corinne privately coaches entrepreneurs and executives on living and leading from their strengths and values. She is the fearless guide for life beyond the comfort zone. She teaches how to maintain the motivation and rock-solid self-esteem required for entrepreneurship. Her clients experience profit with passion. The goal of business is to improve the quality of life while generating revenue.

As a brand and business strategist, Corinne identifies and maximizes core strengths in her clients and their employees to create extraordinary results in business. She designs company cultures of personal leadership, self-development and personal power. Her group retreats and programs teach unshakeable confidence, physical presence, creative visioning and living in the moment as the keys to success in all areas of life.

Connect with Corinne at: CorinneRita.com, TheMaverickCoach.com for private and group coaching, and at: BrazenMaverick.com for personal and professional branding.

CHAPTER 7

THE POWER OF PERSONAL BRANDING TO YOUR MARKET NICHE

BY J.W. DICKS, ESQ. AND LINDSAY DICKS

"Any damn fool can put on a deal, but it takes genius, faith and perseverance to create a brand."

~ David Ogilvy

At a charity auction held on EBay in June of 2011, a frenzied bidding war was made for one particular item. This particular item sold for an incredible $2.35 million the year before. This year, it went for 2.63.

Again, that's 2.63 *million*. So what fetched this incredible price? A ridiculously rare sports car? A private yacht? A solid gold pair of Crocs?

Nope, somebody paid over two and a half million dollars to have *lunch* – with billionaire investor Warren Buffet. A little perspective helps here. At the New York restaurant where the lunch will take place, that much money would buy about 53,000 sirloin steak dinners.

If you want to understand how much power a personal brand can carry, you need look no further than the fact that somebody would pony up seven figures – simply to share a sandwich with someone they saw as the ultimate expert guru in their niche.

You might say that's simply because Buffet is rich beyond belief. But, believe it or not, there are a few other billionaires in the world. You've undoubtedly heard of some of them – but there are also quite a few whose names you wouldn't recognize in a million years, and who certainly wouldn't command that kind of tab for lunch in a public auction.

And that's simply because they haven't created a brand. Of course, being billionaires, they don't really have to care about such things.

But *you* probably should – no matter what business you're in. In this chapter, we're going to talk about why Personal Branding adds value to your business – and motivates your market niche to buy from you.

MAKING YOURSELF MEMORABLE

Before you can even begin to nail down your niche and begin your branding, however, you need to answer one big question…

…Who are you?

We're not looking for your name, address and phone number here. We're looking for two things:

1. What's memorable about your personality?
2. What's your expertise?

We'll start with number one and return briefly to Warren Buffet. What's memorable about his personality is that he comes across as very down-to-earth and uses everyday common sense. His reputation isn't that of a flamboyant show-off who flaunts his wealth. In fact, it's just the opposite – he's a guy who drives his own car and lives in the same house he bought in 1958 in Omaha, Nebraska. In 2011, he was named the third richest person in the world – and yet, when he broke down and finally bought himself a private jet, he named it "The Indefensible," because he felt guilty about the money he was spending on himself.

Now, if you do a 180°, you'll find yourself looking at Donald Trump. Imagine Trump living in the same home he bought 50 years ago. You can't – because Trump is all mansions, luxury condos, extravagant casinos and covering everything that's in them with gold. Everything he does screams "Wealth!" – and yet, his brand is just as effective as Buffet's, even though it's diametrically opposed to it at the same time.

That's because both brands reflect both men's personalities. If one tried to be like the other, it just plain wouldn't work – because nobody would buy it. That's why an effective personal brand has to be authentic. But, let's be clear, there's also a bit of show business involved. We have to believe that both Buffet and Trump work a little overtime at keeping up their respective public images – they know those images work to their benefit and help them in their business dealings.

And that's why we use the word "memorable" when we ask you what your personality is all about. What we're really asking is…how do people remember you? What's the thing they latch onto? Are you always really talkative? Or funny? Or fashionable? Flamboyant? Reserved? When you know how people perceive you and you find the right way to accent that perception in your favor, you've successfully tackled question number one – it's how movie stars make careers. (And why they end up playing the same part over and over – because that's what the public wants to see them do!)

Now, on to question number two. What's your expertise? Meaning… what are you good at? What do you know how to do?

Now, this could be any number of things, but, again, as with your personality, you need to focus on what will make an impact and what you might already be known for. For the moment, it's enough to take inventory and even make a list of those skills.

NAILING DOWN YOUR NICHE

Before you engage in Personal Branding, it's important to nail down what your market niche is going to be – your market niche being the primary group of people you're going to sell to (or to put simplify to the extreme, your customers). Once you decide on what you're going to sell and who you're going to sell it to, the rest begins to fall into place.

Now, let's go back and talk about your particular expertise. The next big question is, what, within those areas of expertise, do you know that other people want to know? And, just as importantly, what do you know that they'd be willing to pay for?

You may be stumped. You may think you don't know anything that's of value to anyone. Dig deeper and you could be surprised.

Say you're an accountant. You may think that you're just another bean counter – how can you create a market niche out of that? Again, dig deeper. Look for a more specific aspect of your business – and a more specific target market – that will match up to create a new and exciting direction for you.

For example, you might have many dentists as clients. And over the years, through working with them, you may have discovered a lot of shortcuts and secrets that help dental practices make more money and save the most on taxes and expenses.

With all that locked away in your brain, you're in a great position to market yourself as an expert in making dental practices super-profit-able. And because you've worked with so many dentists, you already speak their language. Another big advantage of this niche market? Dentists also have the money to hire someone like you – a crucial factor to consider. Let's face it – targeting a niche market like McDonald's workers may only get you a few free Big Macs under the table.

Dentists also have another big niche market benefit – it's a specific profession. The great thing about targeting specific professions is that they're very easy to find and connect with through their professional groups.

You can begin with something as simple as creating a Dentist Financial group on LinkedIn and Facebook, and inviting dentists in other dental groups to join for free advice. By posting blogs, videos and other content that prove you know what you're talking about in these kinds of social media forums, you begin to create interest in who you are and, more importantly, what you can do for them.

A market niche works the best when a group feels as if you know something they don't, that that information will benefit them in a real and substantial way (and *not* necessarily just financially), and that you understand who they are and what their needs are. When your market niche feels as though you are personally and directly talking to them, they respond. That's where your authenticity of personality *and* expertise really comes into play.

POWERING UP YOUR PERSONAL BRANDING

So why do you need Personal Branding if you've narrowed down your niche and you already have something valuable to sell?

Because you'll find that others are also selling the identical thing. Internet marketing is a part of our lives now and everyone does it. The only way you can stand out from the herd is by selling yourself. Not only that, but the old adage, "people buy people," has never been truer or carried more weight. In a crowded marketplace, a trusted and known authority cuts through the clutter like nothing else.

Don't agree? Well, according to a survey done by the international firm of Burson-Marsteller, the Personal Brand of a company's CEO directly influences 95% of investors as to whether they will buy stock in the company. Another study by the University of Pennsylvania shows that when the head of a company's image gains 10% in positive impressions, the company's capitalization will increase on average another 24%.

In other words, the more people like and trust you, the more money will come your way.

Here's a more vivid example of how Personal Branding can really make a business stand out. Recently, the Virgin Atlantic airline celebrated the 25th anniversary of its first flight from London to Miami – and CEO Richard Branson came to South Florida to celebrate.

Branson, known for his flashy, adventurer style, didn't come out in a plain suit and tie to answer questions from the press – no, he arrived at one of South Beach's most exclusive hotels via Cigarette boat with a loudspeaker blaring the theme from "Miami Vice." Wielding a fake gun and handcuffs, he then boarded another speedboat to "arrest" supermodel Karolina Kurkova.

Now, if United or American Airlines ever had a similar public marking of a milestone, you certainly wouldn't see that kind of crazy event – but you also would probably never even know about it, because why would the press or TV news make a big deal out of just another press conference? Branson, with his outrageous antics, gets publicity – and gets more positive press because he makes business a whole lot more fun.

We're, of course, not suggesting you run around with guns and su-permodels, unless that is your lifestyle preference. Richard Branson has earned the "street cred" to get away with such stunts. He's spent decades establishing his credibility, and business acumen, alongside his wild image, so it's expected of him and nobody views it as a negative.

So what's expected of *you* at this point? Well, at the beginning of your outreach to your niche, you need to focus on establishing your author-ity and know-how in your area of expertise.

To go back to our accountant example, if he begins to post in forums designed for dentists and quickly demonstrates he knows nothing about how a dental practice is run, he's through before he actually begins his business. But, because he *does* have the years of experience, that's not going to happen. And he will begin to click with some dentists who want to know what *he* knows. He'll begin to build his all-important fan base by giving them some small useful tips that don't give away too much knowledge but demonstrate he has something genuine to offer.

At the same time, using Personal Branding principles, he also has to give these dentists something to remember him by. Maybe he uses the sign-off, "Creating Tooth Tycoons every day." That's a catchy tag that the dentists will remember much longer than the accountant's name – and it captures his ongoing value to them.

Memorable branding combined with an in-demand service work hand-in-hand to build a fan base that will be the foundation of your business. If our accountant friend does it right, his fan base will boost him and back him as he expands from forum comments and blog posts to estab-lishing his own website for "Tooth Tycoons." Once there, he can offer group coaching services, create a locked paid membership site with exclusive information, and begin to really generate income.

In today's online age, creating the right Personal Brand and choosing the right niche market are crucial to success. And don't worry if the ones you pick are both too specific to start off with – that can be a plus, because you won't be trying to please too many different people at once and it will help you to focus down on your initial business mission. If you're trying to sell too much to too many, your message will be watered down and the impact of your communication will be muted.

As you expand your business, you can also expand your niche market. The Tooth Tycoon can next create Cash for Chiropractors or Podiatrist Profits. The next step should be a natural outgrowth of what you're already doing successfully.

Finally, just remember that your brand and your niche should be an outgrowth of who you are and what you're passionate about. Your potential fan base will sense it if you aren't really engaged in what you're trying to do – and it will ultimately hurt your business, not to mention make you unhappy as you continue to pursue something you don't care about.

Instead, connect with what's authentic about you. And maybe someday, someone will drop a couple million to share a sandwich with you.

ABOUT JW

JW Dicks, Esq. is an attorney, best-selling author, entrepreneur and business agent to top Celebrity Experts. He has spent his entire 39-year career building successful businesses for himself and clients by creating business development and marketing campaigns that have produced sales of over a billion dollars in products and services. His professional versatility gives him a unique insight into his clients' businesses to see untapped opportunities to capitalize on.

He is the Senior Partner of Dicks & Nanton P.A., a unique membership-based, legal and business development consulting firm. JW helps clients position their business and personal brand to take advantage of new vertical income streams they haven't tapped into, and shows them how to use associations, franchises, area-exclusive licensing, coaching programs, info-marketing, and joint ventures to take advantage of them.

In addition to consulting and mentoring clients, JW is also a successful entrepreneur and America's leading expert on personal branding for business development. He is co-founder of the Celebrity Branding Agency, representing clients who want to get major media coverage, marketing and PR, and position themselves as the leading expert in their field. His Best-Selling book, *Celebrity Branding You®!*, is in its third edition and new editions are currently being published for specific industries. He also writes a monthly column for Fast Company Magazine's Expert Blog on personal branding, and has written hundreds of articles, blogs and special reports on the subject.

He is the Best Selling author of 22 business and legal books – including *How to Start a Corporation and Operate in Any State, Celebrity Branding You®!, Power Principles for Success, Moonlight Investing, The Florida Investor, Mutual Fund Investing Strategies, The Small Business Legal Kit, The 100 Best Investments For Your Retirement, Financial CPR, Operation Financial Freedom, Game Changers, How to Buy and Sell Real Estate, Ignite Your Business Transform Your World*, and more.

JW is the editor and publisher of The Celebrity Experts® Insider, delivered to clients in over 15 countries, and provides business development strategies to experts in their field that want to grow their business. He has been called the "Expert to the Experts" and has appeared in USA Today, The Wall Street Journal, Newsweek, Inc. Magazine, The New York Times, Entrepreneur Magazine, and on ABC, NBC, CBS, and FOX television affiliates. Recently, JW was honored with an Emmy nomination as Executive Producer for the film, *Jacob's Turn*.

JW's business address is Orlando, FL and his play address is at his beach house where he spends as much time as he can with Linda, his wife of 39 years, their family, and two Yorkies. His major hobby is fishing, although the fish are rumored to be safe.

ABOUT LINDSAY

Lindsay Dicks helps her clients tell their stories in the online world. Being brought up around a family of marketers, but a product of Generation Y, Lindsay naturally gravitated to the new world of online marketing. Lindsay began freelance writing in 2000 and soon after launched her own PR firm that thrived by offering an in-your-face "Guaranteed PR" that was one of the first of its type in the nation. Lindsay's new media career is centered on her philosophy that "people buy people." Her goal is to help her clients build a relationship with their prospects and customers. Once that relationship is built and they learn to trust them as the expert in their field, then they will do business with them. Lindsay also built a patent-pending process that utilizes social media marketing, content marketing and search engine optimization to create online "buzz" for her clients that helps them to convey their business and personal story. Lindsay's clientele span the entire business map and range from doctors and small business owners to Inc 500 CEOs.

Lindsay is a graduate of the University of Florida. She is the CEO of CelebritySites™, an online marketing company specializing in social media and online personal branding. Lindsay is also a multi-best-selling author including the best-selling book "Power Principles for Success" which she co-authored with Brian Tracy. She was also selected as one of America's PremierExperts™ and has been quoted in Newsweek, the Wall Street Journal, USA Today, Inc Magazine as well as featured on NBC, ABC, and CBS television affiliates speaking on social media, search engine optimization and making more money online. Lindsay was also recently brought on FOX 35 News as their Online Marketing Expert.

Lindsay, a national speaker, has shared the stage with some of the top speakers in the world such as Brian Tracy, Lee Milteer, Ron LeGrand, Arielle Ford, David Bullock, Brian Horn, Peter Shankman and many others. Lindsay was also a Producer on the Emmy-nominated film Jacob's Turn.

You can connect with Lindsay at:

Lindsay@CelebritySites.com
www.twitter.com/LindsayMDicks
www.facebook.com/LindsayDicks

CHAPTER 8

RETHINKING THE OFFICE

BY ALEX WATHEN, ESQ.

INTRODUCTION

S maller organizations are usually the leaders in change. Large organizations are typically less flexible as change usually meets institutional resistance. This chapter discusses how the office is changing from being both the nerve and physical center of a business to being an occasional gathering place.

THE TRADITIONAL OFFICE: HOW WE THINK OF IT.

Before the information age there were still plenty of people who worked outside of the office because of the nature of their job. Sales was typically the area of work where you would travel and be on the road. Organizations that were geographically dispersed with many remote, small locations often had management who traveled a lot. For many people this is still the case. Meetings used to be mostly in person and would often require travel, although teleconferences have been popular for years. If the organization allowed it, you could take papers, paper files, and later computer files home to work on. However, this was usually when you needed to do extra work rather than working from home regularly.

Work has happened outside of the office for centuries. It is not a novelty to work elsewhere, but the office has always been thought of as the center of an organization. It has been where the organization is based;

the center of its activities. When we think of an organization we are probably seeing an image in our minds of the building where it is head-quartered or where the principal office is located. This thinking, while it has always made sense in terms of how to organize our thoughts, is becoming outdated. This chapter proposes a new way of thinking about the office.

GOALS OF THE 21ST CENTURY OFFICE

When it comes to streamlining the traditional office, it is hard to reject ideas that save money. However, there are many other benefits as well. Allowing people to work remotely reduces the need for office space, cuts costs, and reduces energy dependence for the organization. In addition, employees save commuting time, reduce commuting costs (especially with high gas prices), and reduce their stress levels when they are not constantly required to appear at the office. It no longer appears that someone is not working just because they are absent from the office. The whole concept that someone is working merely because they are present between 9:00 a.m. and 5:00 p.m. and presumably not working when they are absent from the office is becoming outdated. While performance has always required more than mere presence, it is the disapproval of absence that is the real curse. Tim Ferriss, in his book "The Four Hour Work Week," describes how he worked 30 minutes a day at one of his prior jobs and had higher sales than those who worked all day; yet he was fired. It is this expectation of presence in the office that must be discarded before any Twenty-first Century office will work.

Besides having a happier and more energetic workforce, many other benefits present compelling reasons for rethinking the office. Employees, free from having to appear at the office, benefit in terms of their leisure. The organization, however, also stands to benefit from people working anywhere. New markets can be served if employees are decentralized. Employees will gain familiarity with new geographic areas or move to their favorite one. Employees who have territories such as managers and sales people can live in their territory and reduce their travel, rather than having to live in proximity of the main office. In turn, clients and customers will also benefit from a more widely dispersed workforce.

THE ROLE OF BRICKS AND MORTAR

Don't think of the office as the nerve center or geographic center of activity in the organization. Think of it only as the legal and official residence of the organization, not the location of its people. We still live in a world where brick and mortar matters. In many businesses you have to have brick and mortar locations or you are not credible. As a bankruptcy attorney I am acutely aware of this bias. I feel compelled to have brick and mortar offices for my firm in order to keep clients and colleagues confident that this is a real law firm. In truth, very little work other than meeting with clients or sorting mail takes place in my brick and mortar offices.

The phones are answered off site and they are answered around the clock. A caller can schedule an "in person" or telephone appointment, receive information, or anything else that can be done over the phone. An in-house 24 hour service such as this is not economical for a small organization, especially in a traditional office. When David Neeleman founded *JetBlue Airways* he pioneered having his reservation agents working from home. This was a first in the airline industry. He had only one-fifth the turnover rate of call center workers and was able to keep high quality people.

It is more and more common that I get hired by clients before I have met them in person. Telephone appointments are increasingly popular because people do not want to fight rush hour traffic or drive across sprawling metropolitan areas when they can meet me by phone. Having a great web presence rich in information, with a personal touch, introduces me to clients before they set up their appointment. Clients often tell me they are ready to proceed because the website explained the initial steps thoroughly. This allows me to focus my time on the important detail-oriented questions clients have for me. That makes all the difference in choosing which course of action to take in a bankruptcy case.

21ST CENTURY OFFICE TYPES

(a) Fully Occupied Office:

We've spoken briefly about brick and mortar offices and while they still have a role in today's society, new office types have emerged. The fully occupied office is similar to a traditional office, but without employees. A fully occupied office is an office where your organization has its own dedicated space and you control the furniture, design, layout, and other physical characteristics. You either own or lease the building or suite, and although it could be shared, it is usually not. Office sharing may be a great way to reduce costs, but it is not a good idea from an internet marketing perspective. If you share the same suite number, local search functions of the major search engines may not properly distinguish you. Even worse, they may not include one of the sharing businesses.

This type of office doesn't require employees since its principal function is to be a meeting place for clients. Typically you would want to schedule select days where you are available for "in office" appointments. Scheduling appointments is done remotely by your staff or a self-service online appointment scheduling system. Other days can be available per your approval. This approach consolidates the scheduling and allows for better use of precious time.

Automattic, the company started by *WordPress* inventor, Matt Mullenweg, has approximately a hundred employees scattered throughout the country while its brick and mortar offices on San Francisco's waterfront have only a handful of employees at most. They even have a virtual water cooler online where employees post about what is happening in their lives and even share baby pictures without the usual fifteen minute shutdown of the whole office and associated loss of productivity that usually occurs at the mention of the phrase "baby pictures".

Referred to as the *Automattic Lounge*, the brick and mortar office serves as a meeting place with decor resembling a sophisticated hybrid of a modern art museum and a college fraternity house. The absence of people, except when having meetings or parties, is the true brilliance of it. *Automattic* functions well by housing its main office in cyberspace and keeping its location a secret.

(b) Executive Suite Virtual Office:

Most large cities have seen a proliferation of executive suites. The greatest benefit to the business owner is the availability of a shared receptionist who can do almost any lawful task for a fee. This system eliminates the obligation of having a full time employee. Conference rooms and offices are available by the hour making this type of location great for a satellite office. This allows you to serve an area where you are growing or have a limited number of "in person" client meetings. The main disadvantage, aside from the lack of environment control, is that the suite number will be shared with a number of other businesses. This can sometimes cause problems with a local search on the internet. These suites are also not very useful for after hours services, however, they can be great for clients who are dropping off signed documents during business hours.

Generally the non-branded, non-chain executive suites offer better deals and will charge less fees for minor additional services. That said, the branded suites often offer a greater list of services. I generally recommend the non-branded suites, but this is a judgment call you will need to make depending on location. Commercial real estate searches on the internet as well as Craigslist will have independent executive suite listings for you to choose from.

Executive suites are generally a creature of large metropolitan areas. Smaller cities under a quarter of a million people rarely have these suites. If you are seeking to expand into smaller communities, approach professional office suites and ask if they would be willing to provide similar services for a fee. Also look for commercial buildings that house a lot of professionals and ask the leasing agents if they would be willing to provide virtual office services. Start with a limited service location in an area you serve until you can find a place with services comparable to an executive suite. In addition, law firms are often eager to rent out their conference rooms by the hour.

Co-working spaces may also be a viable alternative to an executive suite. These locations are less formal and often very casual and artsy, which means a less professional environment. This works better in some businesses versus others. If you serve a community that is more laid back, then these spaces can be a good option. Co-working spaces are usually cooperatively owned. Freelancers, and others who work from home, become members to have a place to meet clients and work with other people on projects. The spaces usually lack receptionists, but they often offer unlimited use for a flat fee. Due to the flexible nature of the membership these spaces sometimes come and go which means you may have to relocate. This could cause you to lose the local internet search capital you have built at that location. In addition to big cities, these spaces are sometimes available in smaller high-tech communities, university towns, or places considered socially progressive.

(c) Limited Service Location:

Bankruptcy courts were the first federal courts to adopt e-filing. However, I am still required to have paper copies with original signatures before I file with the courts. In order to reduce travel time for clients, I have created limited service locations at UPS Stores so they can drop off paperwork. Most UPS Stores will allow you to rent a box for less than twenty dollars per month. Customers can drop off documents or the UPS Store can print them for you if the files are emailed. They will then send you an email letting you know that the documents are signed and dropped off. Other services such as faxing, printing, and mailing the contents of your box are also available. If the client wants a paper form without coming to your office they can print it for them as well. Most UPS Stores are open until 7 p.m. on weekdays and 5 p.m. on Saturdays. My clients appreciate these locations greatly. UPS Store employees tell me that although my firm is not the only business using their locations; my firm is one of the few who fully utilizes their services.

CONCLUSION

Non-brick, non-mortar locations such as your website, virtual phone system, home office, and wherever you travel with your laptop have become the new center of the Twenty-first Century office. If you view working remotely simply as an extension of the office, you are missing the point. You are stuck in that Twentieth Century thinking; that an organization revolves around its physical office. Take off those emerald green glasses. In order to rethink the office you must shed the bias that the center of the office is the physical center of a building. Instead think of an organization as the sum of the contributions of its people regardless of where they may be located.

ABOUT ALEX

Alex Wathen, Esq. helps failing businesses and individuals turn their finances around. He is also a prolific blogger who reports on celebrity bankruptcies and other issues of public importance. He has been featured on CNN, FOX, CBS, and ABC as well as major daily newspapers such as the Houston Chronicle and the Minneapolis Star Tribune. Alex has a bankruptcy blog on FastCompany.com and he is a Top 10 Blogger with the National Bankruptcy Forum. Texas Lawyer Magazine has named him Appellate Lawyer of the Week.

As a business consultant, Alex works primarily on marketing and efficiency of operations. He also helps with public and governmental relations for businesses. Twenty-first century technology is the centerpiece of these strategies. He helps businesses develop their online footprint and dominate the web.

Alex Wathen is a Board Certified Bankruptcy Attorney serving clients throughout the United States. He is based in Texas with offices in Austin, Round Rock, Houston, Dallas, and San Antonio as well as satellite locations in rural and other under-served areas. His Bankruptcy Law practice serves individuals and businesses in bankruptcies under Chapters 7, 11, 12, and 13. He focuses on solving his client's liquidity problems and reorganizing to relieve their financial distress. Alex represents a wide variety of clients. He has distinguished himself by reorganizing construction companies, home builders, retailers, real estate investors, trucking businesses, landlords, and food service businesses. He is also known for representing family farmers in Chapter 12 and by having a nationwide appellate practice before a number of federal appeals courts and the United States Supreme Court.

His notable cases include watershed cases on a utility service in bankruptcy, employment non-discrimination rights of bankruptcy debtors, fighting racial discrimination in jury selection, fighting back against racial profiling, and preventing religious discrimination by the federal government. Alex has the honor of being regularly appointed by federal appellate courts to represent indigent people, *pro bono,* in meritorious civil cases.

Alex, having practiced law since 1998, has been active in bar associations and is a frequent speaker at continuing legal education seminars. He is Board Certified in Consumer Bankruptcy Law by the Texas Board of Legal Specialization where he also serves on the Bankruptcy Exam Commission. Additionally, he is the leading authority on appeals from Texas municipal courts of record.

Alex earned his Juris Doctor degree from the University of Minnesota. He received his Bachelor's degree from the University of Southern California, and his Masters Degree in Information Science from the University of North Texas. He comes from a family of Catholic, Kentucky bourbon makers and some of his relatives still make Wathen's Kentucky Bourbon in Owensboro, Kentucky.

Alex can be reached at: (888) 305-1919 and at: www.abwlaw.com.

CHAPTER 9

THE MORE YOU MAKE, THE MORE YOU CAN MAKE A DIFFERENCE!

BY BARBARA BATT

I f you are a solo-preneur or owner of a small business with under three employees and you:

- Are struggling financially, riding the "income roller-coaster", or having a hard time getting to the next level with your business income
- Often find yourself in a place of worry, fear, or stress
- Feel overwhelmed and never seem to have enough time
- Have trouble making business decisions
- Find it difficult to invest in or benefit from marketing efforts
- Feel like something is missing, or
- Want your business to be in a position to make a bigger difference?

This message is for YOU! You CAN have the business of your dreams and it CAN help you make a difference for others.

How do I know this is possible for you?

Because I did it for myself and I've shown other small business owners how to do it.

After 12 years of owning and operating my own marketing, advertising and design firm, I was still just getting by financially. I was working seven days a week, contemplating shutting the doors and going to work for someone else just to feel some relief. While I loved many aspects of my business, I felt stuck – never really being able to break the glass ceiling and soar.

From the outside looking in, my business appeared quite successful. It had surpassed that deadly five-year mark where most small businesses fail and we were extremely busy. However, I kept wondering when the day would come when I would finally have the financial freedom that I'd felt should come with owning my own business. Interestingly enough, many of my small business clients were experiencing many of the same struggles.

Have you ever wondered just how many years you have to "pay your dues" before you can have that dream business that sustains you rather than depletes you? Well, stop wondering and keep reading because I've discovered a proven formula for helping solo-preneurs and small business owners make more money, create more time and enjoy more fulfillment through their small business operations.

TIME FOR CHANGE

Change the way you look at things, and the things you look at change.
~ Dr. Wayne Dyer

In 2005 I decided to hire a business coach to help me get my business on the fast-track to success. Long story short, 6 months later, my business was in worse shape than it was before I hired the coach. I was in survival mode. It really seemed that closing the doors was the best option. But I just couldn't do it.

Then in October 2006, I started reading authors like Wayne Dyer, Eckhart Tolle, Jon Kabat-Zinn and others. A recurring theme appeared: Our thoughts create our reality. These authors were suggesting that all you needed to change your reality was to change your thoughts. While it seemed a simplistic notion, I decided to give it a try. I didn't know it at the time, but my business and I would be completely transformed by this decision.

While the concept was simple, implementing it was anything but! I spent the next two years avidly studying, so I could develop the discipline necessary to change the deeply ingrained thought patterns that were sabotaging my efforts at success and abundance.

Almost like magic, things started to change in me and my business. In 2008, when many small businesses were perishing or showing dramatic revenue decreases, my business experienced a whopping 40% increase in revenues. Not only that, but I wasn't spending time in worry mode any longer and the sense of being overwhelmed that was once prevalent in my business operations had greatly diminished. This stuff was really working!

I found myself completely absorbed by this idea that our thoughts are directly linked to our business success. So much so that I began performing little secret experiments with some of my clients who were experiencing thoughts of fear, stress, worry and doubt about their businesses. Those that actually took my advice would call me in amazement, exclaiming how things were improving or how they felt good for the first time in years. Now I was hooked! I began the process of putting together a clear formula that would help small business owners achieve the success, peace and abundance that they desired – much more quickly than I had been able to do on my own.

THE BOTTOM LINE . . .

Your thoughts color your decisions which create your business.™

The simple (but not easy!) act of changing your thoughts has more impact on your business than marketing, operations, social media, search engine optimization, or anything else. Until you prepare your mind for success, you'll continue to struggle to "make it."

Consider this example:

A husband and wife team owns a small business in the home improvement industry. After ten years in business, they were putting their home up as collateral against all of the debt they'd accumulated. During those ten years, they'd entertained thoughts like, "What if this business fails and we lose everything?" It was this kind of scarcity thinking that drove them to take projects that weren't profitable so they'd have money in their bank account short-term. Which may have calmed their fears temporarily, but wreaked havoc with their bank account once the jobs were finished and the bills came rolling in. Over and over they thought, "We don't have enough money," so they decided to take every job that came along for the cash flow and created a situation where they didn't have enough money and could potentially lose everything.

Their thoughts colored their decisions which created their failing business. They'd created exactly what they feared most because those were the thoughts they focused on. Simple as that.

Once we got to work creating new, empowering thought patterns, their actions changed accordingly and their business started seeing some remarkable results. More time, more profits, more smiles and more to come!

The program I developed focused on the number one thing keeping me and all these other business owners from realizing their dreams for their businesses—our thoughts. What I saw over and over again in these struggling business owners was the same thought patterns of fear, worry, overwhelm, stress, and doubt. NONE of these thought patterns leads to success. Many business owners will argue that stress is necessary for success or that worry is a motivator. While there may be some shred of truth there (I don't think so personally), you will find it very difficult to experience a sense of fulfillment if you struggle, stress and worry your way to the top. That's a strategy built on suffering and I'm guessing that's definitely not what you signed up for when you started your business. Owning and operating a business is supposed to be your ticket to freedom, not suffering!

YOUR ABUNDANT SMALL BUSINESS

In my seventeen years of experience working with small business owners, I can say with confidence that the number one biggest worry amongst small business owners is money. While the purpose of your business is to make money, there is often a negative connotation around making money that affects many small business owners. So for those of you who might feel like making money doing what you love to do is somehow "bad" or "wrong", here's a new thought for you—The more you make, the more you can make a difference—for yourself, your family, your customers, your employees and your community. When your business becomes a conduit for abundance, <u>everyone</u> benefits.

By "abundance" I mean abundant wealth (no more worrying about money, feeling overwhelmed because you're doing everything in an effort to save money and skimping on your marketing and other business decisions that will make you more abundant), abundant health (no more working 60, 70, or 80+ hours a week, neglecting your physical well-being and skipping rejuvenating vacations), abundant connections (no more playing the wall-flower at networking events, worrying about what others are thinking about you or being afraid of being taken advantage of) and abundant happiness (well, you have an idea of what this might look like).

It's time to stop thinking that making money is bad or that your business can't make a 6- or 7-figure income, and come to realize that you can create as much abundant health, wealth, connections and happiness through your small business as you'd like. How else will you possibly be able to make a difference in your life and in the world?

The only thing keeping your business from creating the abundance that you desire is you. It's not the economy, your employees, the competition or anything else that you attribute it to. You hold the key to your freedom and once you realize this and change your thoughts, you'll open the door to the success that has always seemed to elude you.

If you don't enjoy abundant health, wealth, connections and happiness in your business **right now**, it's time to change.

SMALL BUSINESS - BIG INTENTIONS

Small business isn't analogous to small results, small income, small fulfillment, and it certainly doesn't mean playing small. In fact, there are solo-preneurs out there making 7-figures and "living the life" that most business owners only dream of. The size of your business clearly isn't a reflection on your ability to create abundance.

Adopting big, revolutionary intentions will help propel you toward the success you desire, so don't let the size of your business determine the size of your intentions. Think big and play big and you'll reap big rewards.

This isn't to suggest that there won't be challenges in your business operations, as there most certainly will be. It's how you think about the challenges and how badly you want to fulfill your intentions that will make all the difference in your business success.

Don't misunderstand, this definitely is NOT a Pollyanna, feel-good, bury-your-head–in-the-sand approach. I've seen business owners transform from depressed hopelessness to motivated action with increased profits – just because they changed their thoughts and then acted in new ways based on those thoughts. It's not wishful thinking. It's empowerment and action, and **it works**.

THREE KEY CONSIDERATIONS FOR CREATING YOUR ABUNDANT SMALL BUSINESS

1. Cultivate your revolutionary thinking habits.

- Become aware of your thoughts. If your thoughts don't support your abundance intentions, you'll continue to feel stuck. Once you become aware, you can consciously shift your thoughts so that you can come to a place of solution. Download my free Thought Journal and get more tips on revolutionary thinking in the "Free Stuff" section of my website.
- Remember: worry doesn't improve your bank balance.
- Read or listen to something inspiring for at least 15 minutes every day. See the resources section of my website for ideas.
- Confidence is key. Stop caring about what others are thinking about you and make your own opinion the one that matters.
- Revolutionary business owners invest in education and marketing. Make sure that any programs you invest in are backed by a guarantee. Consider hiring a mentor to help you fast-track your progress and remember that marketing is key to business success. If you aren't willing to invest in yourself and your business, customers aren't likely to invest either.

2. Take ACTION! Many small business owners struggle with procrastination, overwhelm, lack of time and other issues that they know they
need to change in order to be more successful, but they just can't do
it for some reason. How many times have you read books just like
this one only to feel a short-lived burst of inspiration and then go
back to doing things the same old way, with the same old results?
You can read all the books available on successful business practices, winning systems, and even revolutionary thinking, but until
you actually make the recommended changes, nothing happens (or
the same stuff keeps happening). If you are stuck, it's time to "crack
the code" and gain an understanding about what is keeping you from
making the changes you so desperately want to make, but can't for
some mysterious reason. Find more about how to go from stuck to
motivated action in the resources section of my website.

3. Always be of service. Your business, no matter what it is, exists only
because it serves the needs of others in some way. By focusing on
those you serve, you begin the revolutionary thinking process. And
remember, revolutionary business owners think beyond their own
bank account, and include 'sharing their abundance' with those in
need, in their intentions. Once you think in terms of serving others,
you inspire yourself to do what you need to do to succeed.

For more tips and resources to help you make more money in your small
business, please visit my website at: www.BarbaraBatt.com.

ABOUT BARBARA

Barbara Batt is a small business mentor, a respected expert in small business marketing, accomplished graphic designer, author and motivational speaker. Barbara is the owner and founder of U Creative Group™ and most recently launched a new initiative at www.BarbaraBatt.com that promotes a vibrant new vision for American business, where scarcity and competition—which formed the old engine of prosperity—are replaced with a much more efficient and powerful catalyst: a fusion of abundance mentality, cooperation and compassion. Barbara is dedicated to helping solo entrepreneurs and small business owners break through the barriers that keep them playing small, so that they can fulfill their responsibility of creating abundance for themselves and their stakeholders. Connecting these revolutionary business owners and empowering them to make a difference is Barbara's ultimate goal.

To learn more about Barbara Batt and how you can receive the free action guide "Small Business Owners: How to Turn Your Business Around in 90 Days," visit: www.BarbaraBatt.com.

CHAPTER 10

HE WAS PARALYZED AND NOW HE STANDS

BY DR. JILL HOWE, D.C.

HOW COULD THIS HAVE HAPPENED TO ME?

Since I was five, I've always wanted to be a doctor, but it wasn't until a conversation with my mother that I was convinced that if I didn't try, I'd be spending the next forty years working in a career I didn't love. I've been in practice now for twenty years and I'm certain I made the right decision!

When I first considered a career as a physician it was through the eyes of a young child, and a doctor was one of the smartest, most compassionate people I knew; they always made you feel better. As I entered college, the enormity of the undertaking I was considering had me convinced there was no way I could successfully complete the task of medical school. Thank goodness for my mom and her confidence in me!

I graduated with the degree Doctor of Chiropractic, December 1, 1991 and I have never been the same since. My vision of healthcare was based on my upbringing as a generally healthy child from a healthy family. We were never in the hospital or severely ill.

I wanted to put my degree to work and help those people who had the same viewpoint about health that I did. I soon learned that my viewpoint was rare on this planet.

During a particular biology lecture in undergrad, before deciding that I wanted to become a Chiropractic Physician, the specialty of heart surgery interested me. During that fateful lesson on a topic with which I was already familiar, I asked the person next to me what her career path was and she told me about Chiropractic, I was hooked. I realized that I could help patients regain their health before their life was literally in my hands.

Nineteen years after graduating and having established a large multidisciplinary physical medicine and rehabilitation practice, I met Pete. Pete was a fifty-something man who had been in a wheelchair for the last twelve years following a spontaneous paralysis. He was a mail carrier who had hit his head on the overhang of a house one day during his route. He never thought twice about the accident, but a few days later, he woke up paralyzed.

Pete and his family had been to his primary doctor, the Mayo Clinic and every other spinal center available to them to try and get an answer and a solution for their beloved husband and father. To date, their search had been fruitless, and Pete was so weak that he could hardly hold his upper body upright in his wheel chair.

During my first meeting with Pete and his wife, he remarked that he had back pain and that he was pretty resolved to being in the wheelchair the rest of his life. Pete had a good attitude and said he'd love to have any improvement possible with his mobility and strength. A specialized exam revealed several areas of ligament damage and subsequent shifting of his cervical (neck) vertebrae causing pressure on his spinal cord in his neck. His lower back was not without its own degenerative changes and ligament damage as well. Pete stated that no clinic he'd ever gone to examined his neck, and he was very surprised and happy to know that there were other contributing factors to this decade-long paralysis.

Pete's recovery consisted of spinal rehabilitation, spinal decompression therapy, specialized Chiropractic adjustments, as well as natural medical intervention designed to heal those injured ligaments and restore the normal posture of the spinal column which houses the nervous system. Pete was also tested for food allergies and was determined to have a significant problem with both yeast and wheat. The revelation of his food intolerances didn't go over well with him. When you've lost the use of your legs and have to struggle to move any part of your body, your choice of hobbies is significantly limited. Pete made his own beer and was now faced with the choice of trusting me and losing yet another part of his already restricted life or hanging on to something that may be holding him back from recovery.

The day after the results of the allergy test were given to him, Pete came in for his appointment and begrudgingly informed me that he didn't like me anymore and that he'd decided to follow the "stupid diet". Two months and many therapy sessions (both at the clinic and working at his home) after his decision to change his diet, Pete could STAND ON HIS OWN for the first time in twelve years!

In my wildest dreams I never imagined the power of this type of medicine. It was most intriguing for me as a doctor to help a patient go from scared and confused to empowered and healthy, and I'm convinced that this clinic is the model for the Wellness Center of the future. Traditional allopathic medical doctors (MDs) have perfected surgical and chemical intervention while Doctors of Chiropractic (DCs) rely on their knowledge of the nervous system and how it controls every function of the body.

When a patient presents to our clinic, we not only have to be spot on with our Orthopedic (joint), Neurological (nervous system) and Physiological examinations (how the chemicals of the body control bodily functions, where they're made and how they're dispensed throughout the body), but also with the Pharmacological (medications) aspects of our patients' health. While a DC doesn't dispense medication, we must have a strong working knowledge of how the medication affects the body – both positively and negatively – as this helps us understand the nutritional needs of the patient.

As a DC, I have the best of both worlds. The care we provide in our clinic doesn't have any side effects and we get to help patients improve their health while empowering them to lead a healthier and longer life after they are returned to optimal function. We have many families in our clinic who truly realize the value of not only handling their health problems, but also those of their children. These patients entrust their friends, coworkers and families to us in order to help them with a health concern or to prevent one from manifesting.

Twenty years of practicing has allowed me to come up with a system for reproducing this model of our wellness center anywhere and in any financial climate. Anyone who is credentialed to own a medical clinic needs the following things:

1. Thick skin and a willingness to do whatever it takes to create this practice of the future.

2. A systematic approach to running the practice. We have business consultants who train our staff and its owners on procedures and the never-ending paperwork that goes along with health care.

3. The passion to go out and speak to the people of your community so that they can be informed about the alternatives for treating their health problems. One of my favorite functions as the Director of the clinic is to lecture to the public about health problems we successfully treat in our clinic. When the audience members have a realization about a point you're making, it's visible on their faces; you can see they have hope for the first time.

4. Knowledge of what other healthcare practitioners do for the problems you treat in your clinic so you can inform the patients of their options.

5. Know that, as much as you want to, you can't help everyone who walks through your doors. This is probably the hardest lesson for a doctor to learn, but it will cost you immense time and resources that could be more productively utilized to help the 98% of people who can actually benefit from and want your help. The only patient any doctor can help is the one that believes they can be helped, one who is willing to follow the recommendations laid out to ensure a successful outcome. It is very human to want to help the person who presents with the stories that tug at your heartstrings, but those patients have to commit to being a part of their solution or they will remain their biggest obstacle.

6. Being an exceptional clinician means finding a way to let the public know what you do and how well you do it. This is one of the most important ingredients for any business to succeed – Marketing and Public Relations. I'm lucky that my husband is a rock star at this and it comes as naturally to him as medicine does to me. PR should not come off as a self-promotional tool when you're doing it. The public has certain topics that interest them and this tells a good PR person what you should communicate in workshops. People come to presentations to find out what your clinic is about and to feel you out as a doctor; outright bragging isn't interesting to anyone. It's your job when you're wearing this hat to teach (from the origin of Physician); the number of people who arrive in your clinic to be helped determines your grade.

7. It is imperative that you hire and train the best support staff possible as this is the only way for you to excel at your job. Each person in the clinic has his or her own area of expertise. No matter how good you might be at that job, you're the only one who can run the clinic. Train them to do each procedure as you would. Writing up a hat (post or job responsibilities) is a way to ensure that the pertinent information regarding that post is recorded and not left to any one person's interpretation of what's needed or wanted – to successfully inhabit that post. Once you write up all the hats in the clinic, you can easily duplicate this type of practice and ensure that natural healthcare is systematized and has predictable outcomes.

8. The importance of this last point cannot be emphasized enough – the treatment of patients is called "practice" for a reason. Medical breakthroughs happen on a daily basis and from the most unique sources. Through the use of the Internet, patients are most likely doing just as much research as you are. It is paramount in any successful practice that the staff constantly undergoes training in the newest cutting-edge treatments. We train weekly for 2-4 hours on just that – perfecting and expanding our arsenal of therapeutic protocols to restore the human body back to its *factory settings*.

Twenty-eight years after that conversation with my mother in the kitchen, I have completed medical school, been trained by amazing doctors who were ahead of their time and profession fifteen years ago, and married an incredible man who not only had the same vision I did, but the skills to help us accomplish the evolution of the future of medical care as we know it. I'm surrounded by a well-trained, caring and highly motivated staff that assists me in accomplishing a dream I've had for forty years. My family has been beside us this entire time (sometimes actually working in the clinic) and I'm grateful for every patient I've had the pleasure of meeting. I'm proud of this profession and the consultants who have spearheaded new protocols in medicine and the treatment of the human body.

I'm truly grateful to everyone who has helped me with my success and if this information can help another person achieve their career goals, I will feel privileged to have been a part of that success.

The best is yet to come!

ABOUT JILL

Dr. Jill Howe, D.C. has been in practice in Illinois for 20 years. She is an expert in treating chronic health problems such as Fibromyalgia, Neuropathy and Disc Problems. Her health & wellness center is in the top 2% of highest-producing Chiropractic/ Wellness clinics in the country. Much of this success she attributes to the continual addition of new technologies and treatments in her clinic. She utilizes numerous 'state of the art' treatment modalities such as Spinal Rehabilitation Therapy, Decompression, Vibrational Therapy and Medically Integrated Services to handle the real cause of a patient's health problem.

Dr. Howe also works to educate her peers by speaking at National Chiropractic Conventions and frequently participates in ongoing educational seminars.

Giving back to the community is important to Dr. Howe as well. She lectures pro bono at various Park Districts, Book Stores, Police/Fire Departments and Local Fairs to help educate as many people as possible. Dr. Howe is committed to helping her patients eliminate their health problem without the use of drugs or surgery. She believes that while educating her patients about the function and means by which the body breaks down or malfunctions, she can help to create a healthier community.

Born in Illinois, Dr. Howe earned a B.S. in Human Biology as well as a Doctor of Chiropractic from National College of Chiropractic in 1991. She and her husband Larry live in the northwest suburbs of Chicago and are avid dog lovers.

CHAPTER 11

GROWING INTO YOUR OWN FUTURE BEST

BY OZZIE JUROCK

S uccess – by its very nature – is unnatural, achieved by the minority of people, the upper 10%. People that set actual new trends are an even smaller percentage. But we do not have to have an earth-shaking widget/idea to be a *trendsetter*. What we do need to do is be different, lift ourselves out of the crowd and be unique in our own business, in our own area – in our own way. The former Dean of Disney University, **Mike Vance**, said that: *"Innovation is the creation of the new or the re-arranging of the old in a new way."* And he is right. Very rarely do we find something brand new – never seen before. If you do, great, if not…what, in your current business, could you re-arrange in a new way?

I make many speeches (nothing so sweet as the sound of my own voice) and thus spend time in hotels. I noticed one day that my shower curtain rod had been 're-arranged'. It had a decidedly large bend in it, giving me much more room. So what? You say? Well, whoever thought of it… the new curtain rod was "rearranging the old in a new way." The guy who makes curtain rods set a 'trend' in his existing business – curtain rods. I am certain he/she will make a fortune.

In the book *The Plagiarist* by Benjamin Cheever, an advertising executive increased the sales of his client's shampoo. He added the word "repeat" after…'lather, rinse.' Sales soared. Peek at your shampoo bottle next time you are in the shower! You have been trained to 'repeat.' So, take a good, hard look at what you are doing and see where you could improve it. All go-getters are similar. We are entrepreneurs, we want to be on our own, we want to get rid of 'the man' and we throw ourselves into OUR own business with gusto.

We take courses and we are told the clichés:

- You should spend money on classified advertising.
  Does not work.
- You should work on your business, not in your business. Does not work. Maybe when you are a much larger company. And even there...what is Apple without Steve Jobs? Clearly, in the beginning stages of a new business YOU are the business. Not to work in it – is nonsense advice.
- You should 'empower your employees' and let them do what they want. Hogwash. Interesting how many of the 'empowered companies' that we were told to emulate are now broke.
  People do not do what you expect them to do; they do what you inspect...with respect.

Then of course, there is the goal setting exercise and the written business plan. Actually I am here to tell you that North American office drawers are graveyards for finely written – but not acted upon – plans. Do not write down one single goal until you, naked and alone, swear to the universe that whatever that goal is that you wrote down – you WILL do it. The moment you do not do just one of the things you said you would do – your business plan is a waste of time. Throw it away.

We do all that we are told – yet, somehow the new business isn't working as we had hoped. We work longer hours and have more stress. Maybe I am old school, but remember why you went into business in the first place? You thought you could do things better, you had some innovative ideas and if you committed yourself to those new ideas and worked hard you'd make it. And you were right. YOU are the key. YOU...are the trend! YOU are the trendsetter. It is the people that take action, that lift themselves out of the crowd that are in that elusive 10% of successful entrepreneurs. You are here now and can grow into that new best self...the future best YOU. I find that I live a charmed life. I have learned to grow into my future best – always. There is me today and then now at age 67 there are at least another 20 'future best' Ozzies out there.

When I came to Canada, I had little education; I spoke and wrote no English (some say I still don't). I never made a speech in public. I had no car and no money, but I knew that I wanted something else. I signed up as a busboy at the Hotel Vancouver in 1968 and via owning a fish n'chips restaurant, 18 years later I grew into running the largest non-franchise real estate company in the world as president. I led 10,000 employees (7,000 in sales), our gross revenues were over $500 million and we managed to keep over $45 million of it on the bottom line. After I left the big corporation, I grew into a number of *"future bests"*. I started an Internet franchise company, a sign making company. I even ran a construction management company in Taiwan, started offices in Tokyo and Hong Kong. Today, I still run very successful real estate conferences (never less than 700 attendees). Our real estate investment club has 300 members and I still run and write a very successful real estate newsletter with thousands of subscribers. On the way here, I also wrote 4 books.

Whatever I did, I tried to make myself into the best I could be at that stage in my life.

I lifted my head up out of the crowd. I wasn't just a busboy, I was a superb busboy. I came earlier and left later, I studied making better coffee and waiters wanted me assigned to them. Being noticed, I became a waiter and people waited a long time just to sit in my station, because I always had a joke and an 'Ozzie special'. When 2 years later, I was the Maître d'hôtel, I was one of the best Maître d'hôtel's the Hotel Vancouver had ever seen, because I remembered every name (also every large tip!) and introduced serving the first live lobster into a restaurant in Vancouver. Afterwards, when I ran my Fish n' Chips restaurant I always gave an extra piece of fish and grew from selling 150 pounds of fish per weekend to 1,500 pounds. (You have no idea how much fish that is!) When I went into real estate sales, branch management, regional sales and eventually became president, I tried to be the best in each one of those fields.

And when I wasn't yet the best, I made myself tapes and listened to them until I believed I could be and would be and was the best. **You**

see, the price of success is belief. You must believe that there is a better self out there. You can be yourself, but you have to be **your best self.** It is only that best self that others want to touch, see and follow. I know and believe in the marrow of my bones that **everything is possible!** Really, if I could do it, so can anyone else. We all talk about the 80/20 principle. 20% of the people earn 80% of the money. It is a proven, absolutely crystal clear principle. We see it in every industry. We all know it, we quote it and then we still spend 80% of our time with the time wasters and losers. We buy the platitudes: *'The customer is always right.'* No, he isn't and you know it to be true! Some customers need to be 'liberated' to go and annoy other businesses. When you review all of your customers, I guarantee you will find that 20% give you most of your business. You also will find to your great surprise that you spend hardly any time with them. Why do we believe that every customer – even some friends – have the same value, that every hour of the day we spend is equal, that every phone call, every email must be returned instantly with the same vigor.

I would bet that most self-employed people know all of the above instinctively, we understand it all. But we don't realize that **understanding means nothing**. It doesn't! Understanding things is not our problem. Don't we all go see a Tony Robbins or a Mike Vance and we are lifted out of our seats, we take furious notes, we understand clearly the wisdom that is spoken to us, it runs through our veins. And then, 3 weeks later, we open our bureau drawer and find all the notes we took but have not acted on. **Life is all in the DOING,** not just understanding. All the goals and business plans mean nothing until you hold yourself accountable and do something. Winners do not have wings or bigger feet than the losers. Losers understand exactly what to do…the difference is that **winners DO it.** They do that little extra, they create their own trend. You see that great smiling guy or gal behind a hotel desk, or at McDonalds – instinctively you are drawn to that person. He or she is setting the personal trend for themselves. Always do a little more, always go another mile, always be upbeat. We are drawn to the positive but wallow in the negative. And **we attract whatever we focus on**. Good or bad. Birds of a feather flock together, conversely people with money problems are always drawn to other people with money problems.

When I was a busboy, if somebody would have told me that I would run a construction management company in Taiwan…I would have not believed it. I was not ready then… but I did grow into that future best Ozzie just the same. Why? I was upbeat. I gave more, **I kept learning**, I believed that there is a future best Ozzie out there. I firmly believe that whatever you want out of life… the universe is ready to give to you. But you need to have clarity. In today's confusing world everyone is befuddled…you need to be clear, what business you are in, why you are better, what your service call is…and why you absolutely love it. It has to ooze from your pores. If it doesn't …go do something else.

Don't buy the idea that life is somehow limited and your goals have to be realistic. Hogwash. Realistic goals do not drive you. Dream big. Then set goals toward achieving that big goal, but don't fool yourself. To be that trendsetter, to make those extra millions requires a different set of actions than the ones that got you this far.

LIFT YOURSELF OUT OF THE CROWD. Let's face it, most of us in business have a lot of stuff in our head. We have forgotten more than a new person will learn in the next ten years. So use it, but be clear in what you want…the universe wants clarity from us. People buy people they understand. Whether it is adding that 'piece of fish', making speeches about your business, getting on a radio show, writing a newspaper article, start by doing something.

- Where in your business are you better now?
- Where could you be better?
- Where could you 're-arrange the old in a new way'?
- What do people that are better than you do now?

Learn it, study it and ask…where could I become the trend in my industry?

Become the local expert. If nothing else, your classified ads will work better….but over time, you WILL become the trend in YOUR local area.

- Don't think that you could speak in public? Join Toastmasters. Speak at Rotary Clubs. They are very forgiving… there are hundreds of them.

- Learn to write and send one of your business stories. (You have them in your brochures, your industry manuals) to local editors (every local paper needs input) but keep them from being too self-serving.

- Keep sending them. Constant spaced repetition. There will be a time when they have sold more ads than before and they are looking for 'filler'…and there is your story.

- Take a reporter/ editor for coffee…lunch. They eat lunch. Ask them what they are interested in.

- Get into the yearbook of experts. When reporters look for sources, they have a source directory. Get in your national and local ones.

- Join **askanexpert** sites…a lot of them are free.

- Call the **local radio show** hosts and get on as a guest. Radio shows need good local experts. I got on one of the best business shows in Canada, by sending ideas to the host for over a year.

- Get **mentors** but only if they are a lot smarter and have more proven success than you…and if they are accessible. Who cares if you admire them from afar?

- Get into '**Who's Who**'. How do you get in? Everyone does…it is a business! And it is free. It will help in your advertising.

- If you have no credentials, create an **advisory board** (not a Board of directors)… try and get a local alderman or another local business man/ hockey coach to join. Looks good on your letterhead.

- **Challenge all your memberships**…if you don't get any new business…at least you can practice your speeches.

- Is **social media** getting you in front of people that can say yes or no to a buying or selling decision of your product or service? If so, great. If not, don't waste too much time there.

- Use www.linkedin.com for business versus the more personal www.facebook.com

- Learn to advertise regularly in www.craigslist and www.kijiji.ca. It's free, but it must be used regularly.

- Forget spending tons of money advertising…**Promote YOU**… you are the trend. Personal promotion is where it is at and it is mostly free.

- Don't buy advertising calendars, don't advertise on pens, etc. But send Chinese New Year's cards, or Fourth of July cards, 2 foot Christmas cards, be different – don't follow the crowd!

E-mail me at oz@jurock.com and I will send you a free CD (postage you pay) – '**17 success secrets of top producers.**'

Finally, remember that **YOU are your greatest asset**. Look to where you can be unique, where you can become the trend. Always be upbeat and **don't share your doubts**. Put the word **CLARITY** on your sun visor. Look for your quirky side. My *'Salmon Wellington'* recipe is in the *'Chicken Soup for the Soul'* cookbook. My motivational card set *"Grow Into Your Future Best"* is a bestseller. **But most importantly, take more time off**! For the last 15 years I take 2 months off in the summer on my boat the "Proper Tee"…and ski 2 months in the winter.

*Most of the good ideas in our lives come from having the time to think about **growing into our own future best.***

ABOUT OZZIE

Ozzie Jurock (<u>FRI</u>) is the author of *Forget About Location, Location, Location, What, When, Where, and How to Buy Real Estate in Canada*. and *The Real Estate Action Book*. Ozzie Jurock is also president of <u>**Jurock Publishing Ltd**</u>.

- Ozzie is the only Canadian real estate advisor featured in **Donald Trump**'s new book: <u>***Trump: The Best Real Estate Advice I Ever Received: 100 Top Experts Share Their Strategies***</u>

- **Best selling Canadian author Peter C. Newman** in his book *Titans* called him a **Real Estate Guru**

- *Vancouver* **Magazine** called him one of the 45 brightest people in Vancouver

- Ozzie Jurock appears every 2nd Wednesday on the <u>**Global TV Newshour**</u>. See him on http://www.youtube.com/jurockvideo

- He currently writes for the Vancouver Province, Westcoast Homes & Design and he has also written hundreds of published real estate articles in *The Vancouver Sun*, *Business in Vancouver*, *The Calgary Herald*, *The Edmonton Journal*, the *Globe and Mail*, the *Western Investor* and dozens magazines. Several thousand people have subscribed to his monthly and weekly newsletters <u>Jurock Real Estate Insider</u> and <u>Jurock's Facts by E-mail</u>.

Mark Victor Hansen, co-author of *Chicken Soup for the Soul* says:

"Ozzie is one of the wisest money men alive. I love listening to and reading him and so will you. Drink deeply of his wisdom, insights, advice and you'll permanently prosper."

- Ozzie Jurock served in the past as:

- *President of Royal LePage (Res.) in charge of over 7000 salespeople, CANADA*

- *President Royal Lepage Asia based (Taiwan, HongKong and Tokyo). TAIWAN*

- *President of DATUM Real Estate Management Services, TAIWAN*

- *Chairman of NRS Block Bros., CANADA, USA*

- *President of Red Carpet Real Estate, USA*

- *President of ProPhase Inc. Data Corporation, CANADA*

- *President of Signs Now, CANADA*

- *President of FeatureWeb, CANADA*

- *President of Jurock International Net, CANADA*

- *He has served on the boards of the **BC Real Estate Council**, the **Vancouver Real Estate Board**, the **UBC Real Estate Research Bureau** and the **Quality Council of BC** among others*

- *His busy life found him elected **president** of the **Canada Taiwan Trade Association**, serve as a **judge** for the **Ernst & Young Entrepreneur of the Year** award, (also he was a judge at several Real Estate Board building awards) and still finds time to make over 80 speeches a year*

Ozzie Jurock is known as one of Canada's **leading business motivators** and his investor outlook conferences attract audiences of over 700 attendees every time.

Ozzie's mission:

"I want to create environments where people can grow into their own future best"

He and his wife, Jo currently live in Vancouver, Canada.

Ozzie's official home page, social networking profiles and other sites:

OzzieJurock.com	*- Official Home Page*
Jurock.com	*- Real Estate Marketplace*
RealEstateTalks.com	*- Canada's largest Real Estate Bulletin Board*
Reag.ca	*- Real Estate Action Group*
CommitPerformMeasure.com into action	- Thought Starter Cards designed to motivate us
BCRED.ca	- British Columbia's Real Estate Professional Directory
Askanexpert.ca questions.	- Find real estate oriented experts and ask your
Twitter.com/77ozzie	- Follow Ozzie
Youtube.com/jurockvideo	- Latest videos
Facebook.com	- Social network
Linkedin.com/in/77ozzie	- Network of experienced professionals

CHAPTER 12

I WILL MAKE A DIFFERENCE

BY GARY MARTIN HAYS, ESQ.

"One person can make a difference, and every person must try."
~ John F. Kennedy

(...from a speech to a group of students at the University of Michigan
on September 22, 1960 as he was campaigning as a candidate for
President of the United States.)

Within a span of 64 days in 2008, three young women from Georgia or with ties to the state were abducted and murdered. On January 1, 2008, Meredith Emerson was hiking on Blood Mountain in North Georgia with her dog, Ella, when she was abducted, held captive for several days, and then murdered. On March 4th, it was Lauren Burk, from Marietta, Georgia who was a freshman at Auburn University in Auburn, Alabama. While walking across a dorm parking lot, she was forced into her car at gunpoint and later shot and killed. Within hours of Burk's abduction, Eve Carson, from Athens, Georgia, was at her home in Chapel Hill, North Carolina where she was attending the University of North Carolina. She was studying when two men broke into the house and took her at gunpoint. A couple of hours later, she was murdered.

These were three very special young women whose lives were violently cut short. Their murders haunted me as my wife and I have three young daughters. It made me question if I was doing everything possible to make them safe in this world. As parents, we would love to put protective headgear and safety bubble wrap on our children every time they walk out the door. We wish we could be with them 24/7 to make sure no harm ever comes to them. But we can't.

Crime occurs every day in all communities. It does not discriminate based on sex, race, or socio-economic status. We see it in pretty graphic detail when we turn on the television. We read about it when we pick up the newspaper and we hear about it when we turn on the radio. If our kids walk into the room, we quickly reach for the remote to change the channel and hope and pray they did not hear or see the violence. Your child asks you why you changed the channel and you simply respond that you wanted to see what else was on TV.

We know crime exists. But when it comes to our family – to our children – we never like to consider the possibility that something could happen to them. Is ignoring the problem really going to protect you and your family? Do you still think the world hasn't changed since you were a kid? Remember those days? Our parents would leave the doors unlocked at night and the windows open to allow the fresh air to gently blow through the home. This was a time when no one would have considered installing an alarm in their own home. We didn't know about mace or tasers or carjackings. The bicycle was our method of transportation, as we would ride it most anywhere at any time and never think twice about it.

Times have changed . . .

There is nothing like the innocence of a child. They think the world is a beautiful place. Why would anyone want to hurt anyone else – especially them? As parents, we always have concerns for their safety and well-being. But we don't want to alarm them or over-react, nor destroy their innocence or paralyze them with fear.

So we revert back to denying the problem exists. It could never happen to my family or me. Things like this always happen to someone else. "I know how to be safe", and we re-assure ourselves "I never leave my children alone." We are comforted when we remember that they understand the whole "stranger – danger" concept. We reach for the remote, sit back on the couch, and turn the TV to our favorite reality show.

But let me give you a few disturbing facts. According to the Uniform Crime Report detailing Crime in the United States, in 2009 there were an estimated:

- 1,318,398 violent crimes
- 15,241 murders
- 88,097 reported rapes
- 408,217 robberies
- 806,843 aggravated assaults

So we know there is a problem. We realize our children are vulnerable. We know we are at risk. What do we do to protect ourselves and prevent our families from becoming a statistic?

My wife and I considered enrolling our daughters in karate classes and other self-defense courses. But I felt like this was not really addressing the issue. Sure, I would love for our daughters to know HOW TO DEFEND themselves should the need ever arise, but I think it is more important for them to know HOW TO AVOID ever being in a dangerous situation. It is crucial for me to teach my kids – and all children – how to be PROACTIVE vs. REACTIVE. Awareness is the key! Education is the key! All of us need to know how to recognize the warning signs so we can avoid dangerous situations.

One of my favorite quotes, shown at the beginning of this chapter, is from John F. Kennedy:

"One person can make a difference, and every person must try."

To me, that is a call to action for each of us to get our butts off the couch and do something. Imagine what our world would be like if we all sat back waiting for someone else to make a positive change in this world. It would not be a pretty place.

Motivated to make a difference, I started a non-profit – Keep Georgia Safe – to provide safety education and crime prevention training in Georgia (www.KeepGeorgiaSafe.org). Since being formed in July of 2008, our organization has helped train over 80 state and local law enforcement officers in CART (Child Abduction Response Team). If a child is abducted, the first officers on the scene need to have a step-by-step plan of 'what to do' as time is of the essence in safely securing the child. Why? 74% of the children that are murdered are killed within the first three hours of their abduction.

Keep Georgia Safe has also trained over 70 instructors in the radKIDS curriculum (www.radKIDS.org). RadKIDS is the nation's leader in child-safety education. It provides hands-on learning for children ages 5-12 on safety topics from avoiding abduction to Internet safety to bullying prevention. Bullying has been a hot topic and a reason for all parents to be concerned. The radKIDS bullying prevention model curriculum combines self-esteem with realistic physical skills to escape bullying violence. This is a program that not only stops bullying behaviors, but also empowers children to stop violence physically when absolutely necessary – all with the intent to escape and then report, not hide, the encounter. To date, 73 children have used their radKIDS skills to escape an attempted abduction, and thousands more have escaped the bullying, abuse and violence in their lives.

Keep Georgia Safe has been one of the most gratifying initiatives I have ever started and it really has become a labor of love. I started it and I continue to fund it and volunteer because it is the right thing to do. A lot of people questioned my sanity for starting a non-profit in this economic climate and because I was already a very busy individual. In my law firm, I supervise 5 other lawyers and 30 support staff. And I have already achieved great "success" by most definitions of the word in the professional arena. My law firm has secured over $225 million dollars for our clients in settlements and verdicts since 1993. I have been recognized in Atlanta Magazine as one of the state's top Workers' Compensation lawyers. The American Trial Lawyers' Association selected me as one of the Top 100 Trial Lawyers in Georgia and Lawdragon.com selected me as one of the leading Plaintiff's lawyers in America. I have truly been fortunate.

So why should you get involved with a charity? Here are five (5) amazing things that have happened for me and my law firm as a result of Keep Georgia Safe:

1. It shows a commitment to the community.

    Georgia is my home. It's where my wife and I live, where our kids go to school, where our family goes to church. Keep Georgia Safe is a tangible demonstration that I want to do everything I can to make our community – our state – a better place. I have not just given it lip service, but I have done something about it.

Approximately 25 years ago, American Express launched a campaign to increase their cardholder's use of the card and to try and sign up new members. As incentive, American Express promised to donate $1.00 for each new card application to help restore one of the nation's most recognized landmarks, the Statute of Liberty. American Express donated over $1.7 million to the cause. The strategy resulted in a card usage increase of 27% and new applications rose 45%. This campaign clearly showed when a company visibly supports a charity by raising awareness and funds, it can boost sales (American Express, 2003). All things being equal, people will do business with a company that gives back to the community versus one that does not.

According to the Cone Millennial Cause Study, 89% of Americans aged 13 – 25 would switch from one brand to another of a comparable product and price if the latter brand was associated with a "good cause".

2. Opened the door to meet so many incredible, inspiring people.

Because of Keep Georgia Safe, I have had the honor of getting to know some amazing people. Vivi Guerchon, the mother of Lauren Burk, inspired me to start the organization because of her sincere desire to make sure no family will ever lose their child to a violent crime. Ed Smart, whose daughter Elizabeth was abducted from her own bedroom in Utah, has become a friend and very vocal supporter of safety issues and initiatives involving children. He has helped Keep Georgia Safe build awareness for our radKIDS program in this state. Steve Daley, the founder of radKIDS, has helped open my eyes as to the tremendous need for safety education in our country. Sadly, we are too focused on "feel good" programs versus ones that get measurable results like radKIDS.

I have also met so many wonderful people in the State of Georgia that are true influencers – and people that get things done – like Ira Blumenthal, former President of the Captain Planet Foundation;

Vernon Keenan, Director of the Georgia Bureau of Investigations; and so many radio and television personalities that have a chance to make a difference every day that they sit behind a microphone or step in front of a camera.

3. Helped me learn and develop new skills.

I never would have imagined sitting with over 80 state and local law enforcement officers being trained on how to respond in the event a child is abducted in our state. I also never thought I would be helping teach a class of 5 – 12 year old kids on safety topics – but I have done it and I love it! I have honed my speaking and presentation skills through the numerous seminars we have given on safety issues throughout the state.

The media attention our cause has captured has been phenomenal. Our Executive Director, Mary Ellen Fulkus, and I have appeared on 9 television stations, including our ABC, CBS, Fox, and NBC affiliates, 108 radio stations, including the Georgia News Network, and have been in 15 magazines and newspapers. We have made it a top priority to spread the word about being safe to as many people as will listen.

One of the most gratifying stories of success to date happened after one of our appearances on a radio morning show in Atlanta, KICKS 101.5. One of the listeners asked us what we should tell our children to do if they are ever lost or separated from the parent. We told them to stress to their kids to find a mommy or grandmother with children. They will protect that child as if he/she were their own until the parents are located. About a month after the show, we received an email from a mother. She told us about her family's trip to Disney World in Orlando, Florida. To her horror, one of her children became separated from her at one of the resorts. She frantically looked around the hotel. As she rounded a corner in one of the dining rooms, she saw her child standing with a mother and her children. The child had remembered her words of advice and had not left with a stranger. She was very grateful and could not thank us enough for sharing the safety message.

4. Increases a sense of achievement and personal satisfaction.

In the legal profession, it can sometimes take months or even years before a case settles or my client has their day in court. It is the ultimate in "delayed gratification." Working with Keep Georgia Safe, the rewards have been immediate. Parents are so appreciative when we educate them on Internet safety or open their eyes to "out and about" safety issues. The children glow with pride when they complete one of the training sessions in radKIDS and are given positive feedback. I know that every person we touch with our message of safety gains something from it. No one can argue with our mission.

5. It looks great on your resume!

If you are out looking for a job, please do not just sit back and wait for things to happen. Go volunteer. Get out there and make an impact in your community and you will become visible. I hired one of the paralegals at our firm because she showed enough initiative to come and volunteer at one of our fundraisers for Keep Georgia Safe. I was impressed with her drive, her commitment, and the fact that she was not wallowing in the "poor pitiful me" world. Find a charity or mission that inspires you – and go volunteer!

****

We should all take to heart and practice the old Chinese proverb:

"If you want happiness for an hour, take a nap. If you want happiness for a day, go fishing. If you want happiness for a lifetime, help somebody."

So now I ask this final important question: I will make a difference. **Will you?**

ABOUT GARY

Gary Martin Hays is not only a successful lawyer, but also a recognized safety advocate who works tirelessly to educate our children on issues ranging from bullying to Internet safety to abduction prevention. Gary has been seen on 9 television stations, including ABC, CBS, NBC and FOX affiliates. He has appeared on over 108 radio stations, including the Georgia News Network, discussing legal topics and providing safety tips to families. He currently hosts "Georgia Behind The Scenes" on the CW Atlanta TV Network.

Gary graduated from Emory University in 1986 with a B.A. degree in Political Science and a minor in Afro-American and African Studies. In 1989, he received his law degree from the Walter F. George School of Law at Mercer University, Macon, Georgia. His outstanding academic achievements landed him a position on Mercer's Law Review. He also served the school as Vice President of the Student Bar Association.

His legal accomplishments include being a member of the prestigious Million Dollar Advocate's Forum, a society limited to those attorneys who have received a settlement or verdict of at least $1 million dollars. He has been recognized in Atlanta Magazine as one of Georgia's top workers' compensation lawyers. Gary frequently lectures to other attorneys in Georgia on continuing education topics. He has been recognized as one of the Top 100 Trial Lawyers in Georgia since 2007 by the American Trial Lawyers Association, and recognized by Lawdragon as one of the leading Plaintiffs' Lawyers in America. His firm specializes in personal injury, wrongful death, workers' compensation, and pharmaceutical claims. Since 1993, his firm has helped over 25,000 victims and their families recover over $225 million dollars.

In 2008, Gary started the non-profit organization Keep Georgia Safe with the mission to provide safety education and crime prevention training in Georgia. Keep Georgia Safe has trained over 80 state and local law enforcement officers in CART (Child Abduction Response Teams) so our first responders will know what to do in the event a child is abducted in Georgia. Gary has completed Child Abduction Response Team training with the National AMBER Alert program through the U.S. Department of Justice and Fox Valley Technical College. He is a certified instructor in the radKIDS curriculum. His law firm has given away 1,000 bicycle helmets and 14 college scholarships.

To learn more about Gary Martin Hays, visit www.GaryMartinHays.com. To find out more about Keep Georgia Safe, please visit www.KeepGeorgiaSafe.org or call (770) 934-8000.

CHAPTER 13

HOW THE GOVERNMENT, EDUCATION AND LACK OF PARENTING SKILLS ARE ROBBING YOUR CHILD'S FUTURE

BY GARY SCHILL

What Every Parent in America MUST DO TODAY to Ensure Their Child is a TRENDSETTER not a TRENDFOLLOWER.

STARTING WITH THE OBVIOUS:

Let's face it, between our government spending us into record debt, our education system rated 26th in the world, and many parents that are completely overwhelmed, out of touch and living with their heads in the sand, our children are facing the greatest crisis in modern time.

The legacy we are leaving for our children is one of the greatest tragedies I have personally witnessed. I have worked with thousands of families over the past 20 years and I have never witnessed a time where our children have a greater sense of entitlement. They seem to believe that everyone is a winner and deserves a trophy or sticker. Our children are overweight, physically unfit and lack motivation.

Social media and electronic connectivity are providing challenges to our children that we as parents never had to face. For the first time since the industrial age, we cannot give our children advice from personal life experience. We cannot say to them, "When I was I was your age and I had this problem on Facebook or texting, this is how I handled it." Parents do not realize how big this is. Since we did not experience it, we are not programmed to teach it.

This is going to be a very controversial statement, however it is a true statement. I watch foreign nationals from all over the world invest heavily in their children's education. Yet I watch westernized parents spend a great deal of money on toys, flat panel televisions, game systems, cars, vacations and other items that frankly have little to no value to their child's development.

Did you realize that an immigrant to the United States is 10 times more likely to be successful than a child born here?

I LOVE OUR COUINTRY, BUT WE HAVE BECOME LAZY, COMPLACENT, ENTITLED AND IT IS TIME FOR A CHANGE.

However:

I HAVE THE ANSWER! IT IS EASIER THAN YOU THINK AND FRANKLY YOU'RE CRAZY FOR NOT INVESTING IN IT.

The Best Investment in Your Family and Your Child's Future

For more than 20 years, I have worked with families just like yours and mine. As a Martial Arts Master and owner of my own martial arts academy, I see every imaginable walk of life come through my doors. Through my interview process I learn very quickly the dynamics of a family. I learn who the disciplinarian is, who the pushover parent is, if we have a helicopter parent or the parent who just doesn't care. I learn through the children just what type of parenting and life skills the parents bring to the table, and most importantly, why the child is suffering from confidence issues, self-esteem issues, respect and courtesy issues, communication issues and much, much more.

About 9 years ago, I had started incorporating Leadership Life Skills into my curriculum. It all started from a conversation with a group of parents where the conversation kept coming back to: **"I wish I knew that when**

I was younger, I would have done some/many things different."

Through my research, I learned that there are 72 traits that leaders possess. Not all leaders possess all 72 traits; however, there are 12 common traits that all leaders do possess. So we designed a curriculum based upon these 12 traits and incorporated them into martial arts program.

One interesting event occurred as we started working on "Vision Boards", many of the parents called me and said, "Master Schill, I have never seen a 'Vision Board' before and I do not understand how it works." We quickly learned that better than 9 out of 10 people had never learned the leadership and life skill traits we were starting to teach their children. We quickly realized that we had to get the parents up to speed so they could help us help their children.

The "Parents as Coaches Program" (PAC) was started about 30 days later. This program teaches parents success skills and parenting skills that were never passed down or taught to us by our/their own parents. When I had my children, my parents did not provide me with the "Golden Rule Parenting Guide." You know, the one that tells you what every cry means, what to do with every milestone and the most effective teaching and discipline methods.

Breaking the Cycle, Providing the Success Secrets Your Children and You Must Learn

FOUR IMPORTANT LESSONS PARENTS MUST TEACH THEIR CHILDREN TO ENSURE SUCCESS

Our children face challenges that were not present even 5 short years ago. We have to provide them with proven success skills to ensure they are properly prepared for adulthood. To break the cycle your parents passed on to you, teach your children and yourself these four Success Skills I have outlined below.

I. Begin with the End in Mind (Vision): Have you ever created a vision of what you want your child to look like as an adult? What life skills do you want your child to possess as an adult? How many times have you had an idea for a product or invention, then a year or two later you see your idea on the internet or television making millions of dollars changing people lives? The most important difference between success and failure is taking action to turn your vision into reality. Many have great ideas, but most never take action.

This is an amazingly simple but effective technique to help you "Begin with the End in Mind". A Vision Board is great tool for taking your vision ("The Have") and adding the success steps to bring about a successful outcome. This process can be used for many different projects with either short or long term goals. This process teaches them about focus, responsibility, hard work and the rewards achieved by fulfilling your dreams and aspirations.

Below is a sample Vision Board separated into 3 sections. Staring with the "Have" Section, have your child come to you and say I want 'xxxx'. This statement typically starts with an "I". List the item or goal they want in the Have section and add a reasonable date for reaching their goal. Now make up some ways they can earn the "Have" item. These chores, tasks, and jobs are listed in the "Do" section. Fill out the "Be" section with personal conduct and character traits, and then start the process.

Be	**Do**	**Have**
Responsible	Mow Lawns	**iTouch**
On Time and Prepared	Clean Out Garage	Put Down: "Reasonable Date" to completion
Committed to my Goal	Do Weekly Chores to Earn Allowance	Print Out a Picture of the Desired Item or Outcome and Place it on Your Vision Board
Honest	Make a goal and progress chart	

Put the completed Vision Board up on the wall where your child can see it every day. Put together a savings chart to chart their progress so they can see their success. It provides positive, visual reinforcement that will keep them on task and motivated. The results will amaze you. The great thing about this tool is it will work for you and will set an example for your children to follow.

II. Goal Setting: Once you have finished your Vision Board, it is time to define your goals and time lines. Refine your goals using the SMART method.

S = Specific: What is the "Have" on your Vision Board?

M = Measurable: Use a "Success Chart" to track your success.

A = Achievable: Is your "Have" achievable?

R = Realistic: Make the goal within reach. Do not set yourself up for failure.

T = Time Frame: Set an end date. This allows your brain to know when this must be completed.

ONLY 3% OF THE POPULATION SETS CLEAR CUT DE-FINED GOALS

You Always Linger and Never Reach Your Destination

Using a Vision Board and SMART Goal Setting builds habits that ensure your children turn assignments in on time, teaches them the value of money, to manage time, behave responsibly, focus their energies, and most importantly SUCCESS!

III. Preventing the Quitting Habit: I often hear people complain that they "Shoulda", "Coulda", "Woulda". In reality they didn't finish what they started. Many probably didn't realize they had formed the Quitting Habit early in their lives. The Quitting Habit is an easy habit to form, a hard habit to break and the consequences can be devastating to future successes.

Quitting Habits are often developed during childhood. Maybe parents are embarrassed by their child's behavior during a team sport. Maybe practices interfere with a parental activity. Maybe it just becomes too time consuming and the child is allowed, or even encouraged, to quit. Once established, the Quitting Habit makes it easier to quit again and again. Thomas Edison tried over a 1000 times before successfully designing a working light bulb. When he was asked if he was discouraged by so many failures, Mr. Edison's response was "I didn't fail, but I can tell you 999 ways on how not to make a light bulb." <u>Winners never quit</u>

and quitters never win, period!

4 Major Fears that Fuel the Quitting Habit

The Quitting Habit is primarily motivated by "4 Major Fears".

- Fear of Rejection
- Fear of Failure
- Fear of Acceptance
- Fear of Success

The Fear of Rejection and Fear of Failure begin when our children take their first steps. When they fall down, the first thing they do is look to us. Overreacting and hovering over them increases their Fears of Failure and Rejection. By playing it cool, often they are encouraged to get up and keep on going believing the fall was no big deal.

Fear of Success and Acceptance are equally powerful and paralyzing. Can you remember your first visit to a full service restaurant or hotel? You may not have known what fork to start with or how much to tip the porter for taking your bags to your room. Once you have experienced situations like this, you begin feeling uncomfortable because you do not have any experience at this level of success.

Our children face this fear everyday in social situations. Everyone wants to be accepted and, unfortunately, many will compromise their integrity in an effort to be accepted by their peers.

Most of our fears are the same as our parents. Often we unintentionally pass these fears along to our own children. When I started my first company, my mother sat me down at the kitchen table and said, "Honey, you need to forget this idea of starting a business. Businesses fail. You need to get a job and stay with the same company until you retire." That was my mom's reality. Her fear of failure was given to her by my grandfather and it kept her from achieving her full potential. Had I not broken this cycle, it would be affecting me the same way. I would now risk passing this same fear on to my children.

IV. Communication and Public Speaking Skills: Did you realize that 7 out of 10 adults HATE public speaking? With the advent of texting and social networking sites, verbal communication skills are declining quickly. In many schools reading aloud in class is no longer mandatory. No matter how uncomfortable it may be, this required public reading is a child's first introduction to public speaking.

We understand the importance and necessity of public speaking and communication skills. Why do our schools not make this a mandatory skill set? Social Networking and texting allow our children to communicate without ever saying a word. It provides a false sense of security, and they will say things they would never say in person.

It is CRITICALLY IMPORTANT that we build the "Communication" skill set in our children. This improves their social confidence and provides them with skills many of their peers will not possess. This increases their future marketability and chances for success.

There are 72 known traits that leaders possess. Not all leaders possess all 72, but there are 12 success traits that the most successful people in the world have in common. With the 4 I have outlined here, you can make a significant difference in the lives of your children.

I have worked with thousands of families just like yours, and I have seen parents and children improve the quality of their relationships. Children are better prepared for the challenges they will face in life. They develop Success Skills that greatly improve their focus, confidence, self-esteem, perseverance, integrity, communication skills, self-discipline and self-motivation. They possess an indomitable spirit that is impervious to bullying and negative peer pressure. They have become True Peak Performers in every aspect of their lives.

All of these lead to one thing, being a TRENDSETTER, NOT A TREND FOLLOWER

Today the PAC (Parents As Coaches) program consists of 14 different lessons that will successfully guide you through the most important life skills you want your child to possess. It has been featured in USA Today as well as on ABC, NBC, CBS and Fox. We have recently added a faith-based initiative to the Success Lessons and the new program is titled "Parents as Preachers". We added the passages from the bible that correlate with the success lesson taught in the PAC. Both programs are series from our SuccessfulFamilies.com program and can be accessed from the privacy of your home or office.

ABOUT GARY

Master Gary A. Schill is the owner and chief instructor of Peak Performance Training Center. A Child, Family and Professional Coaching Program that provides Personal Development and Success Coaching to children, families and professionals via the Martial Arts.

Master Schill is married to his beautiful wife Paula and together they have 5 children ranging in age from 4-30. The 3 oldest boys all have black belts, his daughter will test for black belt in 2012 and his youngest son is working towards black belt sometime in the near future.

With more than 38 years of Martial Arts experience. Master Schill has developed a revolutionary development program that is proven to develop a child's emotional, mental, physical and social intelligence. Understanding that most parents were never taught proper success traits or parenting skills, he developed a revolutionary Parenting Program (Parents as Coaches – "PAC"). The PAC program provides parents with a new set of Success Secrets that will ensure their children possess life skills found only in the top 3% of the world's population.

Master Schill works with the local school districts teaching anti-bullying, anti-negative peer pressure and abduction prevention techniques to more than 25,000 children annually. In addition, he provides parenting classes to local parents and various organizations.

To Learn more about Master Schill's amazing Parents as Coaches Program, visit: SuccessfulFamilies.com

CHAPTER 14

FIVE WAYS TO USE YOUR OWN PRODUCT TO BECOME A TRENDSETTER IN YOUR MARKET

BY GREG ROLLETT & NICK NANTON, ESQ.

We all know the trendsetters in our market. No matter our profession, there are leaders and experts that are setting an example that everyone else wants to copy. The way they offer their services, the marketing and advertising they do, the partners they have on their side and the general way that their business is growing day in and day out.

Getting to this trendsetter status in your own market is much more achievable than you think and can transform your business from 'just getting by' to superstar, or even celebrity status in your market. Then it will be you who has to deal with copycats and those wanting advice from you.

The fastest and easiest way to do this that we know of is by creating your own educational products (also known as information products). When you have your own original products, it adds another layer of credibility to you and your business.

A great educational product will, first and foremost, help your customer solve a problem that they are having. Every person that buys is either looking to move towards pleasure or away from pain. When your product is the solution, you quickly gain traction in your niche.

Adding products also opens up your business to larger "backend" sales, or sales that you get after the customer has already made their first purchase with you. When someone buys something from you, no matter what the purchase amount, they should instantly be elevated to new status in your business.

No longer are they a prospect; they are now a paying customer. And these paying customers will always open up and allow you to upsell them into higher-priced products and services; ones that will not only benefit them in making their lives and businesses better, but also help you hit your revenue and income goals through greater leverage and higher margined products and services.

Many people really miss this point. One of the most expensive things we all do in business is spend money to attract new customers. When a customer buys from you, it means they like what you are offering. They've opened the door for you to provide them with even more products and services; that will help them as well as your profit margin on every sale. After the first sale, that customer becomes exponentially more profitable, because you didn't have to spend more money to acquire them!

Think about some of the products in your niche and market that really help to solve a problem and have created a buzz. Perhaps a product allowed you to get into the market or business that you are now in. Maybe it was a book, a DVD course, or an event that opened your eyes to an opportunity, and got you motivated to get involved in something similar. We all forget that there really are people out there looking for great education and information on what we do—and we were once those people!

With your own products, you have the power to give that same experience to someone else. And in the process you will grow your business, a business built on helping others, which is the strongest kind of business you can have.

There are five key ways to use your product(s) to transform your business into a trendsetting, customer-acquiring business and make you the go-to person in your market, or industry. Let's walk through them:

1. Separation From Competition

The minute that you publish your informational or educational product you have separated yourself from your competition. The way the product looks and feels, even the graphics and physical space it takes up, alone, gives you an edge in your market because people can now *see* what you know, they don't have to just imagine it.

The reason your competition won't go through the process to have a product created, designed and finally available on their websites? ...or in their stores to sell? They may feel, like you probably did at one time, that it's too much of a process, or even a hassle to create. From deciding what to put into the product, to figuring out a way to record it, edit it and format it—these are just a few of the reasons that immediately come to mind that your competition will never take to create this credibility-boosting, income-generating and freedom-providing product.

Creating a product is nothing more than helping someone solve his or her problem through information. And if you don't know where to start, think of it this way, you can create a simple 4-step framework, leverage technology to record it over the telephone, and have it transcribed and turned into video quickly and efficiently.

When you have a product that you can sell to your customers and web visitors, you immediately have an asset that your competition does not. You can now educate your customers and prospects. When you educate your customers, they become loyal to you because you were the one who opened their eyes and gave them something of value.

In fact, you probably showed them a solution they didn't even know existed, so now your prospect values you even more. You're the obvious answer to their problem, because they didn't even realize some of the problems you addressed existed, so they wouldn't even know where to begin to start comparing what you do with others, as you've just shown them what they don't know!

Having a product that you can sell 24/7 online also positions you to make sales while your competitor's doors are closed. When they lock the doors at 5:00 pm, they are not able to make sales until they come back at 9:00 am the following day. You, on the other hand, can collect revenue from prospects and window shoppers that find you on Google, through social media or word of mouth, no matter the time of day or what part of the world they're in.

2. You Will Create New Partnerships and Associations

There are others who will be very interested in your products beyond your customers and prospects. Businesses in markets and niches similar to yours are always looking for new and exciting complimentary products to offer to their own customers and prospects.

When you find a strong partner, they can essentially do your marketing for you. For instance, if you are a realtor selling an information product on how to buy your first home, there may be a mortgage association that would love to get that information into the hands of their own prospects – prospects who need to learn these tips before they get their first mortgage.

In this example, you can sell your products to the association itself, license your product to them, or have them refer their customers to you in exchange for an affiliate or referral fee.

When the product is delivered to the customer, all parties come out winners. You get a new customer that never would have found your website, the mortgage association wins by helping its clients (mortgage brokers) get more consumers to understand how the mortgage process works and to make better buying decisions, and finally the customer wins as they now have the information they need to create an informed decision about buying their first home.

An example of an added bonus is when you can now take that customer, get them to move beyond the product you sold them and actually get them to return to you for more products and services. In this case, signing on to buy a house from you. As you can see, this is extremely powerful and can help you grow your business exponentially by providing information and value to these consumers.

If you are selling a virtual product, an eBook, a downloadable course or other electronic files you can use networks like eJunkie or Clickbank to find people who are willing to sell your products for you in exchange for an "affiliate" commission. This is just another way to grow your business and position you as the trendsetting expert in your field.

3. You Will Be Able to Grow Your Platform

One of the more exciting things that happen when you create a product and release it to the world is by learning new ways that your business can expand. Beyond the obvious ways of creating income selling your information product on your website, you can leverage your product to open new doors.

The first door is the speaking stage. Having a product to sell and promote at events, seminars and boot camps will help to entice a promoter to put you in front of their audience because if you don't have something to sell, they can't get a cut of the sale—and believe us, that's what they really want, a cut of the sales you make!

Another reason that this will open the door to speaking at local, regional and national events is that you will now have a framework with which to teach from. If you create a 4-part product, or 4-module course, your 4 modules become the framework in which you create your presentation. This will take the people in the audience along your journey and in turn, give them the answers they need.

As we mentioned earlier, you will also have the opportunity to use this 4-part framework to sell attendees your higher-priced coaching or consulting services.

For those that prefer not to travel, you will also have the ability to participate in webinars and other virtual events. Much like the partnership method we spoke of earlier, this method also works wonders, and again, you can use your 4-part framework to teach and add value to online events – whether you are the host or a guest of another promoter.

Other ways to expand your platform include the opportunity to write, contribute or syndicate content to major media sources. Sending a copy of your product to industry magazines, websites, news sources or blogs can give you the social proof or credibility needed to have you appear in these media.

If you've heard us say it once, you've probably heard it a hundred times, but it is worth saying again — "People buy People." One of the biggest reasons that people buy from you is you; by getting your content syndicated in more places, and in familiar places, you are building up your trust and reputation with your audience. This credibility can be added to your website as well as social media in the form of logos or banners.

4. **You Will Have More Money To Spend On Direct Marketing Initiatives**

This may be the biggest benefit to becoming a trendsetting product creator. When you sell informational and educational products, you create new revenue with very low overhead. At the core of it, it allows you to spend more money to make even more.

For example, if you are selling a product for $100 and your cost is $5 for merchant fees and hosting costs, you can afford to spend up to $95 to acquire that customer to break even—because remember in our model above, attracting new customers is the most expensive part of the equation, so you should be willing to spend at least as much as it takes to break even on the first sale to acquire them, because the real profit is in the second sale and beyond to that same customer.

That is a huge benefit to selling digital informational and educational products.

When you have the ability to spend that kind of money to put someone into your sales funnel, you will further separate your business from that of your competition. As you perfect your sales process, your goal will be to decrease the amount of money spent to bring in these customers to begin to profit from the first sale, or add to the "front end" as it's known in the industry, as well as the larger ticket items on the "back-end".

With all of your advertising, you should be looking to spend your money on direct advertising, where you can determine exactly how much you spent to get each lead, and then the cost to make each sale. Some innovative ways to do this are to know exactly who your best customers are and target them with precision advertising – using tools like Facebook ads.

With Facebook you can target your prospect to a T, knowing their age range, where they live, their relationship status, education, workplace, hobbies and so much more. When you know your customers that well, you will find that your conversion from prospect to client through direct marketing will increase, and your cost per lead will decrease.

Other places to market may include renting direct mail lists, magazines, industry newsletters, LinkedIn, Google's Content Network and at trade shows and live events.

All of these places will give you extensive data that is critical to growing your business and will quickly leave your competition in the dust, as they will not be able to afford to compete with you. Having this high leverage product is the first step towards buying customers and bringing them into your sales funnel.

5. You Will Make More Money and Grow Your Business

Let's face it, the more offers that you put in front of the world, the more they can buy – which translates into more money in your pocket.

In order to make money for your business you need to be selling something, whether that something is product, services, coaching, software or anything else that someone will trade money for. Creating an educational or information product adds to your suite of offerings and, like we've mentioned, it will be able to transfer into your customer's hands immediately after purchase, no matter if you are in the office or not, day or night.

For those looking to build a product empire, you can exponentially grow your business with the tried and true methods of upsells, cross sells and affiliate products that compliment your offering. Creating new versions of your products and expanding on the topics sold with new products will help you grow your business by helping more people get the results they desire.

And here's a quick tip: the deeper into a niche or sub-niche you get with your products, the more specialized the knowledge will be, and if there is a demand for that knowledge, people will pay more for this specialized knowledge because the information and education they need is harder to find.

The beauty of a great informational or educational product is that the more people you help, the more money you make. That is because organically, great results speak volumes in both traditional marketing (through testimonials and case studies) as well as through word-of-mouth marketing, that your new, excited and expanded customer base is passing onto their circle of influence.

GETTING STARTED CREATING YOUR PRODUCT

If you are now buzzing to create your own product, here is a quick checklist to get you started. The faster you take action, the sooner you can become the trendsetter in your market instead of being a follower playing catch-up.

(a) Figure out the core problem in your market. Before you can create your product you need to know what your market's desires are. Do this through surveys, paying attention to blogs and social media sites, going to events and shows and reading any and everything you can about your market. Once you have this tied down, it should be evident what the core problem is in this niche.

(b) Solve the core problem. After you know the problem, you need to solve it. If your market's core problem is to lose 20 pounds to prepare for a summer vacation, you need to create the ideal program for them to hit their target goal. If your market's core problem is to get more customers or clients for their business, you need to show them exactly how to get more customers into their business.

(c) Create a framework that takes the person from where they are to where they want to be. You need to create a series of steps that logically take your customer through different actionable phases to help them reach their desired results. In the weight- loss example above, your framework may be 4 weeks to lose 20 pounds. Every week you would essentially help your customer lose 5 pounds and at the end of 4 weeks they would reach their goal of losing 20 pounds.

(d) Record your product. There are an infinite number of ways to record your product from audio to video, in front of the camera to recorded "screencasts," or even writing a book or eBook. Choose the medium that you are most comfortable with and also one that is consistent with what your market is known to use and consume.

(e) Edit, design and package your product. Once you have your product recorded, you want to make it look appealing and stand out whether you are looking to have it online or in physical versions. Look to create cd covers, DVD cases, workbooks and ebooks, or the digital versions of these assets, and package your product accordingly.

(f) Place it online and make it available to sell. Now it's time to get paid for helping people. Price your product based on the value it brings to the customer. The best way to know the right price is to test the price (it sounds obvious, but you'd be surprised how few people do this!). When placing your product online, create enticing benefit-driven sales copy that tells the buyer what they are getting, how to get it and what to do next.

(g) Create a place to consume your product. After your customer buys, you need to direct them somewhere, be it a thank you page, a download page, a members area or even a simple email that tells them exactly how to consume or use the product.

Now that you have all the steps in place, you are ready to start building a business that offers the time and freedom you deserve for helping people live the lives and have the businesses they always desired. Here's to becoming the trendsetter in your market with education and information products—and if you need more help, feel free to visit www.ProductProSystems.com for even more resources on creating and profiting from what you already know!

ABOUT GREG

Greg Rollett, the ProductPro, works with authors, experts, entertainers, entrepreneurs and business owners all over the world to help them share their knowledge and change the lives and businesses of others. After creating a successful string of his own educational products, Greg began helping others in the production and marketing of their own products.

Previous clients include Coca-Cola, Miller Lite, Warner Bros and Cash Money Records as well as hundreds of entrepreneurs and small business owners. Greg's work has been featured on FOX News, ABC, and the Daily Buzz. Greg has written for Mashable, the Huffington Post, AOL, AMEX's Open Forum and more.

Greg loves to challenge the current business environments that restrict people to working 12-hour days during the best portions of their lives. By teaching them to leverage technology and the power of information, Greg loves helping others create freedom businesses that allow them to generate income, make the world a better place and live a radically ambitious lifestyle in the process.

A former touring musician, Greg is a highly sought after speaker having appeared on stage with former Florida Gov. Charlie Crist, bestselling authors Chris Brogan and Nick Nanton, as well as at events such as Affiliate Summit.

If you would like to learn more about Greg and how he can help your business, please contact him directly at greg@productprosystems.com or calling his office at 877.897.4611.

You can also download a free report on how to create your own educational products at www.productprosystems.com.

ABOUT NICK

An Emmy Award-Winning Director and Producer, Nick Nanton, Esq., is known as The Celebrity Lawyer and Agent to top Celebrity Experts for his role in developing and marketing business and professional experts, through personal branding, media, marketing and PR to help them gain credibility and recognition for their accomplishments. Nick is recognized as the nation's leading expert on personal branding as Fast Company Magazine's Expert Blogger on the subject and lectures regularly on the topic at the University of Central Florida. His book *Celebrity Branding You®* has been selected as the textbook on personal branding at the University.

The CEO of The Dicks + Nanton Celebrity Branding Agency, Nick is an award winning director, producer and songwriter who has worked on everything from large scale events to television shows with the likes of Bill Cosby, President George H.W. Bush, Brian Tracy, Michael Gerber and many more.

Nick is recognized as one of the top thought-leaders in the business world and has co-authored 10 best-selling books, including the breakthrough hit *Celebrity Branding You!®*.

Nick serves as publisher of Celebrity Press™, a publishing company that produces and releases books by top Business Experts. CelebrityPress has published books by Brian Tracy, Mari Smith, Ron Legrand and many other celebrity experts and Nick has led the marketing and PR campaigns that have driven more than 300 authors to Best-Seller status. Nick has been seen in USA Today, The Wall St. Journal, Newsweek, Inc. Magazine, The New York Times, Entrepreneur® Magazine, FastCompany.com and has appeared on ABC, NBC, CBS, and FOX television affiliates around the country speaking on subjects ranging from branding, marketing and law, to American Idol.

Nick is a member of the Florida Bar, holds a JD from the University of Florida Levin College of Law, as well as a BSBA in Finance from the University of Florida's Warrington College of Business. Nick is a voting member of The National Academy of Recording Arts & Sciences (NARAS, Home to The GRAMMYs), a member of The National Academy of Television Arts & Sciences (Home to the Emmy Awards), co-founder of the National Academy of Best-Selling Authors, a 6-time Telly Award winner, and spends his spare time working with Young Life, Downtown Credo Orlando, Florida Hospital and rooting for the Florida Gators with his wife Kristina and their three children, Brock, Bowen and Addison.

CHAPTER 15

MARKET RESEARCH REVEALS PROVEN BLUEPRINT FOR OVER 2,140% BUSINESS GROWTH

BY JAY KINDER

"I wasn't the smartest kid in school; I just sat next to him."

~ Jay Kinder

That is my coined "claim to fame" if you will. The funny thing about that quote is that it was true when I was in high school, and to this day, I do my best to surround myself with people who have the answers to my most challenging questions, in all areas of life. I am a relentless 'knowledge seeker'.

I'm going to share with you the "Trend Setter" principles behind my personal quest for excellence, and more importantly, a blue print for you to easily follow – to blaze your own success trail at a record pace. You will find these irrefutable business and life principles undeniably fact. I'm not much for fluff or mindless chatter and babbling, so the content being shared here is the over-arching success formula I have used to earn over 14.2 million dollars in the past decade. What is more exciting is that when you live by these principles and do the research, you will find that doubling your business, and then doubling it again and then again can be the result. You can achieve more than 21 times the result you are currently achieving with this proven system.

The fact is this, multiplying your income is a choice. You either make a decision to have the desire to reach your goals or you choose not to have that desire. You either give up or 'never say die.' One thing that I will guarantee you is that if you choose to follow this formula relentlessly, you will be following the path of the few, not the masses. The way I see it is that if less people want to think big and be true trendsetters then you have less competition in reality, so just go for it. It won't be easy. Nothing worth achieving is easy. Failure is way easier than success. You have to want to win, play to win, and accept nothing less than winning. You must also accept that losing is a part of winning. Trust me when I tell you that you must learn how to lose in order to learn how to win. Be obnoxiously discontent, pig-headedly disciplined, and relentless in pursuit of your dreams!

LAW #1: DESIRE DRIVES SUCCESS

If you've met many celebrities, millionaires or read any books about game-changing trendsetters, you will find a very distinct trend. These trends are what you want to emulate. Sure, you can find the differences between Donald Trump, Steve Jobs, and John D. Rockefeller. The question is have you trained yourself to find the similarities. You won't find it hard to get up early, push yourself harder, or invest more into something that you are passionate about. These men were relentless in the pursuit of their goals. Their desire drove them to success. When the average person would have quit, they kept going. When the average person would have said "this is enough," they kept pushing. Desire fueled their efforts and forced results. They manufactured success by sheer will power.

Of course there will be days that you want to quit, check out, or give in to the temptation to hit the bar early. The only thing that will drive you is your why. What are you trying to accomplish? … what are your goals for yourself? … what do you want to give your family? … that yellow Lamborghini you have as a screen saver? For me, that passion is to help like-minded real estate agents get established as experts, differentiate themselves with proven systems and marketing, and manufacture celebrity-like status in their marketplace while providing advice and experiences beyond their clients' imagination. It keeps me up at night. I wake up knowing that what I am doing is changing the lives of many and that I'm leading a movement that will absolutely annihilate the mediocrity the real estate industry has allowed for the past 100 years. Now, don't get me wrong, I 'dig' the Bentley, go-fast boats, big houses and all that, but what really drives you is *what money allows you to experience*, not the money itself. As I write this, I am sitting by the pool with my laptop thinking to myself – "Man, I really hope you are listening when I say this." Find your "Big Why" and work is no longer work. You will never spend a day of your life working if you love what you do. You can never sacrifice this rule. Do what you love or 'give 'em deuces' and find something you are passionate about. Life is too short to be doing something you don't get excited about every morning.

LAW #2: THERE IS NO SUCH THING AS MONEY?

You heard me right. Money doesn't exist. If you have ever read the book *The Creature from Jekell Island*, then you would know that our Federal Reserve System is not really a bank at all. In fact, it's just an open checkbook and money is pumped into our economy and printed on paper notes we *call* money. The reality is that when you are born, there is a pre-determined amount of money that is "earmarked" to be put into the market – based on the supposed amount of "value" you will bring into the economy in the future. That means that money is a symbol of value and the more value you create in your life, the more money you will create. This is a profound thought and one you cannot ignore if you want to be successful. Focus on bringing the most possible value to one person and then do that over and over again, and you will have all the money you desire. Wake up every day, be thankful for everything you have in your life, and focus on adding value to those you have the privilege to be in contact with. The first second you think about the money and not the value, you will get taken out like a quarterback getting sacked by an unexpected 280 lb linebacker.

LAW #3: GEOMETRIC GROWTH EFFECT

I've seen this in every business that I have personally owned and every business that I have helped someone build. To have geometric growth, research shows that there are only three ways to grow a business:

1. Increase the number of new clients
2. Increase the average transaction value
3. Increase the frequency of repurchase – Get more residual value out of each client.

The Geometric Growth effect is what happens when you optimize all three of these areas of your business at the same time. A mere 10% increase across all areas stimulates an overall growth of 33% in your business. Keep your focus on these three areas and how to improve them and apply the power of geometry to your business.

LAW #4: THE BEST MARKETER ALWAYS WINS

Although I would like to think that I am the best real estate agent in town, the fact is that there are several great real estate agents. So why do I sell over 400 homes and the average agent sells only six? The answer is simple; I'm the best marketer. You must learn the principles of marketing in order to have ultimate success. You can spend the same amount of money on a postcard and have up to 21 times better response with a clear call to action. Here are the marketing principles you cannot ignore:

1. The Headline is 80% of your ads result: Put the benefit, not the feature in the headline
2. Risk Reversal: Offer a guarantee; if you lower the barrier of entry, more people will say yes
3. Social Proof: Add testimonials to your marketing and you will influence more people to buy
4. Call to Action : If you don't tell them what to do, they won't do it
5. Unique Selling Proposition (USP): What differentiates you from your competition
6. Force Multiplier Effect: Use every possible marketing channel to have maximum impact on your target (Direct mail, telemarketer, email, etc...).

LAW #5: DIFFERENTIATION IS YOUR COMPETITIVE ADVANTAGE

This is the foundation of your business, so if you ignore this principle you will surely suffer the slow and agonizing death many small businesses experience. The questions I would like to pose to you are these: Why should I do business with you over your competition? What experience does your client have that makes your business memorable? You can choose to differentiate by having the best price, but that is incredibly dangerous. Besides, who wants to be the least profitable? You have to know your numbers, what your costs are, how much it costs to acquire a client, what is the lifetime value of that client. Most importantly, you have to know what that client would like to experience that nobody else can give them, and you have to give that to them.

Some examples of differentiation in the real estate industry would be creating a proven, successful strategy that is backed by market research to sell a home for up to 18% more money. Services you could provide to execute that could be home inspection, accredited staging services, moving services, and a staff to execute the 80+ variables in the home-selling process. The value you create in this situation creates a significantly higher net profit, therefore making your services unique compared to the competition. Solve this riddle for your business, and every effort, every dollar spent on human capital, every dollar you spend marketing your services will bring exponentially higher return on investment.

LAW #6: MODELING IS THE SHORTCUT TO SUCCESS

You want to be successful and you want to live the life that others only dream about. Who doesn't, right? Remember when I mentioned my thirst for knowledge, well that is one last lesson that I have learned over the years. After attending every conference, buying just about every coaching program, and visiting the offices of most of the top agents in the world, I found one commonality about each and every person that made them *trendsetters*. I saw the same faces at the conferences, they had the same books behind their desk, they spent the same money that I spent.

There is a shortcut to success. Find someone who has done or is doing what you want to do and you learn as much as you possibly can from them. Seek. If you are not where you want to be, if you have a question you want the answer to, if you need to learn how to manage a part of your business that is not working remember this one word. <u>Seek</u>. If you continue to seek until you find the answer, you will find it and you will conquer your current problem and you will move another 10 steps closer to freedom. The sooner you start seeking, the faster the next 10 steps will happen. Before you know it, you will have trained yourself to ask, "Who do I know that is the best in the world at this?" …and another 10 steps and now you have momentum. The quality of life, sense of accomplishment, and freedom you seek for you and your family will be unlocked when you master modeling success. If you would like a copy of my blueprint for success, along with access to a copy of the one book that changed my life and doubled my business twice, go to: www.kinderreese.com/trendsetterjay for a free download.

As we say at Kinder Reese; **We will either see you at the top, or from the top!**

ABOUT JAY

Jay Kinder is a business phenom who went from small town kid to master business growth strategist recognized throughout the real estate industry. Nobody in the tiny town of Walters, Oklahoma, population 2,142, would have voted this notably 'ornery' and average student most likely to be a millionaire, but that didn't stop him from building an impressive real estate brand positioning him as one of the top 10 Coldwell Banker Agents Worldwide, Small Business Administration Young Entrepreneur of the Year, Realtor Magazine's 30 under 30, Wall Street Journal's top 25 agents worldwide, and a laundry list of high achievement awards all by the age of 30 years old.

By the time Jay was 25 years old, he had become a local celebrity and brilliant strategist. By the time he was 28, his passion for real estate expanded as he and his business partner Michael Reese, a top agent that got into real estate after seeing Jay's incredible business success, decided to open the doors to their successful businesses. They began recreating their own success by helping agents like themselves master massive growth and celebrity stardom in their own real estate markets. This new business, Kinder Reese Real Estate Partners has been credited for helping thousands of real estate agents strategically grow their businesses with their proven and market-tested ideas.

Jay and Mike now share a passion for helping growth-minded individuals who have a burning desire to add value to peoples' lives – while enjoying a higher quality of life.

CHAPTER 16

REAL ESTATE TRENDSETTING

BY JENNIFER BLOUIN

’m going to let you in on a little secret. This isn’t like any other secret you’ll be told in your lifetime because I want you to actually tell people about it. After you learn this secret, I want you to run out there and tell everyone you know because this secret is huge. I’m going to tell you how you can actually make money investing in real estate in a down market!

“Stop the madness!” you’ll say. “It isn’t possible!” you’ll cry. I’m here to tell you that it is possible and that there are people out there who are doing it and making money at it. I want you to throw out everything that you might have heard about how bad the market is and listen to what I have to say, someone who is out there doing it right now, in what has been broadcasted as a down market. Let’s face it. Housing prices are at an all-time low right now. America is on sale and people are scared to do anything because the banks aren’t lending. You, my friend, are obviously a contrarian who isn’t buying into the hype. If you weren’t, you would be huddled in your house waiting for things to turn around instead of reading this book and learning how to do something about it. I like that about you. So read on my friend, take notes and learn the biggest secrets out there that I encourage you to spread around!

With banks being extremely conservative about their lending, what happens to all those people out there who need the money to buy an investment property? How are they going to get the funds to buy that single family house or that giant apartment building that's a cash cow? How is that person who is just dipping their feet into the ocean of real estate investing going to get started? It is questions like these that keep most people from taking action and forging ahead with their investing because, after all, if a bank won't give me money, then I can't possibly buy a property. What people don't understand is that the banks aren't the be-all and end-all in the world of financing when you're an investor. There is a plethora of options out there for someone who lacks the funds to buy that one property that will turn the page of their life, one of which is a little thing called:

OWNER FINANCING

If you can't pony up the money to buy the property or you can't obtain a mortgage from a bank right now, then this might be the road you want to take. Beware, though, that most sellers might say no to the request, because they don't know what it is or they don't fully understand it. You will now be able to educate the seller on what it is and why it's good for them.

So, what is owner financing? Simply put, it's when part or the entire purchase price, less the buyer's down payment, is carried by the seller who is providing the owner financing. Instead of going to the bank, the buyer will give a financing instrument to the seller as evidence of the loan and make payments to the seller. If the property is free and clear, the owner could agree to carry all of the financing and in that instance the buyer and seller agree upon an interest rate, monthly payment amount, loan term and the buyer pays the seller for their equity on an installment basis. The great thing about owner financing is that they're negotiable. The seller and the buyer are free to negotiate the terms of the financing. Typically there is no down payment. Many sellers might want a down payment to protect their equity. However, if you structure the terms correctly and in a way that benefits the owner, then a down payment might not be necessary. My husband and his partner are currently working on a real estate deal to buy an apartment building. I affectionately call it his "Unicorn" because he has been working on this deal for over a year. It was a foreclosure that we tried to buy on a short sale and we were sadly unsuccessful. The next option was to buy the note ourselves but unfortunately we were outbid and we lost it again. Now we are trying to buy the building from the note holder, and we are structuring the deal in such a way that is very attractive to the holder. Not only are we asking for owner financing – which the seller has agreed to – but we are also working it so there is no down payment, and in the unlikelihood that we would default on the note, the owner will simply take the property back.

Another type of owner financing is a lease purchase agreement which means the seller is giving the buyer equitable title and leasing the property to the buyer. When the lease purchase agreement is fulfilled, the buyer takes title and will typically obtain a loan to pay the seller after all or part of their rental income is put towards the purchase price.

These are just two of the ways you can purchase a property with little to no money down and without having to go to a bank for a loan.

Another way an up-and-coming investor can make money in a down market is by taking advantage of something called:

SHORT SALES

Foreclosures are at an all-time high and it's predicted that this year will have record foreclosure rates. So how can you get a piece of the action? By getting yourself a property before it goes into foreclosure. Buying it on what is called a "short sale". This is when the borrower cannot pay the mortgage on their property but the lender decides that selling at a loss is better than keeping the note on their books. Banks don't really want these loans on their books because it ultimately affects how much money they have available to lend out. The more bad loans they have the less money is available to them to lend out, so they're eager to get these off their books and we're just as eager to help them.

So how does a short sale work? You need to find a property that is in pre-foreclosure, meaning the owner has defaulted on their loan and they are already a few months behind. Depending on the state that you live in – in my case, I live in Connecticut, so I will use that as my reference – the lender will then file a *lis pendens* which is the formal notice that starts the foreclosure process. This does not mean the property is in foreclosure, it simply means the process has been started and it remains in pre-foreclosure until the day the property is sold at auction. Once you find that property, you can send the property owner what is called a "Yellow Letter". This is a letter that is written on yellow lined note paper in red ink telling the owner of the defaulted property that you want to buy their house and to contact you if they want to sell. It sounds absolutely ridiculous, but it works! My husband and I use yellow letters all the time. We sent a bunch to Key West and within days of sending we were receiving phone calls on the properties that received the letters. Be aware that not all homeowners who are in default will be nice to you on the phone, and conversely, you might get the home owner who pours their heart and soul out to you and actually wants to work with you. When you are speaking to the homeowner, disclosure is key. I repeat: Disclosure is KEY. Make sure you are honest and forthcoming with the homeowner and disclose absolutely everything to them. Three points that they need to know is:

1. They cannot, by law, stay in the house after the property has been sold to you.
2. They cannot, by law, profit from the transaction. If they are in need of some money what you can do is offer to buy some items from the house – appliances, furniture and items like that – and write them up on a separate bill of sale that has nothing to do with the sale of the house.
3. A short sale will damage their credit, but it's not as bad – or as long – as a foreclosure.

Next you will need to contact the bank and request the short sale packet. You can either tell them you are the buyer or you represent the homeowner. The lender will almost always request a hardship letter. This is a letter telling the lender why the homeowner isn't making their payments. Sometimes the bank will request pay stubs, income statements and so on. Be prepared to send the bank everything they ask, otherwise the package will not be accepted. Do not waste time getting the bank the information!! Send everything back ASAP. It takes about 3 weeks or more to get an answer back, so you cannot afford to wait. If the foreclosure is fast approaching you might be able to extend the auction, and in most cases, they will if they know it's a legitimate offer.

The next step is the BPO which is the Brokers Price Opinion. Basically the real estate agent will come out and give their opinion on what the house is worth. This is the key to the short sale! You want to do everything possible to influence the BPO to come down as low as possible. The lower the better, because this is the price you will pay for the property.

Short sales are an excellent way to not only get a house at a great discount, but to help a homeowner out of a sticky situation as well. They take a lot of time and you need a lot of patience during the short sale process, but in the end you will end up with a house for pennies on the dollar that you can turn around and sell for a nice profit.

Finally, the last way to make money in real estate in a down market that I will be talking about is:

WHOLESALING

I saved this one for last because it can be done in any market. While you can do owner financing and short sales in any market, this is the best market to be creative because banks aren't lending and foreclosures are at an all-time high. Wholesaling can be done in an up or down market.

So what is wholesaling? It's a great way to make some cash quickly and easily, and it allows you to become a real estate middleman. Wholesaling is the process of buying and selling real estate quickly. You're putting the property under contract "as-is", well below market value and selling that contract to another investor for a fee. The best thing about wholesaling is you can buy the property for little or no money down! What's sweeter than that?

The first and most important thing you need to do before you even start looking at a property is to build your buyers list! Always, always, ALWAYS find your investor/buyer before you start looking for the house that will fulfill their need by wholesaling them their property. How do you find buyers? You can find them at your local Real Estate Investment Associations (REIA's), Craigslist, newspaper ads. Just make sure you build your list before you start looking. The last thing you want to do is put a property under contract and have no end buyer. That's a 'surefire' way to let the real estate community know you don't know what you're doing and not do business with you.

Now after you build your wholesale list, you'll need to find motivated sellers for your end buyer. These are people who need to sell their property fast. You can find these motivated sellers by posting "We Buy" bandit signs around your town (word of caution: you might get calls from the "sign police" asking you to take them down. I recommend putting them up for a few days at a time and taking them down before they catch you), you can check out Craigslist and local ads in the newspaper. There really isn't a short supply of motivated sellers out there and there is a plethora of places to find them. Another thing you can do is call one of the "We Buy" guys and ask them if they have a large list. Chances are they might have a large sellers list that they can't fulfill, so you can ask them if they'd be willing to possibly sell you some of the names off their sellers list. The great thing about this is if they have a sellers list, they will more than likely have a buyers list that they can hook you up with, so inquire about that as well. Remember: If you don't ask, the answer is no. Now you could probably ask them if they could just give you the names, but most people don't give something for nothing – so offering a little monetary incentive might pique their interest into giving up the goods.

Since the house you're buying is "as-is", your ultimate end buyer (the one who you'll be wholesaling the deal to), will be someone who is going to fix and 'flip' the property, so make sure to market to rehabbers, landlords and of course other investors. Again, these can be found on Craigslist, local newspapers and the "We Buy" guys.

So you've found a property. Now what? You will put the property under contract. In the buyer section, you put your name and/or Assignee (ask your real estate attorney the language that is usually used). This gives you the right to assign the contract to another buyer for a fee.

Here's an example of a wholesale deal:

You spent a lot of time, did your homework and finally found a real estate deal with a lot of equity. You negotiated the terms to quickly get the property under contract. Now you have control of the property and the equity in the property. Let's say that you found a property that's worth $300,000 (you get this by evaluating the comparables in the neighborhood and settle on a price that the market will essentially support). The house is on the market for $215,000 and you know that the house is in need of at least

$15,000 in repairs. This leaves a $70,000 equity position.

You then go to your buyers list and find an investor. This investor can see that the contract you have is worth $70,000 in equity and decides to make a deal with you. You then turn the deal over to him in exchange for cash which is called an "assignment fee". For this example we will use $10,000. You are essentially giving up $70,000 in *potential profit* in exchange for a $10,*000 immediate profit,* and the investor who bought the contract from you is paying you $10,000 because he's confident that he can make more than that on that deal – since there is equity built in.

The deal between you and the investor is called an assignment because you have assigned the contract to the investor. The investor then does his due diligence in making sure the deal is as good as he thinks it is, which, if you've done your homework, you're confident that it is. At closing the investor you assigned the contract to purchases the property and you receive the assignment fee. It takes a little bit of time and some work, but in the end the immediate payoff is worth it, and you now have an investor who will come knocking on your door for more deals – because he's made money and you've made money. It's a win-win-win situation.

That's all there is to it. <u>Just make sure that you have your buyers lined up for the deal.</u> Your earning potential with a wholesale deal can be endless and you can wholesale any type of property and any type of deal. Since wholesaling is a fast and easy way to get cash, it's typically done until you have enough money to purchase an investment property on your own or with other investors.

So that's it: **Three ways to make money with real estate in a down market.** I've only pinpointed three ways, but there are hundreds of ways to make money in real estate. With anything you begin, always remember to do your homework, ask questions of people who are in the business and are successful, educate yourself (something I am doing all the time) and always consult with an attorney. I hope you were able to take at least one of the three strategies to run with and I wish you the best of luck and success in your business.

Happy investing!

ABOUT JENNIE

Jennifer Blouin has been investing in real estate since 2008. Her focus of business is on wholesaling and short sales – as well as buying commercial apartments for cash flow. She invests in properties all over the United States and is looking to branch out internationally as well.

Jennifer is also the owner of a company named DBG Asset Acquisition, LLC which is in the business of purchasing bad debt, judgements, liens and defaulted mortgages. She also does direct sales for a company called Genewize who provides supplements based on your DNA.

CHAPTER 17

VELOCITY MANUFACTURING

BY "DR LISA" LANG

O ver the past decade the United States manufacturing base has weakened.[1] But it is still true that "no economic sector contributes more to creating prosperity than American manufacturing."[2]

"To remain strong players in a competitive world will require continued focus on innovation and productivity gains helped along by government policies that will smooth the path to success."[3]

The challenge will be for U.S. manufacturers to understand that the actions that created productivity gains in the past may NOT do so in the future.

The traditional focus on efficiency and associated measures are old technology and do not serve the kind of manufacturing that we do in the U.S. today.

The manufacturing that has moved overseas was built on the old school thinking that focuses on efficiency. Moving jobs overseas makes sense …

- When millions or billions of the same item are needed.

---

[1] According to the National Manufacturing Strategy Act speared headed by Rep. Dan Lipinski and Sen. Sherrod Brown.
[2] Securing America's Future: The Case for a strong Manufacturing Base by the National Association of Manufacturers in 2003.
[3] Manufacturing Resurgence: A Must for U. S. Prosperity by Joel Popkin and Kathryn Kobe, January 2010.

- When these items will be supplied for an extended period of time.
- When the manufacturing lead-times are relatively short (because the transportation lead-times are long). The combination of the two determines the amount of inventory that will need to be held.
- When holding inventory of the items make sense.
- When little to no customization is needed.
- When the items are not generally needed in a rush for an emergency situation.

And those are the jobs that have gone overseas. Large, long runs of the same stuff with little to no customization can be cranked out very efficiently. Since the items will not be obsolete for a number of years, inventory can be held to deal with the long transportation lead-times.

A NEW MANUFACTURING TREND IS UPON US …

The jobs that are remaining in the U. S. are the toughest, most difficult jobs that need to be delivered in the most difficult of situations.

- Items for which design and/or prototype manufacturing quantities or small quantities are need. And by the way, they need them yesterday.
- Items for which there is fluctuating demand or unknown demand and despite that, delivery is extremely important.
- Custom high precision items that require the best and the brightest.
- Items that typically have long manufacturing lead-times and cannot afford long transportation lead-times as well.
- Items that are too expensive to hold enough inventory to allow overseas shipping, or too heavy.
- Emergency repair items or replacement parts that are needed with no notice.

This means that we have to move away from focusing on mass production efficiency to focusing on flow or what I call *Velocity* in this custom job shop environment.

VELOCITY MANUFACTURING IS THE FUTURE OF U.S. MANUFACTURING

Our lead-times are too long and our due date performance is typically much less than perfect for these kinds of jobs.

Don't get me wrong. We are the best in the world at this. We just need to get better to sustain our manufacturing base.

If we can get a job done on-time, in half the time and we only have a fraction of the transportation lead-time of our overseas competition, there's no reason to lose work to an overseas competitor.

And if you can get a job done on-time, in half the time with the SAME transportation lead-time, there's no reason you can't take market share from your U.S. competitors.

YOU WANT SHORTER LEAD-TIME AND BETTER DUE DATE PERFORMANCE? IT'S ALL ABOUT THE SCHEDULING ...

There's no question that scheduling in this type of custom job shop environment has its challenges. As I said, we're dealing with the toughest, most difficult jobs, which need to be delivered in the most difficult of situations.

Every time we encounter one of the many challenges, our schedule is out of date, and we need to update the schedule. Here are just a few of the common scheduling challenges that cause us to have to continually update the schedule: [4]

1. Clients change their mind, their forecasts are wrong, and they have emergencies
2. Vendors aren't always reliable
3. Mix can vary wildly and so our constraint moves
4. Employees do not always have the right skill and their discipline is lacking
5. Processes are not reliable
6. Machines & tools break

---

[4] Taken from The 9 Challenges to Scheduling Your Job Shop and Why Your Schedule is Dead On Arrival, available at www.VelocitySchedulingSystem.com/ebook.

7. Quality is not near perfect
8. Data is not readily available nor accurate nor communicated
9. Communication between silos is difficult

But there is also no question that scheduling plays a big role in our on-time delivery performance and our lead-time. And our on-time delivery performance, along with our lead-times, determines our competitive position within our industry.

Industry Week reports that its 25 finalists for the "Best Plants" award reported an average on-time delivery rate of 98.7%. And it's no surprise that on-time delivery is a critical aspect in achieving customer satisfaction, loyalty and greater sales.

BUT CUSTOM JOB SHOPS ARE NOT 98.7% ON-TIME

Custom job shops usually don't have the luxury of making the same items over and over again. The mix of work and amount of repair/emergency work a shop has can change so dramatically week to week that their bottlenecks can move, making on-time delivery a real challenge.

It's no wonder NONE of the 25 finalists were custom job shops or machine shops.

So, unfortunately, 1): it's very difficult to schedule a custom job shop; and 2): it's very important that we do it well to be 99%+ on-time and to reduce our lead-times.

That's probably NOT new news. And I'm sure you've tried a number of things to improve your on-time delivery and to reduce your lead-times. You may have updated your ERP or scheduling software, used some Lean[5] techniques, tried Drum Buffer Rope[6], or maybe you've hired an expeditor.

But, whatever you may have tried, my guess is that it may have helped some, but not substantially. And that's because the typical solutions ad-

---

[5] According to an industry study, most machine shops rely on Lean to "improve". But Lean Doesn't Work for Many Shops. According to Taiichi Ohno (inventor of the Toyota Production System from which Lean is based), for Lean to improve on-time delivery, the processes, products and load must be stable for a "considerable length of time". And while this is true in the car industry -- who only allow model changes once a year – this is not the case in machine shops.

[6] Drum Buffer Rope (DBR) and Simplified Drum Buffer Rope (SDBR) the Theory of Constraints approach to manufacturing developed by Eliyahu M. Goldratt, author of The Goal. The problem with off the shelf DBR or SDBR is that for many custom manufacturers and job shops – their constraint can move frequently due to mix changes.

dress the various symptoms, but don't address the root cause.

So now you might be thinking – okay, so how do we address the root cause, what's the secret? How can we *dramatically* improve our scheduling?

THE SECRET IS ....

STOP focusing on efficiency.

And when you are willing to do that, and put a better scheduling system in place, you create a buffer to better absorb all those sources of variability (those 9 Challenges we talked about because we can't totally remove them).

It sounds like heresy, I know – but that's the secret and that's the direction we need to go to increase our competitiveness. The days of mass production are long gone.

The cool thing is that if YOU'RE willing to give it a try and your competitors continue to cling to efficiency – you can create an incredible competitive advantage.

WHAT DOES IT MEAN TO BE EFFICIENT?

The definition of "efficient" from Dictionary.com is "performing or functioning in the best possible manner with the least waste of time and effort." I'd probably add money/cost to that.

One of the ways we typically apply efficiency in a job shop is by keeping all our equipment and/or people busy so that we don't waste any capacity and have the highest possible utilization.[7]

Now, to keep our key resources busy they all have to have a job to work on. And to increase the likelihood that all resources have work, we typically make all jobs in-house available to be worked on.

"Available to be worked on" means included in our work-in-process or WIP.

---

[7] Some shops focus on keeping people busy, some on machines and some try to do both. It doesn't really matter which you tend to do.

This maxes out your WIP and increases the pile of work at every work center. That way ALL key resources have a very high probability of having *something* to work on.

This is particularly relevant in job shops where the mix of work can change from week to week.

That's <u>one</u> of the things we do in the name of efficiency. Now let's talk about the negative effect from the actions that result from just this one thing we do in the name of efficiency.

THE NEGATIVES FROM "BEING EFFICIENT"

According to Little's Law there is a direct correlation between the amount of work-in-process we have and our lead-time. The higher our WIP, the longer our lead-times.

Here's an illustration showing the relationship between WIP and lead-time:

HIGH WIP = LONG LEAD-TIME

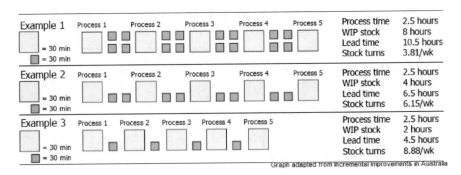

Graph adapted from Incremental Improvements in Australia

The more jobs that wait for their turn the longer the average queuing time, leading to longer production lead-times. Example 1 has the most WIP and longest lead-time. And, conversely, Example 3 has the least WIP and the shortest lead-time.

So, as you increase WIP, you are also increasing your lead-time, not to mention the amount of cash you have tied up in raw materials.

BUT WAIT, THERE'S MORE ... ON-TIME DELIVERY DECREASES

The diagram does NOT include the effect of variability. But if it did, it would show that the variability of production lead-time is increased as the queue grows.

So the effect of high WIP just gets more dramatic the more variability you have – and the more you battle the 9 Challenges.

This directly reduces the on-time delivery because it is more difficult to predict the exact production lead-time and to confirm orders accordingly.

AND ... QUALITY DECREASES

High WIP can also have an impact on quality. Many production failures occur early in the routing, but are detected much later in the production process (usually at final inspection).

If WIP is high, the average lead-time is also high causing a long lag time between the production steps and the final inspection. That means that the final inspection step occurs a long time after the step that caused the failure.

And because so much time has passed, it can be difficult to determine and correct the root cause of the quality problem, making improvement very difficult.

Thus, the higher the WIP, the harder it is to detect and correct quality problems.

All of this brings me to the conclusion that you must ...

STOP FOCUSING ON EFFICIENCY

As you stop focusing on efficiency and reduce WIP (and focus on Velocity instead), here's what happens:

- Queue time reduces
- Lead-time reduces
- Lead-time predictability increases

- On-time delivery increases
- Quality increases
- Cash flow increases

As a result of these improvements, your production lead-time becomes MUCH shorter (if you do it right) than your quoted lead-time. This difference can be used in 2 ways.

First, it creates a buffer allowing you to absorb a fair amount of variability and further enhancing your on-time delivery performance. You can also sell more with the same people and resources – increasing your profitability. And second, the difference is so big that you can also afford to reduce the quoted lead-time to customers.

The combination of these factors creates that competitive advantage I mentioned earlier. That competitive advantage will help you stay or become globally competitive, as well as increase market share here at home.

HOW DOES YOUR GLOBAL PRICE COMPETITIVENESS INCREASE?

When your production lead-time decreases by 50% -- and many Velocity Scheduling System[8] clients have exceeded this number --- then you have effectively reduced the cost of labor advantage of China and other countries vying for US manufacturing business.

Add to this that domestic manufacturing reduces shipping costs, reduces inventory costs, with quicker response times – it is increasingly more difficult for overseas manufacturers to compete on total cost of ownership terms! And that's true even for the jobs I listed earlier on pages 161 and 162 that "make sense" to move overseas.

THAT'S COUNTERINTUITIVE!

Now, all of that is fairly easy to say and much harder to do. It's not physically hard to do, but mentally challenging because we don't have intuition around this approach.

---

[8] Velocity Scheduling System (VSS) is based on the Theory of Constraints Drum Buffer Rope but updated for custom manufacturers and job shops. VSS is the name of Dr Lisa's velocity manufacturing coaching program. You can check it out at www.VelocitySchedulingSystem.com.

To really help the concept stick and to fully explain how to focus on Velocity, I've put together a 47 minute webinar that explains the whole process – of specifically HOW to do this -- nothing is held back. It's called *How to Get More Jobs Done Faster* and you can sign up at www.VelocitySchedulingSystem.com/webinar. There are 2 dates to choose from, so I'll see you there!

This IS the future of manufacturing!

Contact Info: DrLisa@ScienceofBusiness.com.

ABOUT LISA

"Dr. Lisa" Lang is one of the foremost Theory of Constraints experts in the world and a sought after manufacturing expert having appeared in the USA Today, CBSNews' Moneywatch.com, Wall Street Journal's MarketWatch.com, Yahoo Finance.com, About. com, NYDailynews.com, CNBC.com, The Boston Globe.com, The Miami Herald.com, Morningstar.com, and others. She is active in the NTMA, PMA, and AMT communities having helped over 100 highly custom jobs shops to reduce their lead-times and improve due date performance. She worked with Dr Goldratt who is the father of Theory of Constraints and author of the bestselling book, *The Goal*. Dr Lisa is the President of the Science of Business specializing in increasing profits of highly custom manufacturers by applying Theory of Constraints, Lean and Six Sigma to operations with Velocity Scheduling System and to engineering/design with Project Velocity System and to marketing with Mafia Offers.

"A must read. Velocity Manufacturing sets the stage for how manufacturers can reduce Total Cost of Ownership becoming more globally competitive. Dr Lisa is a true expert helping manufacturers to reduce lead-times and to improve due date performance."
Harry Moser, Founder, The Reshoring Initiative www.ReshoreNOW.org

"Is it possible your extremely efficient process is actually preventing you from winning new customers? Dr Lisa thinks so, and she is right! Learn how to increase quality while reducing lead times using Velocity Manufacturing and really differentiate your shop from all the others."
David Landsman, Director MFG.com

"Dr Lisa is a Theory of Constraints expert with lots of experience in the machining, tooling, forming, stamping, and fabricating industries. Velocity Manufacturing is an easy read and will get you started on the road to substantially improving your operations. If you're a highly custom job shop -- you must read this!"
Grady Cope, CEO Reata Engineering, 2011 National Tooling and Machining Association
Chairman of the Board

"With Velocity Scheduling System we increased our due date performance from 69% to 96%. At the same time we shipped more jobs, increasing revenue with fewer people. Being out of survival mode and being out of the chaos and day to day "administrivia" has allowed me to actually enjoy the business and have a personal life!"
Michelle Reichlin, President, Contour Tool Inc.

CHAPTER 18

GIST B U
SUCCESS BLUEPRINT

BY DIAMOND LEONE

What is the price you will have to pay to achieve the goals that are most important to you? I came from a very poor background. My mother was a single parent raising three kids on welfare and my dad was nowhere to be found. I learned at an early age that the price I was willing to pay would be high and worth every penny. It was approaching fall and high school was right around the corner for me. Everyone was getting geared up for school, buying new clothes, new school supplies, whatever. Excitement was in the air. That's when my mom decides to break it to us that we are about to be homeless, again. Being the selfish kid I was, I could only think about what this would do to my reputation...what other kids would think of me. I would be a complete laughing stock. This was serious!

I already had a miserable thrift store wardrobe which everybody made fun of. Not to mention the hysterical laughter I endured when my mom would come to middle school and pick me up in what I called her JE-SUS van. It had "JESUS IS LORD" painted in big letters on BOTH sides of this jalopy. And now with the homeless thing...it was too much for this blossoming princess.

I opted out of high school, faked an older age so I could get various jobs and never looked back. I say "opted out" like there was a form where you check the box or something, but it basically was me saying "hell no" to countless teasing and humiliation. Back then, they didn't have all the fancy "No Tolerance" bullying policies they do now. Where I came from, if you went to school in dirty clothes or wore anything that was worn the day before, better get your ice pack ready. The teasing and name-calling almost always turned to throwing punches.

I worked my little heart out at countless dead-end jobs before realizing there just had to be more to life than what I was doing. I started to read, then read some more. I read Tony Robbins' book "Personal Power" (back then he was Anthony – now he's matured into Tony). I read the "Neuropsychology of Self Discipline", I read Zig Ziglar's "How to be a Winner" and countless others.

I began to see that there was a systematic way to create a better life. It was exciting. I made some pretty good progress over the next 10 years. I put myself through college, bought some investment property, started an IT career, got married, and had 2 kids. I seemed to be checking off all the "life milestones" on my list quite nicely.

Years later, I found myself unhappy but couldn't figure out why. Then I started to do the math. I had given up my career (which left me feeling useless), took a backseat to my husband's demanding work schedule (which left me feeling alone), took care of my two screaming kids all day and was pulling my hair out (which left me feeling exhausted and unappreciated). I was giving and giving of myself yet everything in my life was falling apart, including my marriage. Who was I? What had I become? What happened?

Where am I going with all this, you ask? Well, a few things. First, while I had made progress from where I came from as a poor homeless kid, that was not much comfort to me at the time. I wanted more out of life. I worked so hard, so very hard to have the perfect life, the perfect marriage, the perfect family and it just wasn't happening. And now to top it off, I was a single mom raising two kids alone. Nobody but me to pick up the pieces and move on. BOO-HOO, SNIFF, SNIFF – that's right, I was having my big pity party for one. For those of you who have been through a divorce and started your life over, you know what I'm talking about here.

Second, I remembered a saying "If it is to be…It's up to me." This statement shifted my mindset. I went back and re-read all the great books

I read previously in my early life and a lot of new ones too. The skills I learned like goal setting, defined purpose, planning and persistence changed my life. Looking back, I realized that I was working really hard in life, but I didn't have a plan. I was merely taking care of the immediate priorities and obligations and before I knew it, the day was over. The next day, I would do it all over again.... like a robot. This is the common "grind mode" in which so many of us get caught up, in everyday life. I began to research a way that I could systematically apply all these great things I learned to my life, and be able to measure my results within an organized framework.

Several years of research later, through trial and error, I created the "Success Blueprint" System. It changed the way I look at life. It allows you to clearly define every area of your life and create goals for each of those areas. This way you will not leave any area of your life unmanaged. You know exactly where you want your life to go. You feel more in control and you are happier because, unlike other methods out there, this one allows you to see your life's big picture.

Had I only known about this earlier, I could have applied it to my life sooner. I could have avoided being the sacrificial mother and wife. I would have had clear goals for my own life and knew where I was going. But the amazing thing is that it's never too late to apply it.

Here's how it works:

There are five basic areas of your life.

Success in these areas is crucial to your feelings of happiness. They are:
1. Your Health/Personal growth
2. Your Finances
3. Your Career
4. Your Family/Relationships
5. Your Spiritual Connection/Contribution to others

To say that you want to be happy in these areas is not enough. You have to know exactly what your goals are in each area so you can measure your progress. To be successful in your life you need to have a plan. A life plan. Without a plan, your dreams will remain dreams only. A life plan serves as the blueprint to help guide you from where you are today in each of the above areas, to where you want to go. You can't hit a target that you can't see. By knowing exactly where you are supposed to go, it's easier to stay focused.

In short, a life plan is a written blueprint for success that helps you to:

    a.   Clearly see who you are and your life's "Big Picture"
    b.   Define and set realistic goals
    c.   Create a measurable time-table with deadlines to achieve those goals
    d.   Develop an action plan to get started and keep going
    e.   Create easy steps to review your progress to make sure you stay on track

But it does not have to be that complicated.

Your Success Blueprint should answer three basic questions:

- Who are you?
- Where do you want to go?
- How will you get there?

1. WHO ARE YOU?

The first step to creating your Success Blueprint is to find out your behavioral and personality type. You must have a firm understanding of what makes you tick. There are many types of tests you can take to figure this out such as the DISC test, Meyers-Briggs Type Indicator, Enneagram tests, etc. These tests help you gain insight and better understanding of the strengths and challenges of your behavioral style. Knowing this information will assist you with goal setting, career planning, making decisions, managing your time, understanding your social interactions with others and much more.

One of the most popular tests is the DISC test. Try the following websites to take a DISC test. However, if the links are disabled, just Google "FREE DISC TEST" and you will find one:

- www.mytotal.net
- www.discprofile.com/disctests.htm
- www.onlinedisc.com/sitemap.htm

2. WHERE DO YOU WANT TO GO?

What do you want out of life? More simply, what is your big "WHY" in life? Your big WHY is the reason for everything you do. You need to know this before you can set goals because it is the reason behind your goals. If you're not sure what you want out of life, than let's go over some questions that may help you clarify your purpose in life:

(i) What are your core life values? Your values determine what is most important to you, your big "WHY". For me, it's my family. For some, it could be their careers or financial status. For others, it could be helping people. It works like this: whatever is most important to you, you must center all your goals, all your decisions in your life around that. If you don't, you will be perpetually unhappy and you won't understand why. I teach a course on helping people to clarify their life values. If you need help with this, go to www.diamondleone.com and contact me. The reason is that you must know what your values are in order to complete your life plan. Your whole life plan and all the goals you set revolve around your core life values.

(ii) How does your Eulogy read? I know this sounds kind of disturbing, especially since you are still alive, but you should always begin with the end in mind. This exercise will help you figure out what's really important to you and what you would have wanted to achieve in your life.

Get out a piece of paper and answer these questions:

a. How do you want to be remembered?
b. What is your definition of success?
c. What makes you eternally happy?
d. What would your perfect life look like?
e. What was your major contribution to the people you loved and to this world?

Now that you have:

- Clarified your values – which are the areas of your life that are most important to you

- And you know how you want to be remembered

You should have a really clear idea as to where you want your life to go. Remember your passion is your purpose. If you are still not sure what you want to do with your life, go to www.diamondleone.com and sign up for my coaching program. I will help you sort this out.

3. HOW DO I GET THERE?

Now it is time to set your goals in each of the five areas of your life. Goals are the engine behind your whole success life blueprint. It is what defines each step you need to take and helps keep you focused and on track. Each goal must be a "SMART" goal.

A **SMART** goal is:

Specific – A specific goal has a much greater chance of being accomplished than a general goal. A Specific goal must answer the 5 W's below:

- What: What do I want to accomplish?
- Why: Specific reasons, purpose or benefits of accomplishing the goal.
- Who: Who is involved?
- Where: Identify a location.
- Which: Identify requirements and constraints.

Measurable – You must establish solid criteria for measuring your progress along the way to achieving your goal. What good is a goal that you can't measure? If goals can't be measured, you will have no way of knowing if you are making progress toward their completion. When you measure your progress, you stay on track. Ask yourself:

- How much?
- How many?
- How will I know when it is accomplished?

Attainable – Goals must be relevant and attainable. Your goals cannot be set too high or too low otherwise they become meaningless and you will ignore them. You can obtain almost any goal you set by planning your steps wisely and set a timeframe that allows you to carry out those steps. Goals that previously were out of your realm of possibility will eventually move closer and be attainable. This happens because when you list your goals, you develop a positive self-image which helps you to grow and develop the personality and traits that allow you possess your new goals.

Realistic – A goal must be within your available resources, knowledge and time. You want to keep your goals manageable enough and relevant enough to what your overall objective is so that you can achieve them. For example, if you are obese and want to lose weight, you wouldn't want to set a goal of running 5 miles a day. That is not a realistic goal to start with. Maybe eventually down the road you might have this goal, but keep your goals realistic at the time you set them so you will be more likely to accomplish them. Ask yourself:

What conditions must exist in order for you to achieve this goal?

Time based – A goal must have a target date by which to complete it. This is a very important step in goal setting. Goals that do not have a deadline will be overlooked in the day-to-day crises within your life. When you have set a targeted deadline for a goal, you will continuously feel a sense of urgency. Ask yourself:

• When must this goal be completed?

See the Success Blueprint Diagram below for illustration:

Now that you have answered the three important questions:

1. Who am I? – You have figured out your personality type, what makes you tick, what drives you.
2. Where do I want to go? – You have clarified your life values. You know what your big "WHY" is, meaning you know why you get up each day and what your purpose in life will be.
3. How do I get there? – You have identified the 5 key areas of your life and set SMART goals in each of those areas and given each goal a deadline.

Finally, all you have to do now is TAKE ACTION! You will need to have a system of monitoring your progress. I suggest every week you sit down and review your goals. Make changes if you need to but always stay with it.

I have a limited amount of slots left for those of you who would like me to personally help you design and implement your Success Blueprint system. I can also help you on a weekly basis to stay on track by offering my one-to-one coaching services. Please go to www.diamondleone.com or diamondleone@gmail.com to contact me. I look forward to your success!

ABOUT DIAMOND

Diamond Leone is an author, speaker and founder of GIST B U. Gist B U is a movement and brand designed to creatively inspire, educate and empower people to reach their own best potential through mediums such as fashion, the arts and health and fitness, to name a few. Diamond's story is one of triumph over adversity. She was raised by a single mother, grew up in some of the poorest areas of DC and Maryland and her family found themselves homeless and hungry many times throughout her childhood. These defining moments in her early life, coupled with her strong faith in God, gave her the tenacity and compassion to want to help others rise above their current circumstances and go after the life they dream of and deserve. After putting herself through college, her career experiences ranged from business management, real estate investing to project management. Although these successes were rewarding financially, they simply didn't fulfill her need for creative expression. She began a journey to discover her real passion of being creative and to help others.

She spent years studying the works of giants such as Tony Robbins, Brian Tracy and Zig Ziglar, and other top personal development teachers. This information was powerful and exciting but there seemed to be a piece of the puzzle missing. There needed to be a systematic way that could help people figure out who they are, then identify what was important to them and yet still apply the skills they learned to their lives and measure its effectiveness.

Using her creative talents, she developed The Gist B U Success Blueprint program to fill this need. This unique Blueprint helps you to understand who you are and what values are most important to you. It identifies the 5 core areas of your life, helps you to set goals in each of those areas and incorporates a method to measure your progress along the way. By following this program, you can clearly see your life's "Big Picture". You will know how you want your life to unfold as well as the actionable steps you must take to achieve your goals.

To contact Diamond directly and learn more about the exciting new things that she and her team are putting together, go to www.diamondleone.com or email: diamond@diamondleone.com

"To truly enjoy life, you must be willing to look deeply inside yourself.... and laugh."

Diamond Leone

CHAPTER 19

AMAZING REMARKABLE BUSINESSES – DOMINATE THEIR MARKETING!

BY JAMES (JIM) P. ENGEL

New Customers, Thousands of Them – Wanting to Buy from You… One Problem…They Don't Know You Exist….Yet!!!

You Will Find Out Here: The Top 4 Most Powerful Secret Formulas that the Top 2% of Businesses in the World Use to Dominate, and How You Can Help Those Unlimited Amounts of New Customers <u>Find You</u>, and <u>Buy from You</u> – Now!

The Simplest and Most Efficient Way that I can Teach You How to Attract Unlimited Amounts of New Customers is to Answer What You and Every Business Owner Always Wants to Know:

Question: What Are These Top 4 Most Powerful Secret Formulas?

1. <u>Eyeballs + Hearts + Brains = $$$$$$ Dollar Signs $$$$$$</u>
2. Q.Q.R.: <u>Quality, Quantity, Repetition</u>…(of Your Message).
3. The Most Powerful Law in the Universe: "<u>The Law of Reciprocity</u>"
4. The "<u>Power of FREE</u>" (Always Give Your Customers Massive Value!)

** By the End of this Chapter You will Also Understand why I Give

Away $3,478.00 in Free Gifts to My Best Prospective Clients!! I'll Give You a Hint: It Relates to the # 3 Most Powerful Secret Formula – "The Law of Reciprocity"

More on This Later…

But, Before I Open up Pandora's Box and Share these Business Transforming Secrets with You, I would like to see if You have any of these Business Owner Pain Points that I find by Talking to Thousands of other Business Owners Just Like You!

Talking to Business Owners Today, You Hear the Exact Same Half a Dozen or So Pain Points – ALL of which Go Away with Proper / Successful MARKETING:

These Business Owner Pain Points Are:

1. Our Business is Down with the Economy!
2. How Do We Fill Our Slow Times During the Day, Week, Month, and Year?
3. We Don't Know <u>HOW</u> to Market / Advertise!
4. We Don't have <u>TIME</u> to Market / Advertise!
5. We Don't have <u>SERIOUS MONEY</u> / $100K + to Market / Advertise!
6. We Don't have <u>ENOUGH CUSTOMERS</u> Calling or Walking In Like we Used To!
7. We Can't Cover our Overhead and Make a Decent Profit!!
8. I Don't Know if I can Continue Like this, or If I Even Should Keep the Business Open!

Any or All of These Challenges Sound Familiar to You as a Business Owner?

I am guessing You have experienced Many of these Challenges if You are Striving to have a Top 2% "Amazing Remarkable" Business!

Alright, enough of the Challenges and onto the Record Breaking Success You Deserve in your business.

Let's get down to Brass Tacks with –
<u>"The Top 4 Most Powerful Secret Formulas to Business Success"</u>:

SECRET FORMULA #1:

Eyeballs + Hearts + Brains = $$$$$$ Dollar Signs $$$$$$

_The Formula for Attracting an Endless Supply of New Customers is:

Eyeballs + Hearts + Brains = $$$$$$ Dollar Signs $$$$$$. This Formula, or Equation as it were, is what the 95% of Businesses that Failed.... Never Even Considered: It is Completely Missed by Most Every Business Owner to the Shock and Horror of Top 2% Business Owners!

Eyeballs: is the Amount of People that See Your Message. This Must Be Tens of Thousands or Hundreds of Thousands....NOT Whom ever Happened to be Driving by Your Business!!! (Or Whomever Saw Your Flyer).

"The Law of Large Numbers" DOES Apply Here!!

Next is Hearts: You MUST get them Engaged Emotionally!! This is Achieved with Your "Amazing Remarkable" Offer. If they Don't get Excited to Buy, They Will Not Buy!!

YOU MUST HAVE AN "AMAZING REMARKABLE" / "IRRESISTIBLE OFFER"!!!

In the Earth Shattering Book: "The Irresistible Offer" Author Mark Joyner Explains what an Irresistible Offer is by Stating:

"The Irresistible Offer"

"Once you get it, you'll be absolutely and utterly unstoppable. It would be impossible to fail!"

"The "Irresistible Offer" is an identity-building offer central to a product, service or company where the believable return on investment is communicated so clearly and efficiently that it's immediately apparent you'd have to be a fool to pass it up!"

The irresistible offer cuts through all of the noise and clutter. It creates an itch that the buyer has to scratch. Such an offer makes doing business with you so easy and obviously beneficial that you stand out clearly from the crowd. People remember you. People can't move quickly enough to give you their money. The irresistible offer sparks the customers imagination and creates an urgent, got to-have-it-now BUYING FRENZY!!"

Wow, No Further Explanation Needed Here!

LASTLY; After Hearts Comes Brains…..After Someone See's Your Message, THE EYEBALLS, and Gets Attached Emotionally, THE HEART, they will Need to back it up Logically with THEIR BRAINS before they will Open Their Wallets and Buy from YOU!!

With Your "Amazing Remarkable" Completely "Irresistible Offer" (Per Mark Joyner once again) You Must Answer "THE BIG FOUR QUESTIONS":

A client will buy from you ONLY if you answer their Inner Dialogue of these Unspoken BIG FOUR QUESTIONS:

The Big Four Questions Are:

    1: What are you trying to sell me?
    2: How much?
    3: Why should I believe you?
    4: What's in it for me?

P.S. In Future Chapters I will Go Much More Deeply into the Magical Marketing Mystery of: "**5W's and an H**":

"What, When, Where, Why, Who, and How" to Show You how to be "Amazing Remarkable" to Your New Customers!

****** The Fatal Mistake Most Businesses Make with Secret Formula #1 is they NEVER Get Adequate EYEBALLS Looking at their Offer!!! At "Amazing Remarkable" it is Our Job and Only Goal to get Your "Amazing Remarkable" / "Irresistible Offer" out to 300,000 Local Consumers – That is 600,000 EYEBALLS!!!

Number of Eyeballs Looking at Your Offer is KING!

Erasmus of Rotterdam once said: *"In the Land of the Blind….The One-Eyed Man is King."*

If the One-Eyed Man is King, What does 600,000 Eyes Make You??
$$$$$$

If You Really Get This and Really Do This: EYEBALLS + HEARTS + BRAINS = $$$$$$$

You will be Completely Unstoppable as a Business and Achieve Any and All of Your Dreams and Goals!!!

SECRET FORMULA #2:

Q.Q.R. : Quality, Quantity, Repetition...(of Your Message)

YES, it All Boils Down to Q. Q. R.

The First Q Represents:

QUALITY OF YOUR MESSAGES!!!

You Must have a Quality Message with an Amazing Remarkable / Irresistible Offer!!

Without a Quality Message to Begin with, Your Offer will be Completely Tuned Out by Extremely Busy "Would-Be" Consumers!
QUALITY IS KEY # 1 !!

The Second Q Represents:

QUANTITY OF YOUR QUALITY MESSAGES.
You Must have Many Messages, In Many Different Formats, and In Many Different Marketing Mediums if You Really want to Dominate Your Market!!

QUANTITY IS KEY # 2 !!

Lastly, The R Represents:

REPETITION OF YOUR QUALITY & QUANTITY OF MESSAGES, OVER A LONG PERIOD OF TIME!!

AGAIN, You Must have QUALITY MESSAGES, MANY MESSAGES, In Many Different Formats, and Many Different Marketing Mediums....REPEATING THEM OVER A LONG PERIOD OF TIME if You Really want to Dominate Your Market!!

REPETITION IS KEY # 3 !!

Q.Q.R.:
QUALITY MESSAGES,
QUANTITY OF QUALITY MESSAGES,
REPETITION OF QUALITY & QUANTITY OF MESSAGES OVER
A LONG PERIOD OF TIME = COMPLETE AND UTTER MARKET
DOMINATION!!!!!!!!!!!!

Here's the "Secret Within the Secret" Right Here: Q.Q.R. Is the #1 Best Predictor of Business Success over Business Failure. If You get This Q.Q.R. Formula Right, the others are a Bonus!!

SECRET FORMULA #3:

The Most Powerful Law in the Universe: "The Law of Reciprocity"

"The Law of Reciprocity" – AKA: Also Known As:

"The Golden Rule"
Childhood Lesson.

"You Reap What You Sow"
Religious Belief.

"*Quid Pro Quo*"
Latin

"Something For Something"
Latin Translation

"Karma"
Cultural Belief

"You Scratch My Back, I'll Scratch Yours"
Working Class Definition

"Yin & Yang"
Eastern Cultural Belief

"A Good Exchange in Value for My $$$ Dollars"
Customer Belief

My Mentor Always States it as:

"Being a Student of the Painfully Obvious"
Common Sense

If You Really get to the Heart of the Matter – Emotions, Thoughts of Value, Balance, Fairness, This is Really what Everyone – Including You as a Business Owner, and Your Customers / Clients are Looking for as Well: <u>Reciprocity!!!</u>

Massive Deposits into Others *Emotional* and *Financial Bank Accounts* Really Do Pay Off!!

Give them a Fair Shake, Maybe Even Over-the-Top Value on Your End – and You've Got a Customer for Life!!

Look Yourself in the "Business Owner Mirror" and Ask Yourself:

Am I Delivering Over-The-Top Value, an – "Amazing Remarkable" / "Completely Irresistible Offer"??

If Not, Create an "Amazing Remarkable Offer" Immediately and See Your Profits Soar!!

Possibly the Best Book Ever Written on the topic of being "Amazing Remarkable" or "Completely Irresistible" was just written by Marketing Master – Guy Kawasaki in his Masterpiece Book: "Enchanted!!" Being "Enchanting" is how Guy took Apple to the Top of the Marketing World and being "Enchanting" / "Amazing Remarkable" / "Completely Irresistible" is how You will take Your Business to the Top as well!!

SECRET FORMULA #4:

The "<u>Power of FREE</u>"! (Always Give Your Customers Massive Value!)

Lastly, and Ironically – Possibly the Very First Questions You Should Think About Are:

Q1: Do I Really Enjoy My Business and Attracting Hundreds or Thousands of New Customers?

Q2: If Someone Showed Me the Way to Double, Triple, Quadruple My Business – Would I Jump on it and Make it Happen? Better Yet, What if they could Do It For Me?

Q3: What is my LTVC: "Lifetime Value of a Client?" Meaning: Dollars a Client Spends with me a Year – ie: $1,200 (X) Times the Average Amount of Years I Retain a Client – ie: 30.

Do the Math.........$1,200.00 / Yr. X 30 Years = LTVC of $36,000.00

Knowing that Your Lifetime Value of a Solid Customer is $36,000.00 – Answer the Following Questions:

Q4: What Would I Be Willing to Pay for a New Client? Many New Clients?

Q5: If I Gave Away Some of my Goods and Services for Free, How Many New Clients Could I Attract?

In his Book: "FREE – The Future of a Radical Price" Author Chris Anderson – Also the Author of the New York Times Bestseller "The Long Tail" Chris Lists Fifty Business Models Built on FREE. Want a Shocker? Most of the Companies that Started out "Giving it Away – for Free" are Hundred Million and Billion Dollar Companies.

Please See if You have heard of Any of these Companies:

Google	Travelocity
Microsoft	Match.com
Apple	Craigs List
Amazon	Costco
Adobe PDF	LinkedIn
eBay	Zillow
Skype	TurboTax

Services Such as:

Free $100.00 to Open Checking Acct.
Free Software with Computer
Free Internet Search Forever!
Free First Night's Stay
Free Shipping for Orders over $25
Free Meals for Kids with Adult
Free Cell Phone, Charge for Minutes

These are All some Pretty Amazing Companies and Many are Now Billion Dollar Plus Companies, but one of my Personal Favorites was Featured in "INC. Magazine" Cover Story – July / Aug. 2009 in which it Told the Story of Larry Leith – Owner of 18 "Tokyo Joe's" Restaurants in Denver, CO. These 18 Restaurants Now Average $1.3 Million Each per Year in Sales, but the Humbling Back Story is that Larry Leith was "Beyond Broke" – as he states in the Article; Paying his $1,000.00 Home Mortgage on his Credit Card the Day of Opening his First Restaurant– So he put out a Coupon Mailer that Lunch and Dinner on Day One were FREE!!!

RESULT? "Tokyo Joe's" Ran out of Food by 7:30pm after serving nearly 800 Meals…and with That a Vibrant, Loyal Following Was Born!! 13 Years and 18 Restaurant Locations Later…Not to mention the $23,400,000.00 in Annual Revenue – Larry Leith Still Looks to that First "FREE Food Day" as his Best Decision Yet!

What Could You Do at Your Business to Create an "Amazing Remarkable" Offer like Larry and Build a "Tribe" (Seth Godin's Book) of "Raving Fans" (Harry Beckwith's Book) and Customers?

Q6: If Someone Brought 100 New Clients to Me and My Business – How Many Could I Retain? #_____

Honestly Jim, Are You Really Asking Me this Question as a Confident Business Owner?

Yes, The Answer is Yes – and I will Tell You, Answering this Question is Trickier than You Think!!! Why?

FACTS, Let's Cut the B.S. and Look at FACTS:

FACT 1: You have Done Your Math and Figured out that Your LTVC / Lifetime Value of a Customer is: $_____

FACT 2: You Know (NOW – After Reading this Chapter) That Many of the Largest Companies in the World Started with an "Amazing Remarkable / FREE" Offer.

FACT 3: You Know (NOW – After Reading this Chapter) That an 18-Restaurant Chain with $24.3 Million in Annual Revenue Started on their First Day with Free Food All Day!

FACT 4: You Now will Know that there is a Firm like "Amazing Remarkable" that can Bring You Hundreds or Thousands of New Customers… Quickly – Through 58 Different Marketing Channels and Technologies.

FACT 5: NOW, Take Your Average LTVC (X's) Times Hundreds of New Customers and Honestly Tell Me that is a Number that Excites You!!!

This Number Will be FACTUALLY in the Hundreds of Thousands to Millions of Dollars!!! $_____

We are getting Close to the End of our Life Altering Business Success Transformation and I have just shared with You – The Top 4 Most Powerful Secret Formulas that the Top 2% of Businesses in the World Use to Dominate, and How You Can Help Those Unlimited Amounts of New Customers Find You, and Buy from You – Now!

I would Like to Do Two Last Great Things for You as a Future Top 2% Business Owner:

NUMBER 1: Share with You some Insights from a Few $100 Millionaire Marketers…and One Billionaire:

Mr. Dan Kennedy – $100,000,000.00 Marketing Genius – Quotes (Paraphrased):

"The Person that can make the Customer come through the Front Door has the Highest Value!"

"The Worst Number in Marketing is 1! Having 1 Marketing Strategy Always Fails.

Having Multiple Marketing Strategies Sells…and Many Marketing Strategies Sells Big!!"

"The Difference between Broke and Rich boils down to Marketing!"

"Invest Heavily to Get Clients – this will give You Income at Will, a Toll Booth type of Wealth Generation!"

"The Doing of the Thing is the Least Valuable of All Things in the Business!!

Riches are Found in "Marketing That Thing" VS. "Doing That Thing!"

D.O. Flynn: (My Personal Favorite Quote)

"The Haves and the Have-Nots can be Traced Back to the Dids and the Did Nots"

Bill Glazer – Top 5 Marketer in the World: *"If You want the Same Mediocre Results as 95% of All Entrepreneurs and Business Owners – Then just follow the Herd"*

Peter Drucker – Process Management Genius / Pioneer:

"The Best Way to Predict Your Future is to Create It!"

The Worlds First Billionaire – John Paul Getty:

"I would Rather get paid on 1% of the Efforts of 100 People than 100% of my own effort."

NUMBER 2:

Even More Importantly – Prove To You that I Practice What I Preach – By Proving to You that: The Most Powerful Laws in the Universe are "The Law of Reciprocity" and "The Power of FREE" by Always Giving Your Customers Massive Value! I have a "Dozen + 1" FREE Gifts I would Like to Give to You that have a Value of $3,478.00!!

1. $1,000.00 Free Local Marketing for Your Business.	$1,000.00
2. Free $500.00 Video Shoot for You and Your Local Business.	$500.00
3. "Google Search Engine #1 Ranking Secrets Revealed" 29-PageWhite Paper.	$100.00
4. "Social Media Secrets" 31-Page White Paper.	$60.00
5. $1,000.00's of Dollars in Free / Discounted Local Goods & Services.	$1,100.00
6. "Secrets of the Millionaire Mind" Book by Harv Eker.	$20.00
7. Multi-Media Computer Disk with Latest Customer Presentation Technology.	$27.00
8. "10-10-4 Video Secrets FAQ's & SAQ's" 11-Page White Paper.	$50.00

9. "Pre-Meditated Success" – "Success Secrets of a Simple-Minded Irishman"Book by Tom Murphy. $30.00

10. Free Audio Download of this Book Chapter: $15.00

11. "Secrets to Shooting Compelling Video" White Paper. $30.00

12. I am an "Amazing Remarkable" Ahwatukee Business Owner and I would Like to Write a Book Chapter like this for my own Business / Customers. (Notes, Instructions, Webinar, Tele-Seminar, CD, DVD) $450.00

13. I am an "Amazing Remarkable" Business Owner in Ahwatukee and I would Love You to Send Me One of Your "Wow Boxes"   Please Do!! $96.00

*** Bonus: After Studying All of These "Dozen Plus 1" Marketing Gifts from "Amazing Remarkable" –

Please Call me Directly – Jim Engel at 480-505-2525 and I will get You a Copy of "Enchanted" by Guy Kawasaki!!

Congratulations!! Your Business Life Will Never Be the Same After Learning these Concepts!!

FOR YOUR "POWER OF FREE" GIFTS – GO TO:
WWW.AMAZINGREMARKABLE.COM/TRENDSETTERS

ABOUT JIM

James (Jim) P. Engel: Creator and Owner of Four Businesses Built from $0 to over $1 Million in Earnings a Year from Each Business.

Creator and Owner of the # 1 Ranked Mortgage Branch at his Firm in the State of Arizona for 12 Years.

Creator and Owner and Ranked # 1 Real Estate Office in the Country out of 125 Real Estate Offices – Generating Earnings of $1 Million Dollars a Year from Each Business!!

Previous to his 12-Year Ownership of these businesses, Jim was ranked #1 Stock Broker at his Stock Brokerage Firm and Retired Exceeding his Firms Goals 15 Times Over.

With these Amazing Achievements came A lot of Hard Work and ALOT of Hours…

BUT, This Isn't About Jim….It's about YOU…. and Your Business Going Forward…

There's Only <u>ONE KEY ASPECT</u> (<u>MARKETING</u>) that Jim credits All of his Success to more than ANY other factor.

Ultimately, He decided to walk away from his old businesses and start a New Business solely focusing on that <u>ONE KEY ASPECT</u> (<u>MARKETING</u>) to which he owes all of his success…to Benefit <u>Your</u> <u>Business</u>!!

For Your "<u>Power of FREE</u>" Gifts – Go To: www.AmazingRemarkable.com/TrendSetters

Unknown: ***"Everyone who Makes A lot of Money Defies the Industry Norms and Enjoys Doing it!"***

James (Jim) P. Engel: Jim@AmazingRemarkable.com OR 480-505-2525 OR www.AmazingRemarkable.com

Twitter: Amazing_Remark
http://twitter.com/Amazing_Remark

FaceBook: Amazing Remarkable
http://www.facebook.com/pages/Amazing-Remarkable/211087597136

YouTube: AmazingRemarkable
http://www.youtube.com/userAmazingRemarkable?feature=mhw4

LinkedIn: Jim Engel
http://www.linkedin.com/pub/jim-engel/15/14a/922

www.AmazingRemarkable.com   www.AmazingRemarkableDealsAhwatukee.com
www.AmazingRemarkableTV.com   www.AhwatukeeTV.TV

CHAPTER 20

BATTLING BAD FAITH

BY STEPHEN K. BROOKS, ESQ.

*"Here's my Golden Rule for a tarnished age: Be fair with others, but
keep after them until they're fair with you."*
~ Alan Alda

To me, a trendsetter means someone who leads the way, bucks
the odds and makes a difference for those in his or her circle.

That's our defining philosophy at The Brooks Law Group. Any significant case has everyone on the firm working as hard as possible to make sure our clients receive the justice they deserve. That's why we describe ourselves as "people first" lawyers; we defend victims who may have lost their health, their homes, their peace of mind, their jobs and/or their loved ones as a result of an unexpected accident or disaster that came out of nowhere. Being able to help them to recover as much of what they've lost as we can is always our ultimate objective. In the course of doing this my clients become my friends.

In most cases, we're up against large insurance companies who are unwilling to pay what our clients are entitled to. That means we're incredibly outmatched in terms of resources and manpower. To prevail against them requires a certain amount of "out-of-the-box" thinking, as well as the patience to deal with cases that may drag out for years and years (of course, as I will discuss in this chapter, sometimes those insurance companies can be their own worst enemies by forcing litigation). Fortunately, we have proven ourselves successful in many of these David vs. Goliath struggles. For the past two years I was honored to be included in membership of **The National Trial Lawyers. The National Trial lawyers** is a national organization composed of the Top 100 Trial Lawyers from each state. Membership is obtained through special invitation and is extended only to those attorneys who exemplify superior qualifications, leadership, reputation, influence, stature, and profile as trial lawyers, both civil plaintiff and criminal defense.

I'm also proud to say that I am a member of the Million Dollar Advocates Forum, one of the most prestigious national organizations for attorneys. Less than 1% of America's lawyers make up the membership, which is limited to lawyers who have achieved significant awards for their clients in complex and difficult cases.

These are not just my honors, however – each of the dedicated people who make up our law firm play a crucial role in affording our team these opportunities.

FINDING MY PASSION

If you knew my family history, you'd be surprised that I actually did become a lawyer. The reason is that I come from a long line of doctors. My father was a doctor, my uncles were doctors, my grandfather was a doctor, and even my great-grandfather was a doctor. But there must have been something in the water in our house – because there was a big sea change when it came to my generation's chosen profession. Not only did I become a lawyer, but so did my brother – and my sister also happened to *marry* a lawyer. My father used to joke that, if anyone ever sued him, he'd at least be judgment-proof with all these lawyers around.

So I didn't become a doctor. But, if you knew me as a teenager, you might have thought that I was really born to be a real estate tycoon. While most fourteen year-old boys have yet to even think about what they're going to do for a living, I was already buying real estate. And to tell you the truth, that's just what I kept right on doing for a couple of years out of college.

Everyone, however, continually told me that I would be a good lawyer – so I decided to go to law school. My original intent was to become a real estate lawyer. And at first that's what I did. But an incident that

196

happened while I was still in law school stuck with me. I was driving when my car was struck by a truck – the driver had fallen asleep.

Although I was okay, with the exception of a fractured ankle, the accident still haunted me – because I now knew firsthand what it was like to experience that kind of frightening and totally unexpected mishap, and how easy it would have been to have been seriously injured or even killed through no fault of my own. It sparked my initial interest in personal injury law.

Which was a good thing, because real estate law was, frankly, not very gratifying for me. I had a good friend who was a personal injury attorney and I talked about what he went through with those kinds of cases; I liked what I heard and decided to make the switch.

I began my own firm in 1992 with just me and one assistant, and, four years later, my brother, who was with a larger law firm, decided to join me. He had been a family lawyer, but also had an earlier incident not unlike mine; he was driving back from Virginia, looking at law schools ironically, and a drunk driver had hit him head-on. After that, he too knew what it was like to be in the victim's seat – so he was happy to give personal injury a try.

Frankly, that kind of personal experience is key to what we do. It allows you to empathize with your clients. To me, the best part of my job is the interaction with people. When a client comes to me, that person is usually at their worst. An accident may have caused them to lose everything good in their lives. To be able to step into a person's life at that point and help them through that process and find justice is satisfying in a way that real estate law never could have been. It's especially rewarding when I can help those I know when they find themselves in a tragic situation.

For example, a close friend of mine lost his 9 year-old daughter in a car accident and I walked through the ordeal with him both on a professional and a personal level when the insurance company gave him problems. Luckily, I enabled him to obtain a substantial recovery – roughly 20 times the amount of the available policy coverage. In another instance, an acquaintance lost his wife in a helicopter crash and I was able to help resolve part of the case for a large settlement.

Emotionally, this is obviously a very difficult process for those who suffer the death of a loved one – and someone who can calmly guide them through their options can be an invaluable resource. I feel lucky to be able to serve that way.

DEALING WITH BAD FAITH

One of the big reasons for my firm's success in our legal battles with insurance companies is our understanding and application of the Florida Bad Faith law. Third-party common law bad faith has been around a long time. Additionally, Florida enacted 1st Party Bad Faith, also known as the civil remedy statute, back in 1982. Bad faith is an important tool used to level the playing field when victims and their lawyers come up against insurance companies' immense legal apparatus.

If you're unfamiliar with the legal concept, bad faith simply means that the company has a duty to act in a fair and honest way towards the insured. They're obligated to investigate claims thoroughly, and apply a reasonable standard when interpreting policies. They're also not supposed to make an unreasonable delay towards making payments and they should not attempt to under-settle or "lowball" a claim.

In other words, they need to act honestly and fairly in resolving a claim. When they don't do that, they're opening themselves up to litigation that could require them to pay a whole lot more than the amount their policyholder was insured for. When they act in bad faith, they expose themselves to legal judgments that could cost them millions instead of tens of thousands of dollars.

Most good lawyers, a category that includes those at my firm, give an insurance company every opportunity to resolve a claim in *good* faith. When that doesn't happen, the Bad Faith Laws of the State of Florida are there to protect the common man. In most cases, insurance companies play on the fact that people involved in accidents are desperate for money and don't have time to wait to get paid. Many times, the insurance company fails to even properly investigate a claim. Insurance companies will delay claims, offer low offers of settlement and generally drag things out to force a "throw in the towel" moment on a financially-desperate injured person.

I believe that many times insurance companies take the calculated gamble that most plaintiffs do not have the staying power to take them on by pursing their case through trial and then a bad faith claim. It can be a long process. In rare cases the insurance company is not trying to get away with something – bad faith often occurs just because of disorganization or a lack of communication due to the bureaucracy of a company. As a result, they end up taking action that denies our clients' legitimate claims and qualifies as bad faith.

BAD FAITH IN ACTION

It's really hard to explain why insurance companies allow some bad faith cases to progress. As I noted earlier, claims that might only have cost them five figures often end up costing them six or seven.

For example, in 2004, Florida was hit hard by a series of hurricanes. One homeowner sustained mold damage as a result. She met the insurance adjuster at her house where the mold was clearly visible. The insurance policy covered mold damage and there was no exclusion of mold coverage. But, the adjustor took the hard line position that mold was not covered by the policy. We pointed to the contract language again – it was obviously covered. No, the adjustor said, it *wasn't.*

That claim could have been resolved right then and there for about $50,000. Instead, our firm ended up having to sue the insurance company resulting in a jury verdict around $100,000. The insurance company then had to pay our client's attorney's fees – that was another $259,000. Our client was also awarded $26,968 in prejudgment interest. Additionally our law firm was awarded $25,282.15 in prejudgment interest on the attorneys' fee award of $259,000. Our bad faith lawsuit then resulted in another $300,000 recovery. That took the bill up to $711,250 – over 14 times the original claim. And that $711,250 doesn't take into account the insurance company's own legal or expert witness fees.

Close to three quarters a million dollars – all because the insurance company refused to acknowledge what was right in front of their eyes. They left my client no choice but to pursue the proper remedy under the law. This had nothing to do with "greedy lawyers" and everything to do with my client not being treated properly for a legitimate claim, forcing her to seek legal representation.

In another one of our cases, a car accident left a passenger with $250,000 in medical bills – and she was also forced to watch her 42 year-old daughter, who was the driver, die. The insurance company for the other driver involved in the accident said there was no liability on their end and they were not obligated to pay policy limits of $50,000.

After filing suit, we discovered that the insurance company had no idea that the driver they were saying was blameless had been found permanently criminally incompetent by five judges in the county in which the accident took place. The defendant driver also had not been using her medication for about five months, had a meth substance abuse problem and also suffered from audio and visual hallucinations. Not only that, but this same driver was also diagnosed as suffering from significantly impaired cognitive functioning by both the Circuit Court of the county and the Social Security administration. And, to put the icing on the cake, she had also been convicted of multiple felonies.

In the insurance company's mind, they made a reasonable investigation of the case – but never uncovered any of the above facts, *which were all part of the public record* and which we easily discovered with a little research of our own. Now the defendant owner has been exposed to a multi-million dollar judgment because of her own insurance company's failure to adequately investigate this claim. And again, only because the insurance company refused to pay the $50,000 of coverage as laid out in the policy.

WHY BAD FAITH LAWS ARE NECESSARY

Earlier this year, the Florida legislature briefly debated a drastic overhaul of the current bad faith statute, but, fortunately, that notion did not progress much beyond the talking phase. I say "fortunately," because losing that tool means consumers lose a lot of protection.

For instance, in another state that does not have a strong bad faith provision in the law, someone was in a car accident and became a paraplegic as a result. The insurance policy limit was $25,000. But then, the insurance company refused to pay even the $25,000. Because of no bad faith law, if the person were to sue them and obtain a $2,000,000 verdict, the insurance company would still only be on the hook for. $25,000. If the insurance company has no consequences for dealing with you in bad faith, then in many cases they will not deal with you in good faith.

In Florida, because of a strong bad faith law, the insurance company would have to deal with the actual value of the claim if they refused to pay, not just the policy limit.

The other advantage our firm has, besides having the law on our victims' side, is the fact that we do actually try cases. Insurance companies do research law firms – and are much less willing to offer a reasonable settlement if the attorneys aren't willing to go to trial over it. There's no real incentive to do so.

Again, my firm and I are proud to help these people recover what is wrongfully denied to them by insurance companies. And we intend to keep doing it for years to come.

ABOUT STEPHEN

Stephen K. Brooks, Esq. practices at the Brooks Law Group with offices in Tampa and Winter Haven, Fl. He can be reached at steve@brookslawgroup.com or 1-888-We-Mean-It. You can read more about Steve and the Brooks Law Group at brookslawgroup.com.

Steve received his B.A. Degree from Stetson University and his law degree from Stetson University College of Law. Stephen also had the opportunity to study at Oxford University through an arrangement with Stetson University College of Law. He then joined a six-member law firm. The diverse experience he gained there has been invaluable to his own firm. It is the basis of a wide pool of practical knowledge and personal contacts from which he continues to draw.

Stephen devotes all of his current practice to "people" problems, personal injury, wrongful death, and social security disability. His widespread success in these areas is quickly creating a reputation of a force to be reckoned with. Yet he is easy to talk to and his sincerity quickly turns clients into friends as well.

One of the reasons for Stephen's success is immediately apparent. He is the rare combination of a "can-do" individual with a no-nonsense approach to getting things done. He cares about the people he represents... and it shows.

Raised in the Winter Haven area, Stephen maintains his close ties in the community. He currently serves on the Board of Directors of Tri-County Human Services, Inc. (http://www.tchsonline.com/home/). He has also served on the Board of Directors of Meals on Wheels. Steve is a member in the local Chamber of Commerce and on the professional side, he is a member of The Florida Bar, An Eagle member of The Florida Justice Association and The Polk County Trial Lawyers Association.

Stephen K. Brooks was selected in 2009 and again in 2010 for inclusion as a member of the American Trial Lawyers Association "Top 100 Trial Lawyers" for the state of Florida.

Stephen K. Brooks is a member of the Million Dollar Advocates Forum. It is one of the most prestigious groups of trial lawyers in the United States. Membership is limited to attorneys who have won million and multi-million dollar verdicts and settlements. There are over 3000 members throughout the country. Fewer than 1% of U.S. lawyers are members.

CHAPTER 21

WELCOME TO THE WORLD OF HAIRDRESSING

BY KAREN BENNER

This is the greatest job in the world! Where else can you be whoever you want to be, dress however you want to dress, establish your own working schedule most of the time, and make so many people happy, changing their look and improving their outlook on life! Doing hair, makeup, facials, and nails can indeed be a wonderful career.

You may work in a salon, teach at a cosmetology school, represent major companies, be a platform artist, work in the television and film industry, travel doing off-site jobs such as model shoots or movies, specialize in bridal hair and makeup, or even work in the resort or cruise industry. I'm writing this to help the new hairdresser (consider an alternative term if you want) understand what to expect in this fascinating field that I've been involved with for so long.

THE PSYCHOLOGY OF HAIRDRESSING

I never thought, all these years, that I would earn a PHD in psychology. However, a Professional Hair Dresser is just that. You learn to help people by listening to them, and over the years you start to hear the same situations over and over again. You hear what mistakes people made, and what they did to solve the problems. And these clients do count on you to give them advice! Your clients are sitting in your chair under your calming, yet artistic hands, and they will tell you things they won't even share with their own family.

You must have knowledge about some of the subjects that clients confide in you about, so I strongly suggest having access to a computer. When in doubt, Google It! Clients trust you, so, just like a doctor or lawyer; you must never reveal their secrets to others!

Oh yeah, I could definitely write a book about all of the stories that I have heard, and all of the people who I have counseled. And as a matter of fact, years ago, I was approached by a major publisher to write a tell-all book about what happens in the salon since a stylist hears all juicy gossip. But in honor of my clients I turned that down. I have respect for my clients and would never tell their stories (and some are real steamy)!

One of the hardest things to do is to know how to handle crimes and abuse. I'd recommend familiarizing yourself with the location of the nearest women's shelter in your area to offer as a recommendation to clients when needed. You will definitely run into this problem in the course of your career.

Please listen carefully to their stories. Don't waste their time on your problems, that's the fastest way to lose a client! They don't want to hear about what bar you went to, or who you took home last night, and how good the sex was... I've have heard that story so many times from the chairs around me, and well, it's embarrassing <grin>. I want nothing to do with your scandal! So if this hairdresser is next to you, please speak to them in the back room about their behavior, since they might not realize how it seems in public. Always have positive things to say to your clients, and, when appropriate, tell them about your accomplishments. They will always ask you about what's new in your life the next time they are in your chair. It is this attitude and these positive vibes which will inspire them to return every time, unlike the attitude of a Debbie-Downer or Sally-Scandal.

SEVEN STEPS TO BUILDING YOUR CLIENTELE

We, as hairdressers, have a huge advantage over most working people. We can work just about anywhere, in just about any town. But what happens when you move, or much worse, you lose your job? How are you going to build the clientele again? During my career, I have moved out of town several times. However, starting over isn't as hard as it may seem. To help you understand what is involved in starting fresh, I have set forth the following steps to establish a new clientele, in order to get your calendar booked up and packed with clients.

1. Get known in your community

Establish a relationship with those people in your surrounding area through things such as neighborhoods, churches, local businesses etc. I found that when I was involved in my neighborhood women's club, I was very active and involved in all of the charity events. When the ladies within the club got to know me, they started coming to me to get their hair done.

2. Volunteer in your community

Doing good things for others will always come back to you tenfold! When you volunteer, a lot of good will come your way. You can help others that are less fortunate, and you will become known within your community as being a helpful person. There are so many people within your community that need assistance, and you can spend anywhere from an hour to a couple of days per week to help those who are in need. Look for charity events, and support causes that are meaningful to you, or causes to which you can relate.

3. Get educated and stay educated

I have always continued my professional education, focused on my industry's latest and greatest services. When you know your craft inside and out, you have an advantage over the next hairdresser. Go to at least two tradeshows a year. There you will often find free classes that will show you the latest styles and trends of color, cutting, styling, and even the latest chemical services in our industry. Of course, going to a trade show can be, well, overwhelming. Because of this, you have to have a plan a strategy, so to speak... These shows can be like a twenty-mile marathon, and you need to have a plan of attack.

I would recommend that you get plenty of rest before a tradeshow starts. Normally, a few of the larger companies will have a big party or fundraiser the night of the big show. My advice is to please be kind, and donate the ticket and don't go or just go for a short time and not drink.

Tradeshows can be overwhelming if you don't feel good the next day. Read the show program, as well as the class schedule, and plan which vendors you want to visit. Be sure to purchase tickets ahead of time, since the classes sell out quickly (although there are a lot of free classes given, so all is not lost if you can't get into the one you want). Make a list of the products and tools, scissors, brushes, and other items you might need for your professional needs. Remember that the last day of the show vendors usually have some great deals so walk the floor and take notes to go back to those booths.

4. Not Busy? (How to find more clients)

In this new economy, life has been rough for a lot of hairdressers. People just aren't spending the kind of money on themselves that they once have. Beauty is often the last thing on their to-do list. If you have breaks in your day, please don't sit around complaining how slow it is. Instead, go outside and offer to do hair on people who will act as models. Offer a free hair cut and style, and that doesn't cost you anything except for your time. In many instances, they will come back to you, and they will remember you the next time they need their hair done.

5. Do your promos

I think the best way to find new clients when you're starting out is the models that you are doing for free. When you finish their hair tell them that you need them to help you grow. Most of the time they will help you, especially if you gave them an exceptional haircut or color. Simply ask them to send you three friends to get their hair done; for every three they get one free service. This can be not only haircuts but other services: color, foil service, perms, straighteners, hair extensions, etc. So essentially those core people could have free services for a long time!

6. Join a networking group

When you're involved with other business people like yourself, you feed off each others' ideas and help each other with strategy about growing your business. You then automatically have a base clientele list because everyone in the group is supposed to refer clients to each other.

7. Have passion

Have passion for whatever it is that you do as your job. Obviously, you should love to go to your job. If not, you should be doing something else, or working somewhere else! Why go through life being unhappy or frustrated every day? Instead, find what makes you passionate and work your butt off to make lots of money and enjoy the fruits of your labor!

ADDITIONAL TIPS TO HELP YOUR CAREER

a. Fashion

Fashion plays a very big part in our industry. Hair and makeup are essential but how you present your fashion sense is crucial. There are so many kinds of salons and clientele, and how you dress usually predicts your future clientele. So in the beginning when you're establishing a client base you should take in consideration how you want to look. As an example you wouldn't want to go to an upscale salon wearing jeans and a t-shirt to apply for a job. Same with exposing too many tattoos, or too much skin showing. You must achieve trust among your new clients and let them get to know the artist in you and then you can truly be yourself in the long run. Also, many salons have dress restrictions on the new stylists until they are established.

b. Choosing the right salon for you

There are so many choices of different clientele, but where do you fit in? You must do some research into several salons in your area. Are you willing to conform to the lifestyle and rules of the establishment where you want to work? Are you qualified to do the clients in that salon? Do you fit in to the group of people working there? Most salons are a very close knit group and already well suited for each other. You should get to know some of these people before making your decision of the salon you want to work at. Remember our job is a very social one so choosing the right place to land your clientele is important.

c. Mentoring

After you graduate Beauty School, there's nothing more you want to do than have your own chair, right? Most schools only teach you the basics, although there are a handful of schools that give an awesome background and foundation. While I was in school I was in a hair competition and won first place and I was offered to work as an apprentice in the best salon in town. This was not a chair, but as in every job you have to start at the bottom. With that said I received the best education possible. My boss took me under her wing and molded me into the artist I am today. Now for the past twenty years I go to the beauty schools and grab one of the students to mentor for a year at a time. Then when they graduate usually they are experienced enough to have a chair of their own.

LIFE AFTER HAIRDRESSING

I've been standing behind this chair for thirty-three years, and I'm wondering, when do I retire? During the birth and raising of my son, I have taken a hiatus so to speak…

Several years ago, I opened a salon in our area and it was an interesting project. We had more than twenty employees and were very successful. A few years into it, my husband and I decided to sell the salon and now I am working as an independent contractor, for a few days a week.

With that being said, I'm a Hairdresser. We are known to make a lot of money, but what they don't teach us in beauty school (or practically anywhere else) is saving for our future! At twenty years old, I was earning more than $120,000, and I spent it all! I had a great apartment, a great sports car, and my closet was to d-y-e for (hairdresser term). I went on great trips to far-away places (for beauty competitions mostly), and had no worries.

Well that is the mentality of most of us hairdressers. Make a lot of money, pay the bills, have nice things, and spend the rest! Nothing about saving, so at fifty-some years I have not enough money to retire so what do I do to re-invent myself?

I'm going to listen to The Paul Mitchell mantra "Work Smarter, Not Harder". What can I do to save the kind of money to keep me going, well into my golden years, and without working my hands to the bone?

I'm thinking about making something happen in my own industry. I can't yet say what it is, but in all industries people who are on the 'inside' come up with products to fill needs that they see, which other people will also want. I am hoping my product will fulfill a need that I see. Maybe I can tell you about it in a future book!

ABOUT KAREN

Karen Benner has been in the cosmetology field for more than thirty years, and has been at the top of her industry almost since the beginning of her career. She has won numerous awards for artistic achievement at both the state and national levels, and has owned and operated some of the most successful salons in the greater Orlando area. She has appeared on television and has been featured in the Orlando Sentinel newspaper several times. She is also a platform artist and educator, representing some of the industry's top companies.

Aside from Cosmetology, Karen has many other interests, including designing and creating costumes and knitting. She has also been a ballroom dancer for the past three years and has won more than fifty awards in this short amount of time.

To learn more about Karen Benner or to contact her, you may go to her web site at: www.KarenBenner.com

CHAPTER 22

CREATING OUR OWN RULES FOR DATING OVER 40

BY KATHY VAN LIERE

etting back on the dating scene when you're over 40 can be scary. Especially if you've been out of the dating scene for many years like myself.

I had been married for over thirty years when I found myself divorced, 25 pounds overweight, carrying a lot of mental baggage from my marriage and divorce, and I had low self-esteem. I was the complete package…I was a complete mess! I wanted to move forward, but I thought to myself, "Where do I begin?" I certainly needed to get my act together before even thinking about getting into the dating scene. Wow, was that a scary thought! Dating again! And, what about sex?

I had to do some of my own 'Personal Development.' Unfortunately, the idea of me taking care of myself was totally foreign to me. I was brought up thinking that taking care of yourself first was actually selfish…it's crazy, but that's how many of us had been brought up. I've since learned it's selfish not to take care of myself first. If I didn't take care of myself first, I didn't have the best of myself to give to a new relationship, my children, friends, co-workers, my community or anyone else.

I lost the weight. I got my head back on straight. I was a much happier person again.

It was about a year after my divorce when I finally felt I was ready mentally and physically to date, but where do I start? I had friends lining me up with a few blind dates. I was nervous about getting onto the online dating sites. I was also nervous about having sex for the first time with someone other than my ex-husband.

I took myself out of my comfort zone and just went out there and started dating again...I found myself making tons of mistakes. I broke all the dating rules. I didn't even know there were dating rules! I didn't seek out to be a dating guinea pig, but that's what happened to me. Early on, I did 20 dates in 30 days! Not because I wanted to date that much, I was just naïve. I've certainly had my share of frustrating, crazy and sometimes even scary dating experiences. Oh, the stories I could tell you, and I will share with you!

When you're trying to find that special someone, dating can almost feel like a second career. While online dating gives us the ability to meet people we probably would never have had a chance to meet, it's time consuming, and can be addicting for some people.

As I became clearer about what I wanted in a man and a relationship, dating became much more fun. I found myself creating my own rules for dating and it was liberating! I'd like to share some of my dating rules with you.

DATING RULE #1: PARK YOUR BAGGAGE AT THE CURB!

If we're not willing to park our life's baggage at the curb, we struggle and get frustrated in the process of finding that special person in our life. I carried a lot of baggage from my own life experiences. I had been physically abused as a child and emotionally abused throughout my life. I certainly didn't want to bring a man into my life if I couldn't get past my own baggage.

I've asked several men over 40 about why they preferred to date younger women. Most of these men said they'd actually prefer to date women closer to their own age. However, if they had a choice between a woman closer to their own age who carries a lot of baggage and a younger woman, they'd choose the younger woman any day. I'd ask these men, "You'd date a younger woman even if you run the risk of having more children?" They'd say "yes!"

Now, women over 40 don't corner the market in the baggage department, but we sure do seem to hold our baggage much longer than men. I've worked with some divorced women who were so bitter, even six, eight years after their divorces. They'd still act like their divorces happened yesterday! We all have our pasts that contribute to who we are and our outlook on life. However, if we don't get past the baggage that comes with our pasts, we most likely will continue to draw to us the same-old crap!

One of the ways I got past my mental baggage was to play games while I walked. Walking not only helped me lose my weight, but it was also very theraputic for me. I'd walk while listening to a playlist of my favorite music and as I walked along the homes in the neighborhood, I'd find something I appreciated about each home I passed. I'd also watch for something I'd never noticed before, even though I'd walked the the same path many times. This helped me to stop focusing on all the negative stuff!

DATING RULE #2: GET YOUR PACKAGING IN SHAPE.

For myself, being physically out of shape added to my mental baggage and lack of self-esteem. I wasn't very disciplined to make sure I exercised as much as I needed to, in order for me to get back into shape and stay in shape. I needed to have someone else push me so I hired a personal trainer. Now, if you can't afford a personal trainer, find an exercise buddy.

When you're dating, you're marketing yourself. It's all about the packaging. We're influenced by the packaging when we shop, the same goes for dating. I had one guy meet me for the first time with toilet caulking all over his shirt and shorts. He'd just come from one of his rental properties where he'd just replaced a toilet. He didn't get a second date from me!

I also hired a wardrobe consultant to work with me after I lost my weight. Now that I was mentally and physically in a different place, I wanted to figure out my wardrobe style. We figured out my style leaned more toward sexy sophistication. Although, I still love to wear workout clothes while hanging around the house. What's your style?

DATING RULE #3: BE CLEAR ABOUT WHAT YOU WANT.

What does that special man or woman that you want in your life look like? I've found the more clear I am about the special man I want in my life, the closer the men I've drawn to me fit my ideal man. As I actually meet the men, I find they may have everything I'm looking for, but the chemistry isn't there. Or, they may help me to better define my special man.

Now you may be thinking I'm being unrealistic. Nobody is perfect. That perfect man or woman isn't out there. Well, 'perfect' is in the eye of the beholder. What I may describe as my perfect mate may be something completely different from another's description. Our imperfections are perfect for that special person we want to attract.

If you don't know what you want in a mate, how will you know he or she is 'the one?'

DATING RULE #4: BE HONEST! DON'T START ANY RELATIONSHIP WITH A TALE OF LIES...BE HONEST WHEN WRITING YOUR ONLINE PROFILE.

I've been on a lot of 'meet and greets' where I've found out the men had lied about their age, their height, their body type, and/or used pictures from when they were much younger. I even had a guy use someone else's pictures in his profile! If it can be lied about, many did!

I had one man say he was 5' 6" tall; I'm 5' 4". I wore my flats when I met him for a drink. I thought something was up when he didn't get off the barstool to greet me as I approached him. After we talked and had a drink, we got up to leave. He came up to my eyes!

I also had a guy tell me he was 60 years old, and his pictures looked like he was 60. I got to the restaurant ahead of him. I was a little hidden so as he walked into the restaurant, he called me on my cell phone. A frail old man in his late 70s walked toward me as we talked on our cell phones. It was hard for me to hide at that point. Nice trick!

Another man represented that he was 'available' by being on an online dating site. At our first meeting he said he was looking for a monogamous relationship. There was enough sparks on our 'meet and greet' to continue seeing each other. The chemistry between us continued to grow after several dates and intimacy, I found myself starting to cross the emotional threshold with this man. Then he got a guilty conscience and admitted to me that he was in a serious committed relationship. I wasn't going to be the 'other woman.'

I'd had men ask me on the first 'meet and greet' if I was dating anyone seriously, was I emotionally available. After my experience of being the 'other woman,' I knew why the men were asking me these questions. I actually started asking the same questions, but not until around the third date. I don't go past a third date if there aren't enough sparks to start having the potential of a relationship. I don't want to lead anyone on.

I have so many more stories like these. If the men lied in the profiles, no second date from me! Certainly lying in profiles goes both ways because many men I met online or on a blind date would be relieved when I showed up for our first date because I actually looked like my pictures. They'd then tell me about their horror stories.

DATING RULE #5: FOR BLIND DATES AND ONLINE DATES, SCHEDULE A FACE-TO-FACE 'MEET AND GREET' AS EARLY AS POSSIBLE AFTER COMMUNICATION STARTS.

I started to refer to this dating rule as ripping off a band-aid; you just need to get it over with quickly! Ouch! After some hard lessons, I also learned to just say "no" to meeting a man who was avoiding meeting me reasonably soon after we started communicating. Is he hiding something?

In one case for me, a guy was hiding a pretty serious drinking problem. He showed up to our first date drunk. While we were at the restaurant, he started to sit down on his side of the booth about three feet away from the seat. As he tried to catch himself, he grabbed the top of the table and the two full glasses of red wine we'd just ordered spilled all over me! It was certainly a memorable first date!

It's hard to tell from emails, phone calls and even Skype, that someone has a drinking problem. So if a man doesn't want to meet me early on, he really isn't for me and I'm not for him! I've learned to allow a couple of emails to go back and forth and then have a phone call. Before meeting, I like to talk on the phone to see if the communication is easy and to listen to the man's voice, the phone voice test.

It's amazing how we'll naturally gravitate towards certain phone voice types. For me, I want to know if I would enjoy listening to this man's phone voice if a relationship developed between us. A whiny voice, or a weak phone voice isn't appealing to me.

DATING RULE #6: IT'S OKAY TO ENJOY SEX, EVEN IF YOU'RE OVER 40!

Besides being a dating guinea pig, I do a lot of research reading. One day, I was reading some entries in an online forum when I came across an entry from a woman in her early 50s. She was recently divorced. She said she wasn't ready to date yet, but she wondered if men over 40 like to have sex. Now having come from a loveless relationship myself, I can understand why she was asking this question.

The first 2 times I had sex with men after my divorce were a disaster. The first guy had trouble performing and the second guy stopped in the middle of having sex and said, "you're not ready." I was totally into our love making…in fact, I had initiated the sex, but I was being told I wasn't ready? You can imagine how this made me feel…I was thinking, "What's wrong with me?" There wasn't anything wrong with me, nor the men. Perhaps I was being a little naïve.

Although I made the first guy feel okay that he wasn't able to perform, I've since discovered there are things I could have done to help him actually perform. This of course assumes there wasn't a medical problem. There was a power struggle going on with the second guy. It was about him, not me. Since my divorce, I've been fortunate to have some men who made me feel very safe sexually and ultimately I experienced incredible sexual growth and pleasure.

I'd been with one man when he asked me if I'd do a blow job. I had to admit to him I'd never done one before. The sex had been incredible, but I sucked at the blow job! (Pun intended!) He asked me at the end of the weekend of love making if I'd be willing to go online and read about doing a blow job. I said "yes," but I would still have considered myself a sexual prude at that time. I told him I'd do it as long as I didn't get on a porn site. I did my "research." I found some stuff online. As my confidence grew sexually, I started talking about sex with my friends. I wanted to know what their secrets were for doing and receiving a great blow job. Practice makes perfect!

Sex over 40 can be an incredibly wonderful, freeing experience. It doesn't have to be a taboo subject. Open communication with your sexual partner can lead to a much more pleasurable experience for both partners. With one partner, I found myself saying, "Don't Stop! Stop! Don't Stop!" because of the ectasy of multiple orgasms on top of another. He hit that G-spot! We may be over 40, but we're not dead yet!

I've learned so much from the countless hours of research, reading and talking with men and women over 40 who are dating, and getting back into the dating trenches myself. I enjoy sharing my stories, my experiences and the tools I've learned and used myself to leave my baggage at the curb, enjoy dating, enjoy sex, and enjoy the relationships I've had with men. We can create our own rules for dating over 40!

To learn more, and receive a Free report I've written about the "Top 5 Myths You've Been Led to Believe about Sex Over 40" go to www.DatingOver40Club.com.

ABOUT KATHY

Kathy Van Liere has been seen on ABC, NBC, CBS, and Fox. She's an author of two upcoming books. She has a book coming out in late 2011 about dating and sex for singles over 40. Her second book is for business leaders: "De-Stress Your Business and Your Life, and Increase Your Bottom Line."

Ms. Van Liere is also a CPA and a highly sought-after business consultant. She's worked as Chief Financial Officer for a variety of companies for over 20 years.

CHAPTER 23

SMILE YOUR WAY TO WEALTH AND SUCCESS

BY DRS. ALLEN AND KELLY SMUDDE AND HUGH SMITH JR.

"We shall never know all the good that a simple smile can do."
~ Mother Theresa

S tudy after study validates what society already instinctively knows: A great smile can help to bring us happiness, wealth, and success. From infancy on, we learn that smiles illicit endearing responses from our loved ones. Babies learn that when they smile, it brings them much desired attention and affection. One of the first things people notice about another individual when being introduced is their smile. It is one of the most powerful non-verbal communicators that human beings possess. When you smile, a subconscious message is sent out that exudes self-confidence. In fact, your smile alone is capable of instantly welcoming a person into a conversation. According to Dan Pashman in his book *Smile! It Just Might Help the Economy*, when encountering salespeople in a store, shoppers tend to be drawn toward those with friendlier dispositions, and those salespeople tend to do better in business. Studies show that people tend to remain in stores longer and spend more money when their salespeople are smiling at their customers. Salespeople quickly learn that their charisma subconsciously magnetizes other people towards them and they, in turn, become more profitable and successful in their jobs.

The power of a smile is such that it radiates outward and can almost magnetize people toward you. In fact, a great smile can even persuade people to your way of thinking. As an example, no one seemed to use his smile more effectively than our ex-president, Ronald Reagan. For this reason he preferred to meet face-to-face with foreign dignitaries and seemed to instantly bond with world leaders. His smile coupled with his personality gave him a persuasive edge that he used to good advantage to sway people to his point of view. Whether people agreed with his political convictions or not, he was undoubtedly able to non-verbally give them a sense of warmth and comfort during the stressful Cold War period of his presidency. He used the formidable power of his smile, among other attributes, to attract others to him and eventually change the course of world affairs.

As we've seen, smiling is a non-verbal method of putting people at ease and getting them to lean toward your point of view, but there are also health benefits associated with smiling. Physiologically, smiling is actually good for your health. Smiling releases endorphins into your bloodstream and throughout your body. Endorphins are the body's natural "happy peptides" that have a chemical structure similar to that of morphine. According to Dale Anderson MD, "Smile, Laugh, Connect: The Key to Increased Morale," the physical benefits of smiling include "lessening of tissue inflammation, reduction of pain, relaxation of muscles, suppression of the appetite, and enhancement of the immune system." Enhancement of the immune system means that those who smile more often get sick less often. The endorphins produced help the body to fight off illness, especially those involving tissue inflammation, like arthritis. Endorphins also make you less hungry, take away pain symptoms, and relax you. Dr. Anderson goes on to say that, psychologically, endorphins cause a sense of euphoria that counteracts depression and anger. People who smile more and who have higher endorphin levels "tend to be friendlier, optimistic, humorous, creative, confident, popular, and yes, more successful and wealthier." Thus, an expression as simple as a smile can enhance your life by making you healthier and wealthier.

Speaking of success, most people who are successful in our society work on making their smiles as aesthetically pleasing as possible. It is easiest to make these observations with celebrities because of the volumes of "before and after" photos circulating in print and on the web. If you look at celebrity photos from before they were famous and compare them to the after photos, you will notice spaces between their front teeth, crooked teeth, and dental problems all present *before* they achieved fame, but with very few exceptions, not in the *after* photos. Celebrities will try to achieve dental perfection in order to get parts in movies, or in order to solidify their persona as "successful". Since most people are not born with perfect smiles, they would require the help of their dental team to enhance their smile. The technological advancements in dentistry have made it much simpler and quicker to enhance one's facial appearance. Most dental treatments can be completed rather quickly and can leave people feeling more confident in their appearance. For those people who are apprehensive, many dentists offer varying levels of sedation to allow a more comforting dental experience. There are several different ways dentistry can enhance every person's social status.

It might be beneficial at this time to lay out the most common dental issues that society perceives to indicate a lack of success in a person. The three most common (and easily correctible) dental issues are bad breath, tooth discoloration and crooked teeth.

First, and most importantly, every person who wishes to have any level of social success needs to eradicate bad breath. Most interpersonal social interactions occur within a smelling-distance of 18 inches to 4 feet (*Anthropologist Edward T. Hall*). Bad breath, or simple chronic halitosis, is caused by the waste products of bacteria that live inside our mouths. One such bacterial by-product is volatile sulfur compounds (VSC) that evaporate readily as you exhale and discharge a rotten egg odor. Other notable bacterial byproducts that emanate from our mouths are isovaleric acid (sweaty foot smell), Putrescine (decaying flesh smell), Cadaverine (decaying corpse smell), and skatole (fecal matter smell). Bacteria can easily break-down and hide underneath the gums, between crooked teeth, and within the smallest amounts of plaque the thickness of a piece of paper. If you wait too long after a meal to brush your teeth, there is food accumulation inside your mouth that feeds the bacteria and causes halitosis. This is more common in people who only brush their teeth once or twice a day. Flossing removes food particles that get caught between teeth and helps reduce halitosis as well.

Most of the time, brushing and flossing alone do not remove bacterial plaque and calculi from your teeth. This is why frequent visits to your dental hygienists are imperative to your social success and health. Plaque hardens within 48 hours and eventually becomes calculus, which is so tenacious and adherent to tooth enamel that it is nearly impossible for a lay person to remove. Plaque and calculus create a sometimes-visible film around teeth that allows for an ideal environment to harbor noxious anaerobic bacteria. The bacteria then release acidic by-products and demineralize, or break down, the gums and bones that hold your teeth and jawbone into place. This causes periodontal disease and further propagates halitosis. Only a thorough dental cleaning can properly reach below the gums and around the six surfaces of every tooth to remove the toxins. Going for months without a professional dental cleaning is a recipe for bacterial accumulation that leads to bad breath, among other issues. With the amount of times that we eat and deposit food and pathogens into our mouths, most people need more than two professional dental cleanings a year to maintain their smiles.

Second, one of the easiest and quickest ways that people can enhance their smiles is to whiten their teeth. Ever since 2000 BC when the Egyptians first tried tooth whitening, the world has had a desire to cosmetically whiten their smiles, as it is natural for teeth to darken and stain as we age. The foods we eat and drink cause a natural build up of organic pigments that discolor our teeth through the years. Along with certain medications, smoking, and drinking wine, this darkening effect compounds over time. Cosmetic dentistry has come a long way since ancient Egyptian times. Professional whitening only takes a few minutes for a dental office to fabricate custom whitening trays for you. The trays last many years and only need to be worn a few times a year to maintain white teeth. In-office whitening requires only a few hours in a dental office to initiate. The most natural look is to have your tooth color match the color in the whites of your eyes. This also accentuates your eyes as well as your teeth when you smile. Having your teeth and your eyes match in color gives you a more powerful smile which unites your face together more harmoniously.

Third, numerous studies show that society as a whole perceives people with straight teeth to be more intelligent and of a higher socioeconomic status than those with crooked teeth. In addition, they are perceived to be more attractive, kinder, more successful, wealthier, and more attractive to the opposite sex. As well as not being as attractive as well-aligned teeth, crooked teeth are also not as healthy. Misaligned teeth allow toxic bacteria more surface area in which to hide and eventually to destroy other teeth and surrounding structures. Gums can be more inflamed around crooked teeth, and the increased bacterial load can cause a higher incidence of periodontal disease. Dental decay is also more prevalent around misaligned teeth because the bacteria can get trapped in hard-to-clean crevices. Since there are so many more opportunities for bacteria to get trapped around misaligned teeth, cases of bad breath are higher than in patients with straight teeth. Fortunately, straightening teeth is more convenient now than ever before. Patients can choose from conventional braces or clear braces or clear aligners. Tooth straightening can typically be done in a matter of months. There are so many options that can be discussed with your dentist or orthodontist that can easily change your smile for the better.

For people who want a straight white smile without the months of waiting, veneers, crowns or bonding are alternative methods. These are acceptable options when whitening and straightening will not be enough to achieve an aesthetic result. Typically, a smile can be restored in two weeks or less with veneers, crowns and bonding. These are ideal if you are unhappy with the structure or have cavities or trauma involving your front teeth. If your smile is affected in a way where your front teeth are missing, then removable dentures, bridges, or implants are other options to restore your aesthetics. All three options fill in gaps with natural looking teeth. Your dentist can discuss the option that is best suited for you.

Since visual aesthetics (how attractive you are perceived to be) are so vital to our success in today's society, you literally cannot afford to deny yourself a beautiful smile. As a practicing dentist, my patients have told me time and again that by improving their smile, they have in effect literally changed their lives. A healthy smile has physiological as well as socioeconomic benefits for you. The sacrifice of a few hours in a dental chair can easily change how you are perceived in society, and more importantly, how you feel about yourself when you look in the mirror. Also, that time in the dental chair will have been well spent once you begin to climb that corporate ladder on your way to "the big corner office" that is the dream of most corporate employees.

One of the most honorable privileges of being a dentist today is being able to make such significant contributions to the smile. By simply doing the job we were trained and educated to do, we are able to alter the way a person is viewed by society, and thereby enhance that person's quality of life, their happiness and their well-being.

Beauty is power; a smile is its sword. ~ John Ray

ABOUT DRS. ALLEN AND KELLY

Drs. Allen and Kelly Smudde are a husband and wife team practicing in Valencia, CA. They were both born in Indiana and met in Chicago at Northwestern University. Dr. Allen moved from Terre Haute, IN to La Canada, CA when he was ten years old, and Dr. Kelly grew up on a farm in Valparaiso, IN. It was not until they were at their wedding reception on Dr. Kelly's farm in Indiana that they realized that their fathers had a mutual roommate while at Indiana University Dental School, and all were reunited at their wedding.

They both come from a long line of dentists in the family. Dr. Allen's father and several family members are dentists, and Dr. Kelly is a fourth generation dentist. They both started learning dentistry from their earliest memories onward. They both spent many hours in their parents' labs hand-sculpting teeth out of wax and hand-making jewelry.

They are continually building upon the foundation of skills that they learned as children, so that they can provide you and your family the best dentistry has to offer.

Education:

Dr. Kelly Smudde attended Culver Military Academy for eight summers. Her family has attended Culver for over 70 years. Dr. Kelly attended Saint Mary's College in Notre Dame, IN and is a Fighting Irish Fan. Dr. Kelly then went on to attend Northwestern University School of Dentistry in Chicago. She did her residency at UCLA Sepulveda VA in LA.

Dr. Allen Smudde attended Flintridge Prep for high school in La Canada, CA, then Glendale Community College, and Humboldt State University in California. He then went on to attend Northwestern University School of Dentistry in Chicago. Dr. Allen did his residency at Northwestern Memorial Hospital VA in Chicago. (He likes the Fighting Irish too.....along with The Northwestern Wildcats!)

Drs. Allen and Kelly Smudde can be reached at: YourValenciaDentist.com, or by calling 661-259-4474. Their address is 27450 Tourney Road Suite 250, Valencia, CA 91355.

ABOUT HUGH

Hugh A. Smith, Jr. is a technical writer at Dell, Inc., where he has worked for the past 11 years adding to the knowledge-base used by technicians and customers alike. He lives in Round Rock, TX and is an avid reader who enjoys quiet days spent at Lake Travis and quality time spent with family and friends.

Hugh received his Bachelor of Arts in Slavic Language and Literature from Indiana University, Bloomington.

CHAPTER 24

LAUNCH LESSONS

BY KEN GRANGER

All the research and planning in the world could not have prepared me for what would happen when I first launched emailStationery.com.

We unveiled emailStationery.com at 7:50 p.m. on September 30th, 2007 and soon after the first real orders flowed into the system. We had been providing email branding as a service under our sister company for a couple of years – but we were not prepared for what happened next.

We expected that our customers would make their purchases online and within a few days have their email stationery up and running. What we found is that a very large percentage of our customers bought email stationery and completely forgot about it! The clients would give us their money and disappear for weeks or months. This was a huge problem in our scheduling and workflow. We built our order management system anticipating the design process would last just a few days – in reality our clients were causing a huge traffic jam and some projects were taking months.

This also impacted our marketing. Our model was to encourage emailStationery.com to go viral. Every client who uses our email stationery would be sending hundreds if not thousands of emails per week to their clients and more importantly their colleagues. This meant that for each stationery that we installed, we would make an impression on hundreds of other potential clients. If our customers never completed their order, there was no way for them to help us grow the brand.

Just a couple weeks after launch we had to rework the entire order process. We scrapped the off-the-shelf e-commerce platform and began building a custom order management and customer relationship management application; one that could help us solve the problem of customers getting busy and forgetting about us. Over the next few months, we poured hundreds of hours into development of a custom system that helped us keep track of our customers, keep emailStationery.com top of mind, and ultimately roundup the clients who went astray.

With new systems in place we reserved a booth at our first industry tradeshow. It was close enough to our headquarters in Orlando that we could pack up the SUV, a cooler with some refreshments and the staff. We arrived about 4PM on a Friday afternoon and began setting up our ten foot by ten foot exhibit. A few minutes into set up, we noticed something wrong; the paper banner above our booth had our company name spelled with an "a-r-y" at the end instead of "e-r-y." We were not too concerned because our exhibit covered the sign, but just a few moments later the show management dropped off a copy of the exhibitor guide. I panicked – 10,000 guides were printed with our name spelled wrong – "for more information or to order your own email stationary, visit www.emailstationary.com!" We did not own emailstationary.com – and someone else already registered it.

We took several hundred orders at the show, and felt it was a success. But something inside of me could not stop thinking that there were 10,000 people walking around with information on how to contact us with the wrong website address. I knew I had to do everything in my power to secure emailstationary.com. I did some research and found out it was owned by a gentleman in the Cayman Islands. I sent a very generic email from my Gmail account (not wanting him to know we owned emailStationery.com) inquiring if he would consider selling the domain. To my surprise he responded quickly and said he would sell the domain but only if I would be willing to pay $20,000. My heart sunk - as a small new start up, how could we afford to pay $20,000 for a domain name that was a misspelling of our own name? I used Google trends (trends.google.com) to discover that sixty percent of Americans spelled 'email stationery' wrong. So, that meant that sixty cents of every dollar we would be spending on marketing would be wasted if we did not own the misspelled domain name. Over the next 2 months, I aggressively negotiated with the domain owner and $8,000 later, we owned emailstationary.com.

We will never know the true cost of this oversight – and honestly, if this had not happened, I don't know if I ever would have thought to check to see if emailstationary.com was available. While $8,000 was very painful financially – letting the domain fall into the hands of a competitor would have been a disaster.

As emailStationery.com began to mature and find its rhythm, we learned several other valuable lessons, which can be summed up in six simple steps:

1. PROTECT YOUR UN-BRAND

Most small businesses go to great lengths to protect their brand – by registering trademarks, securing their domain name with .net, .info, .biz and others – but don't forget to protect your "un-brand." Register the common misspellings of your domain name. If your domain name has repeating letters register variations of that too, and register both the singular and plural versions of your names.

Above all register the .com for common search terms. For example at emailStationery.com we own domain names – like email-branding.com or e-mailtemplates.com and over 100 others just like these. Owning these domain names help us rank in the search engines for common search terms and also keep our competition from sneaking up on us and gaining market share.

2. LEARN FROM YOUR EARLY ADOPTERS

Until you actually have customers, you only think you know what's best for your product. Your first customers will be excited to help you build your company. Ask them for candid feedback and listen to what they have to say.

Don't be afraid to tell your customers that you're a new company, or that your product offering is brand new. Most early adopters like to discover something new – and if you take good care of them, they'll be shouting your praises from the rooftops.

3. BUILD FLEXIBLE SYSTEMS

At emailStationery.com, we started with an off-the-shelf e-commerce program. It worked for about a week before we realized that we needed something more robust that gave us the ability to customize our work-flow. There would have been no way for us to predict this other than getting live orders in the system and learning from real-life scenarios.

Years later we are continuously updating our order management sys-tem. We regularly survey our staff to get feedback on what we can do to improve the systems they work with. Some suggestions are as simple as moving a link to a more logical place – if it saves a few clicks dozens of times per day per staff member, we will make the change.

4. SIMPLE SELLS

We learned in the very early days of emailStationery.com that the best way to sell was to focus on the simplest of product features. In fact, if some of the more advanced features were excluded people would still buy stationery from us. The more complicated your product offering is, the more difficult it will be for the average consumer to make a buying decision. You could have the most amazing product offering – but one too many cool options or features could confuse your buyers. A con-fused buyer is not a buyer at all.

5. DELAYS ARE DEADLY

Soft-launch as quick as possible. Delaying your launch can be a death sentence for your business. Until you have real orders and real custom-ers, you're making decisions based on speculation – which are most often wrong!

I'm a big fan of budgets and proformas. Sit me down in front of Excel for a few minutes and I can make a beautiful spreadsheet where we can make millions of dollars. If only it were as easy to make that kind of money in real life! You can make money on paper all day long, but until you launch your product and start getting real customers, your budget and revenue projections are really just fantasies.

At launch, immediately start collecting real data and grow your busi-ness with real orders, real customers, and real numbers.

6. SAVE SOME OF THE GOOD STUFF

Resist the temptation to include every feature in version 1.0. Save some of the goodies for upgrades. This gives you the ability to continually generate buzz by announcing new features. Your loyal customers will appreciate that you regularly add value and your new customers will recognize that your product is not stale.

POST LAUNCH ANALYSIS

So now that you've launched your business, or new product or service, how do you know if it was a success? Maybe you hit your revenue projections. Maybe your expenses were far better than you had budgeted. Maybe you signed on customers faster than you expected. All of these successes would make a business owner feel proud. But what if you did not hit your revenue projections? What if you did not sign up as many customers as you had hoped? What if your expenses were higher than you anticipated? Would you still consider it a successful launch?

It all depends on what you learned from your launch.

In the early days of emailStationery.com we would attend trade shows and industry events to increase brand awareness and we were shocked that potential clients just didn't get it! They didn't understand what email stationery was or what branded email meant, or that you could drive traffic to your website from an email. We found ourselves selling a product that our average customer was not ready for. We missed our revenue projections. Our expenses were higher than we budgeted, and we did not sign up as many customers the first few months as we hoped.

We were pioneers – *trendsetters*. The company was navigating in unchartered territory and it took a bit longer for customers to adapt and learn the new technology. The first year emailStationery.com missed every goal we had set – but we did not give up. We knew our revenue projections were a fantasy and the reality we were living in was giving us more data and actionable items to work on to make our business stronger.

We learned from our first customers and made them loyal fans and sources of referrals. We adjusted our tradeshow strategy so that people sought us out. We made adjustments to our internal systems to better serve our customers, and today, we are a much stronger, nimble and profitable company because of it.

ABOUT KEN

Starting a company is hard work; can you imagine five startups before your 30th birthday? That is exactly what Ken Granger has done, starting his first business at the age of 18. Ken is continuously coming up with new business concepts and ideas.

By age 22, Ken was running a multi-million dollar nationwide retailer at theme parks such as Walt Disney World, Disneyland and Universal Studios. He grew the company to over 60 employees and nine retail locations. Through this experience, Ken has acquired the ability to manage a large team while working toward a common goal, and maintaining the highest standards of quality and service.

While successful in retail, Ken's true passion is technology. In 2005 he started an IT service company that provided network design and support to small businesses. He sold the company in 2010 so that he could focus solely on helping small businesses develop their brand and online strategies through Arranging Pixels and emailStationery.com.

Ken is a sought-after resource on branding and design, and is often called a "technology super-hero." He lives by his mantra – *help business owners improve their quality of life through branding and technology.*

To learn more about Ken connect with him online:
facebook.com/KennethGranger
twitter.com/KennethGranger

CHAPTER 25

THREE KEYS TO UNLEASHING YOUR LEADERSHIP SPIRIT

BY DR. BENNY MORRIS

Leadership is the ability to influence others through inspiration driven by passion, born by a vision, achieved by conviction and ignited by purpose.

~ Dr. Benny Morris

My life has been devoted to seeking my own individual purpose and teaching and coaching others to do the same. I have found that the key to being an accomplished and effective leader is to find your God-given gifts and talents; there is where you will discover the area in which you are meant to lead. My last book **The Valeo Method™** is a 480 page life success guide anyone can use to truly find and live the dream of their soul, their purpose. I thank God that it is changing lives all over the world. I attribute the success of The Valeo Method to the fact that so many people are lost and struggling to find their way, and this simple five-step process is giving them a beacon of hope and a plan to follow.

When I decided to be a contributing author to this amazing book, I wanted to address the subject of leadership. I speak to audiences ranging from high school and college students to Fortune 500 companies with a passionate challenge to all of them to discover, ignite and unleash their own leadership spirit and to help others do the same.

A lighthouse keeper was given a monthly supply of oil to maintain the lighthouse on a rocky and dangerous coastline. Being near a small town, many curious guests visited the lighthouse. A woman with small children begged the keeper for oil to keep her family warm. A friend borrowed some oil for his lamp. A mechanic convinced the keeper to give him some oil to lubricate his equipment. By the end of the month before the next delivery of oil the lighthouse keeper ran out of oil. That very night the light went out and several ships wrecked and many lives were lost. Upon investigation by the authorities, the lighthouse keeper was very regretful. In response to his remorse he was told, "There is no excuse for this tragedy; you were given just what you needed to keep that light burning!"

Each of us is given gifts by a benevolent Creator. It is our responsibility to discover our gifts and to have dominion over our gifts and keep our lights burning! It is also our responsibly to lead in our particular area of gifting. When you discover your gift and develop it, people will line up to pay you to receive the benefits of your gift! The great writer Solomon, the wisest and richest man of his times said, "A man's gifts will make room for him."

If you are not getting paid for sharing your gift and leading in the same area, I want to make a prediction. My experience tells me one of three things:

1. You haven't sought hard enough to find your purpose and your gift (because everyone has one).
2. You know your purpose and you are not telling enough people about it, so those whose purpose is to help you manifest greatness can't find you.
3. You found your purpose and you are doing it but you aren't using your gifts to share with others. As a result, you are not reaping the size of harvest you are intended to enjoy.

So where do you fall in these three examples? When we discover our gifts we enjoy a life on purpose. A life on purpose links us to another gift that comes with our purpose and that is called "potential." We should always remember that God would not give us a purpose without giving us the potential to carry it out! Singing legend Pearl Bailey had a nice way of looking at it. She said, *"When you have man-made talent, you have to really work at it to be good. When it is God-given talent, you just have to touch it up once in a while."* When you discover your purpose you discover the secret gateway to finding your leadership spirit, making a difference and leaving a legacy.

KEY NUMBER ONE: LEADERSHIP IS AN ATTITUDE, NOT A TRAIT

You have to believe you can be a leader. True leadership is an attitude rather than a title. It inspires rather than manipulates. It is rarely an ability that is inherited; instead it is an earned skill. I don' t believe there is any such thing as a born leader, but one thing I am totally convinced of is this: every one of us is born with a spirit of leadership. Peter F. Drucker, one of this generation's foremost authorities on leadership, puts it this way, *"There may be 'born leaders,' but there are surely far too few to depend on them. Leadership must be learned and can be learned..., 'leadership personality', 'leadership style', and 'leadership traits' do not exist."*

The challenge is most people never activate their amazing innate leadership spirit gift; they just die with it still inside them. Sadly the result is, most people settle for average at best, and when this happens we rob each other, our society and future generations of our hidden gifts. Just look at politics and the state of the economy. Look at the financial fallout, the pain and loss from the poor leadership on Wall Street. Sadly integrity is becoming a vanishing commodity today. The true secret to rising and not falling is integrity-based leadership. When people are in a place of leadership because it is their job and not their passion, it reflects in the organization, team or company they lead.

Top to bottom, inside out, what you see at the top you see at the bottom. Just walk in most businesses and look at the attitude of the employees. If you see great customer service, cheerful attitude and commitment to excellence, it is coming down from the top. If you see poor service, poor attitude and lack of commitment to the business, guess what? That bottom line is being affected by the top of the organization.

When we put leaders in political positions where they must run an office and they have never started, developed or run a business, what should we expect? If a leader can go home at night and forget about their charge as a leader, he or she is not leading with spirit. They are leading with a title only. I am not saying you can't relax and enjoy time off, I am saying leadership is an attitude not a trait. So how do you wake your leadership spirit?

KEY NUMBER TWO: TRUE LEADERSHIP COMES FROM VISION FROM THE HEART, NOT THE EYES

Visionary Leadership is the ability to cause others to see a vision of their future bigger than their current ambition. Our sight can be an enemy to our vision (success). I love what poet Maya Angelou wrote, *"One solitary fantasy can transform a million lives."* True vision comes from the heart and is a vital part of a true leader. Vision is the key to your life having meaning and unleashing your leadership spirit. Purpose is what you were born to do; vision is how you see it. Your eyes show what is, vision shows you what could be.

Effective leaders have the ability to see with vision and convey with sincerity to their followers, team or company their vision. Vision awakens the spirit of leadership in a person causing them to develop an attitude that separates them from followers. It feeds the development of attraction power. Sadly most people have lost their passion or desire for leadership, because they have been drawn in by the negative energy of the collective consciousness of society, the news media, and the state of the economy and their personal environment. As a result many potential leaders are discouraged instead of encouraged to have vision and to desire to lead.

Vision comes from God's deposit of purpose in you. Vision demands the destruction of barriers; and vision can see beyond barriers. In fact, the greatest gift God ever gave any of us is not our sight, but our vision. Why would I say that? Because your eyes are the enemy of your vision. Eyes show you what is, vision shows you what could be. Vision releases you to think and dream of the endless possibilities of what could be!

Vision is truly a function of your heart. Sight is limited to the capacity of the eyes. Vision disturbs your sight. I encourage you to live with your eyes closed. The problem with your vision is your eyes! What you see is blocking you from what is waiting for you.

With all my leadership programs I teach people how to develop authentic vision, because when you have authentic vision things happen. If you have no vision, there is nothing to tie your dreams to.

KEY NUMBER THREE: TRUE LEADERSHIP COMES FROM INSPIRATION, (FROM SPIRIT) NOT MANIPULATION (FROM MAN)

True leaders have discovered and understand who they are, that they have a purpose and they know what it is. There is no more powerful inspiration. Too many leaders today are acting under manipulation of man and not of spirit. An example: This is what has to be done, it is your job, whether you like it or not, just do it. That may work in a perfectly-defined job, but not with top notch leadership. When we have leaders who are influenced by their environment alone instead of influencing their environment, we have mediocre to poor leadership.

Saint Paul said it this way, "In his grace, God has given us different gifts for doing certain things well." When we are seeking our gifts and working with our gifts we are creating and attracting an environment to lead in our particular area of gifting. Another way of looking at true leadership is this: It has little to do with what you do; it has everything to do with who you are. As an aspiring leader, your charge is to manifest yourself into the leadership capacity and environment you were born to lead in.

Here is some more "good news," just like your purpose is bursting to get out of you and take its role in God's cosmic play, so is your leadership spirit, which comes as a package deal with your purpose. Here is the only catch: For purpose to be realized, and your leadership to be unleashed, you have to do something. You have to activate your potential and put demands on it, you have to take action and exercise your potential gifts!

Just like bones lose density, muscles atrophy. The old "use it or lose it philosophy is alive and well here." Most people as they get older, lose courage as fast as they lose muscle tone. If you are going to be a powerful and effective leader, when would "now" be an effective time to start? The saddest part of life is not death; it is a person with no purpose. King Solomon put it this way, "A man is better off being stillborn, than being born without a purpose." That is a powerful statement. In other words, once you are born you have a purpose and it is your obligation to the Creator that you fulfill that very special purpose He created specifically for you.

If your life isn't working, and you are having troubles and aren't effective as a leader, I challenge you to "slow down to go fast." Ask yourself, "Do I really passionately love what I am doing? Would I do this even if I wasn't getting paid?" If you are stuck and you know what you are doing is not your destiny, stop and rethink what you are doing right now! Life is too short and sweet, you deserve to live your purpose and lead others in your area of gifting. Here is the truth I promise you my friend, after working with thousands of people in this area, no matter what happens, until you make this discovery, and find and live your purpose, the dream of your soul, I promise there will always be something missing.

THE IMPORTANCE OF TEAM IN LEADERSHIP:

How can we change the cycles of loss, disappointment, and emptiness in so many people's lives today? Here is what I believe and have seen inspiring the organizations I work with. We need to help and encourage each other toward finding our purpose; unleashing our gift of the "leadership spirit" and building more "team" into our lives and businesses. I specialize in working with organizations to develop leadership skills by creating an environment where people are happy to "lead without title" because they are so proud to be on the team they represent. We need so much more of this attitude in our companies, schools, organizations, churches and government today. People are literally starving to be a part of a team.

Recent studies show employee morale at an all-time low. Front page USA Today reads: Four out of ten people in America are considering leaving their jobs and are putting in applications and sending out resumes. Also, a recent Gallop Poll shows the number one reason for leaving jobs? Not paycheck, not benefits, no! The number one reason people are leaving is because they want to be appreciated! That is a clue!

I teach team-building and encouragement programs to all types of companies and organizations and the response I see from employees and students of all ages touches my heart and soul. People need encouragement now more than ever. They want to be appreciated, recognized and know they make a difference. What is amazing is it doesn't take much, and it goes a long way.

My challenge to you here is to stop being robbed of your destiny. Wake up and unleash the leadership spirit that is inside of you. Take charge of the gifts almighty God has given you, and lead in them. I challenge you to honor yourself by discovering the beauty, the mystery and the glory that is your destiny through your leadership spirit and help others do the same.

ABOUT BENNY

Dr. Benny Morris, also known as Dr. Encourage, is the author of the groundbreaking new book and five-step process called *The Valeo Method*™. A sought after keynote speaker, team building expert and leadership coach, Benny ignites the hearts of his audiences, clients, seminar and webinar attendees by challenging them to discover new levels of confidence, courage and hope.

Benny has been seen on ABC, NBC, CBS and Fox affiliates and interviewed as an expert on how to overcoming limitations and challenges and to create breakthroughs in life. He has spoken to organizations like ATT, Caldwell Banker, Bank of America, Equitable, ReMax, Century 21, Metropolitan, John Hancock, Prudential, United First Financial, Numis Network, United First Financial, The Equitable, and the United States Department of Energy, Oak Ridge. From intimate workshop groups to audiences of twelve thousand and from keynote speeches to entire weekend events, Benny customizes his presentation to encourage and inspire his audiences.

Benny is known for taking folks in the toughest situations in life and coaching them to amazing turnarounds. Benny is also an expert weight-loss coach. He teaches his clients the non-solution to weight-loss obesity. Benny found himself battling an ever increasing waistline until he was 80 pounds overweight. Using *The Valeo Method*™ he lost the excess weight and has kept it off for years now. He coaches his weight-loss clients in how to do the same.

Benny's weekend seminars and one day events are a big hit in the corporate arena. His teambuilding training helps companies who want energize and excite their employees, help them understand core values, work together better and excel as a team. Participants leave invigorated, committed and ready to take on a challenge.

Benny has been a successful inspirational speaker and trainer for over 20 years. His success as a consummate entrepreneur and team builder makes him uniquely qualified to understand and adapt to the challenges and potentials of any business or organization. Benny has built and sold a successful multi-line insurance agency (recruiting over 100 agents), a real estate development company, a health club, a home health care franchise, the #1 Anthony Robbins franchise in the nation and a successful restaurant.

His educational background is theologically based and he is currently finishing his second doctorate in spiritual counseling psychology. Benny is also a certified personal trainer and an instrument rated pilot.

Benny can be reached at: 1-888-996-3902 or: info@DrEncourage.com

His website is: www.DrEncourage.com

CHAPTER 26

STOCK MARKET SCHLOCK MARKET:

QUIT GAMBLING YOUR RETIREMENT FUND WITH PIN STRIPED SLICKSTERS!

BY JOEL SANGERMAN

L ife is good. Life is very good when you are making a generous salary in corporate America and doing quick-turn real estate deals on the side for kicks, grins, and huge paydays. The "phat" Vegas MTV-like crib, the Porsche, Caddi, BMW and Harley motorcycles, plus a garage full of other toys inflates a sense of accomplishment and security that makes life feel very, very good. Living among A-list celebrities was the "bomb!" Who knew the stock market A-bomb was about to blast America's retirement savings to smithereens?

The title of this chapter might be better called "I survived the great stock market crash of 2008-2009. Now what?" That is the question I asked myself after following Jim Cramer's sage-like advice by getting the hell out of the stock market when we hit Dow 9000 in early 2009.

Prior to that, almost 20 years of company matched 401K contributions and easy money real estate profits diversified into various stock classes created a velvety soft retirement cushion. Watching life savings grow like a chia pet on steroids through the stock tickers flashing green across the bottom of every plasma TV in the house was intoxicating and addictive.

Margin accounts with brokerages and credit lines on properties enabled immediate funding and fast-payoff on highly profitable real estate deals. It was like having my very own "private bank". It allowed for cherry picking of the best deals and created six figure profits on several deals. Those kinds of paydays totally rock!

By the middle of 2007, you did not have to be a rocket scientist to see danger on the horizon. Properties I bought in 2003 doubled in value by 2005. Properties I bought in 2005 launched towards the moon in value. Anyone could get a mortgage. You did not even have to have a down payment. You did not even have to verify your income. Huge banners in mini malls of Las Vegas read "NO DOCUMENTATION" loans. This lending environment made it very easy to sell and very easy to sell at high prices.

How could a 1000 square foot condo, in a four-story stucco building four miles south of the Las Vegas strip overlooking a liquor store and a few cacti, be worth $350,000?

Things were too damn good to be true! My female intuition took over. I am a man, but I have female intuition.

It was time to sell. I went in to liquidation mode and it felt good. Cha-Ching, Cha-ching went the email notifications each time I was sent a final HUD 1 from the title company. Green ticker symbols flashed "euphoria" on my Crackberry.

As the Dow raced to the moon nearly all the major brokerages licked their chops. We should be "cautious" but we could "always" expect growth over the long haul. Expecting returns of 8% to 11% was reasonable depending on how one balanced their portfolios. After all, according to "the experts", there was never a long term period that failed the stock market investor.

We hit 14,000 on the Dow. That was way cool! I had a Ruth's Chris Cowboy Ribeye Steak that night with my daughter, Liv, who pronounced the lobster bisque "monster soup".

Later in 2008 Lehman Brothers fails, Bernie Madoff scams are revealed, cooked books are opened, and publicly traded companies are exposed.

Bam! Dow 11,000! I'll never forget Bill O'Reilly's hysterical look on the hotel's muted TV that night. The look on his face suggested to me that he may have been a bit top heavy in stocks. I was at the Disney-world hotel with my girls getting dressed to have dinner with Belle because Cinderella was booked. I was thinking that I should buy Disney stock the next day. DIS has thought of every possible revenue stream they can squeeze out of the patrons. My kids love the place and oh what a business model!

Brokers made calls to measure client temperament and to assure the bosses that nobody was too spooked. Email newsletters exclaimed, "Weather the Storm"! "Be a Long Term Investor", "Don't Time the Market", "Stay the Course", "Buy and Hold; Don't Fold". This is also what we heard from most of the talking heads on the financial cable channels.

Dow falls below 10,000! I think I saw Art Cashin, my personal favorite, wearing a 'DOW- 10,000-by-yr-2000' baseball cap. It was the 4th quarter of 2008. The redness in his cheeks made me suspect libations were on board! I know I wanted one myself.

Again we hear the "Stay the Course" cries from the pin striped slicksters vested in the market's success.

Dow falls below 9,000!

That was enough for me. I was done watching this mess. It was to be expected and as I converted to cash, all I could think about was that I should have bought "put options" that would have made a bundle on the downswing.

A little bit less enthusiasm was now coming from the talking heads about the merits of "Buy and Hold". The "Fast Money" program even had a whole show on the "Death of Buy and Hold". Daily panic selling rumbled through Wall Street, ultimately leading to a March 2009 low of 6,547.

General Motors, one of the largest car companies in the world hit a market cap of less than Mattel. Mattel is the company that makes the little matchbox cars found at Toys R Us.

In slightly more than one football season, we saw fortunes take 53% nose dives. Retired people were sent back to work while others had their retirement nest eggs fried and scrambled.

This chapter is being written on April 29, 2011 as my baby Brooke is turning 2 and the Dow is flirting with 13,000. What a run up!

I guess staying the course may have been good advice at Dow 9,000 but when the unthinkable occurred, a 53% pull back to 6,547, we didn't hear a lot of "stay the course" talk.

Can it happen again? Many of the talking heads say it will and many say it can but "probably" won't. Each side makes economic arguments that seem well thought out and credible. My position is they are all very smart, very likeable, and they are also all completely full of – - – - ! Nobody knows what is going to happen next with the stock market. It is somewhat of a gamble.

Let's face it. Most of us do not even know the names of the top companies we buy everyday in our 401Ks and IRAs, much less what they do and who is managing them. The value of a stock on any given day is subject to the mass psychology of the stock market which can change dramatically as we have seen happen favorably and not so favorably. Yet, we are all invested in stocks like a bunch of sheep certain there is no big bad wolf around the corner to devour us. This includes yours truly. I have a lot of money on the stock market roulette wheel. I just have a lot less than conventional wisdom might suggest I should have.

There are too many financially dead carcasses that still litter the roads from Wall Street to Main Street as a reminder. And I am just not into road kill.

Of course, there is no doubt that a fortune can be made in the stock market. Speculators do every day and will continue to for a long time to come. You can even bet on declines. In very recent times bets on declining stock prices won jackpots. I use gambling words like "bet", "win", "jackpot", and "speculating" because, to a certain extent, that is what we are doing when investing in the stock market.

Having lived in Las Vegas for years, I can tell you that the Wall Street casino is one that I personally love to play in. However, we might consider very seriously if we want most or all of our retirement money invested there; even if well diversified. Diversification did not help that much when all hell broke loose in 2008 and 2009.

If we are going to speculate with our investments, stocks are not the only option. Some buy art, classic cars, or even baseball cards and actually enjoy their investments in their daily life. This is a bit too risky for me. Then, again, is it really that much more risky than having your money in some Wall Street Schmendrick's computer surfing the wave of mass psychology that is the American stock market? It probably is, but I doubt hanging quarterly statements over the fireplace is as enjoyable as a Picasso or Lou Gehrig's Jersey!

My two daughters have a great grandfather who is in the baseball hall of fame and his card, issued by the US caramel company in 1932, is valued at over $200,000. His Hall of Fame Ring was up for auction in 2003 and I got outbid because my computer froze as I tried to "snipe" the last bid. Yikes!! I wish someone was selling it again!

Wayne Gretzky bought the famous Honus Wagner baseball card in 1991 for $451,000 by phone at a Sotheby's auction. He was not a collector. He bought it as an investment and sold it to Wal-Mart for $500,000 who used it in a promotional gambit. In February 2007 the card was bought for $2.35 million by an investor and 6 months later it was sold again for $2.8 million equating to a 35% annualized return. I used to "flip" baseball cards, but never like this!!

Had Gretzky kept that card all 16 years through the last sale he would have had a 12% annualized return! Of course, he would have had a massive tax bill on the resale too! While an asset class such as art or baseball cards is subject to tax, quite candidly, that is the kind of tax problem you would like to have!

While those types of "collection investments" may not be appropriate for everyone, it is definitely appropriate to consider true diversification of at least some of our stock, bond, and CD holdings.

Despite the alarmism surrounding stocks, the real estate and stock market combination has always been a very successful tandem for me. However, that tandem got a divorce after the stock market crash of 2008-2009.

Both investment vehicles were cheating on each other. Real Estate deals found a better partner. Her name is Ms. Roth-IRA. She is way sexier and she makes a mean chicken pot pie!

One very hot real estate strategy investors employ today is to use a self-directed IRA as the buyer for their real estate. However, not everyone wants to be a real estate investor.

Everyone, however, does want a better return on their money without increasing risk.

This largely unfilled need has led to a White HOT trend as savvy investors look for alternatives to potential future stock, bond, and CD fiascos.

Enter the self-directed IRA.

A self-directed IRA is technically no different than any other IRA (or 401k). It is unique because the available investment options include real estate.

Anyone can set up a self-directed IRA and take back some control of their money and retirement savings.

Using a self-directed IRA to invest in assets other than stocks and bonds is not discussed as frequently by many financial planners, because most of the firms offering to be custodians of IRAs are banks and brokerages. They focus on mutual funds and CDs because they have vested financial interests in you choosing those investments from them. As a result, there is a common misperception that stocks, bonds, CDs, etc… are your only retirement investment options. This is certainly not the case.

As with stocks, investing in real estate with your IRA provides tax-free or tax-deferred returns that leverage the magic of compound interest.

There is around $4 Trillion invested in IRAs, 401Ks, and other qualified programs. That figure is way out of balance favoring stocks, bonds, and CDs. It is interesting that financial planners pronounce the virtues of diversification yet have so many of their clients fully invested in only the instruments they offer; namely stocks, bonds, CDs. True diversification would include diverse assets such as real estate, or low loan-to-value notes and mortgages that have significantly higher yields than what is traditionally offered.

With real estate, you do not even have to go out and buy real estate to have your IRA invested in it. You simply fund some of the purchase money used to secure the real estate with your self directed IRA. These funds are placed as a first lien on the real estate at low loan-to-value ratios. Your principal (the loan amount) earns interest that is directly deposited to your account. Returns are guaranteed by the real estate as collateral. You can choose to ensure the real estate has far more value than the amount of the loan. This creates tremendous safety and security for your investment. Your principal remains on the property for as long as you like or until the property is sold or paid off entirely.

What kind of return on investment can be expected?

Percentage returns on your IRAs investment can range from 7% up to 15% or more. Those are sweet tax-free returns in a Roth IRA or tax-deferred returns in a traditional IRA.

Just how safe is this sort of investment?

If you were to loan money at 50% of a home's value with the first lien on it favoring you how would you sleep at night with respect to concerns about your money?

I might "lay me down to sleep" praying that I DO NOT get paid. At 50% loan to value I might rather get the house that was collateral than my 7% to 15% interest payment! Yes, that would be better financially, but no, that's not really something to wish for – getting paid monthly is cool too. The point is that your collateral makes it extremely difficult to lose; especially if your loan is on a piece of real estate with competent ownership from an experienced real estate investor.

The beauty of this investment vehicle is that the IRA owner retains the ability to be "hands-off" with their investments and watch the returns safely compound to retirement wealth. It is an opportunity to take some of your retirement account and dictate terms and conditions in the same way banks do. Pretty powerful stuff! As CEO of your "bank" you decide who gets to borrow your money and under what terms. You negotiate the interest rate and the repayment schedule.

Here is the real question: Would you rather have a 7% fixed return for the next 5 years or would you rather let it ride in the stock market? We don't know the right answer yet as a certainty. We do know that 7% will earn 40% total return over 5 years. We also know the stock market could be up or could be down in that same time frame.

By the way, the stock market (DJI Avg.) from April 2006 to April 2011 (the time of writing of this chapter) provided a slightly negative return. That would be a 40% difference in returns during that time frame.

Today, we need to be smart enough to learn from the lessons of complacency. Lehman Brothers, Bear Stearns, Merrill Lynch, and AIG should be examples we don't soon forget. Knowing that some very smart people depended on people like Bernie Madoff and lost fortunes should ring reminder bells in our head that we ought to pay attention to our investments.

One of the lessons learned is that we should "self-direct" some portion of our assets and know exactly what we are investing in. This is why I am a huge fan of truly balancing out a retirement portfolio and connecting with knowledgeable real estate investors to get a self-directed IRA investment in place.

If my company, DMC Equities, Inc., can be of any help please feel free to contact me personally. I can be reached at: joel@ibuyrealestate.com.

ABOUT JOEL

Joel Sangerman is a dedicated professional in the field of health-care economics. He began investing in real estate as an asset diversification strategy in the 1990's. In 1997 Joel formed DMC Equities, Inc. and began buying and selling properties in Chicago with later expansion to Las Vegas. Closing his first $10 million in real estate deals using many different types of purchase and sale methods refined his expertise across several different investment strategies. Being interviewed for blockbuster real estate educational courses and being included as a contributing author in Trendsetters are great honors, given his approach to real estate investing has been secondary to an exciting corporate career. In the spirit of what Joel calls "personal bandwidth" he is currently applying some of the same creative business skills honed in the real estate arena to the pursuit of improving the nation's healthcare delivery system. Joel is one of many dynamic leaders participating in the national discussion on healthcare payment reforms that will revolutionize healthcare delivery in the USA over the next few years. This dual passion for career and entre-preneurial pursuit is what drives Joel's success in both endeavors.

Being able to operate successfully on a part-time basis is one of the major benefits of adding real estate investment to a portfolio of life activities. Joel has counseled hundreds of friends, colleagues, and contacts on developing the multi-tasking ability to accomplish real estate success without compromising careers or involvement in other passions. Joel offers specialized coaching to new real estate investors with a no-nonsense approach. On a larger and less personal scale, Joel is a highly-engaging public speaker taking the podium at various real estate investment conferences and healthcare industry meetings.

For a limited time, several bonuses are available to readers of "TRENDSETTERS" who may desire help in the following areas:

Setting up self-directed IRAs and opportunities for low-risk, high-yielding real es-tate investments.

Not-for-profit groups and organizations may inquire about booking 'no fee' speak-ing engagements.

No charge consultations on real estate matters may be scheduled on a limited basis.

There is tremendous need throughout the country for homeowners to get competent help navigating the process of selling their homes as a "short sale" or in modifying existing loans to be more affordable. This is a highly specialized area of real estate that is evolving and ever-changing. Joel will take a personal interest in helping hom-eowners needing this sort of help.

Joel is authoring a new "reality" book and DVD series and is recruiting participants. Inquiries from "Trendsetters" readers about participating in this exciting and unique project are welcome.

Please feel free to contact Joel directly through his website at: www.ibuyrealestate.com or via email at: joel@ibuyrealestate.com. Live assistance may be obtained at 702-364-2323.

CHAPTER 27

ONE CHICK MILLIONS

BY KAREN LEUNG

Glorify the Lord with me; let us exalt His name together.
~ Psalm 34:3

MY STORY

On January 23, 2009, I was attending the regular Friday night fellowship and gathered with my friends in one of the families' house as usual. My tummy experienced a deep pain around 11 p.m. I went to the upstairs bathroom. My internal organs were cramping and I experienced severe deep pain. I sweated heavily and the last thing I knew I was lying on the floor calling my friends downstairs for help using my mobile phone.

Half an hour later, the Paramedics arrived. Two men with uniforms were kneeling beside me and helping me. One checked my blood pressure and the other gave me the EKG test. After all the tests, they put me on a stretcher with an IV and wheeled me out of my friends' house to the La Palma Hospital.

Once I arrived in the hospital, I was staying in the ER. As soon as I was attended by a nurse, I requested an excuse to go to the bathroom. I ended up giving out a lot of blood in the toilet bowl. I could estimate the amount of blood I gave out could fill up two medium rice bowls.

As soon as I saw blood coming out from my body, I requested help from the nurse. After she went inside the bathroom and saw my blood in the toilet bowl, she immediately ordered all kinds of tests and scans for me. A certain kind of medicine was given to me immediately and it went to my blood stream via my IV. I was relocated to another ward for hospitalization.

There was a doctor who specialized in intestinal gastroenterology visiting me the next day. He told me that he ordered a colonoscopy for me. After the colonoscopy, the doctor suspected that I was attacked by E. coli. I could see one-third of my small intestine was damaged by E. coli.

I thanked God that He provided all the help I needed when I went through this life- threatening situation. If I had gone home and continued to bleed like I bled in the hospital, I could have died by now.

After I recovered and my health recuperated, I decided to write this book to inspire women not to give up hope of their dreams. They will succeed.

Success doesn't come by accident.

DON'T GIVE UP

If you have a great idea, pursue your dream and don't give up. One day you will succeed. It takes a lot of perseverance. But mark out the perseverance, you will win the race.

Look at one of our foremothers in this great American Land, Madam C.J. Walker (1865 – 1919). She was born in Louisiana. She was an African-American. She had plenty of life challenges at her young age. She was an orphan at age seven. She was married at age fourteen, it was reported that she had escaped the abuse that she was suffering at the hands of her brother-in-law. She became a mother at age seventeen, and a widow at age twenty.

She supported herself and her daughter by picking cotton on a farm, by being a laundress, and by working in a barber shop. From what I can tell, the most she ever made during that time was $1.50 a day.

But it got worse…

At around twenty-five years old, she began to develop a condition that caused her to start balding. Can you imagine? As if she didn't have enough to deal with – now the poor lady's hair is falling out. It shouldn't surprise you that she quickly became a student of how to fix her balding problem.

In fact, she researched all kinds of treatments, and eventually discovered that sulfur could abolish the scalp disease that was causing people to lose their hair. (Apparently, people lost their hair a lot back then because they didn't bathe as much. They would get some nasty scalp infection and their hair would fall out. But if you treated the problem with sulfur, you could knock it out.)

So she did the only logical thing to do, which was to start her own business selling a product called "Madam Walker's Wonderful Hair Grower." Keep in mind, she was just starting out and didn't have a big budget (probably NO budget at all) so she had no choice but to ... Go Out, Grab The Whole World, And Bend It To Her Will!

And the first thing she did was to go door-to-door, selling her hair product. Listen – nobody really embraces a door to door sales person with open arms these days, you know?

But imagine what it must have been like for Madam Walker in the racist and male- dominated environment she was working in back then.

...That took some *cojones.*

- How many times do you think she was rejected?
- How many doors do you think were slammed in her face?
- How many insults did she hear?

I'm willing to bet she even was threatened ...regularly. But did that stop her?

Hell No! Not only did she survive ...she thrived.

Madam Walker hung in there and sold more products, developed new ones, and finally opened up a factory in Indianapolis. By 1913, she was traveling around the world training other women to sell her products.

...And by the time she died in 1919 at age 51, she had become the

World's First Female Self-Made Millionaire!

Recently (April 28-May 1, 2011), I attended the Glazer-Kennedy Insider's Circle "2011 Marketing & Money-Making Super Conference" at Rosemont, IL. Kathy Ireland was invited to be the featured Celebrity-Entrepreneur guest speaker on April 30, 2011. Her title was "What It Takes to Build a Big Business from The Ground Up."

As I listened to her story, I was greatly inspired by her success. How she thrived through all these objections, rejections, and the worst economic situations! How she got her idea from… A pair of socks!

You got it right… Just one pair of socks! When she talked to people about her idea, they laughed at her. But she embraced other people's criticisms. However, she wouldn't let the negative comments hinder her progress.

She went door-to-door telling people about this pair of socks and selling to them. Can you imagine…

- How many times do you think she was rejected?
- How many doors do you think were slammed in her face?
- How many insults did she hear?

But did that stop her? Hell No!

But things got worse…

One day, she received the news that the billion dollar manufacturing company that manufactured her socks went belly up. She and her partner contacted the manufacturing company's bankers to discuss the manufacturing company's debt. The bankers agreed to meet with them over a lunch meeting.

During the lunch meeting, the bankers disclosed that Kathy and her partner were solely responsible for the manufacturing company's debt. If they did not handle it correctly, this might lead to the foreclosure of Kathy's house to pay for the manufacturing company's debt. A debt she was not responsible for.

Did she survive? Not only did she survive …she thrived.

Kathy Ireland has developed a $1.4 billion multi-product, multi-channel design and merchandising empire. This empire is NOT just licensing her name, but actually building businesses.

Today, Kathy Ireland Worldwide works with a variety of Brand-Partners, creating and marketing over 15,000 products in 29 countries. Products include cosmetics, skin care, apparel, jewelry, home furnishings, furniture, lighting, and many more…

You don't have to possess a skilled talent. You may have knowledge concerning something that you enjoy very much. Possibly you possess a curiosity by which you enjoy examining items, and doing so is the obscured passion. Think about something you are very intelligent about because you choose to be, not because you are required to be, at your job.

Most of the best occasions in your life may be the passion you would like to have again in your lifestyle. You might have been a runner and always wanted to win the New York Marathon, but now you are an adult and have carted that fantasy off many years ago. That doesn't mean you cannot get back into shape and go for your big dream.

Absolutely everyone is excellent at something. If you don't possess a pastime such as building candles, beaded jewelry, sewing, quilting, painting, or photography on the weekends, it doesn't mean you don't possess a talent. This simply means that you haven't fairly figured out what your talent is yet. You want to understand what it is that drives you. The majority of people are great at what they do when they take pleasure in it.

If you are having a difficult time figuring out what your true passion is, it may be standing right in front of you. You may have collections of figurines, periodicals, leisure pursuits you like to do on weekends and far more. Consider a look around your house and see if most of your things are a clue to what your true passion is. You may be shocked that you have surrounded yourself with these things and not even recognized it.

Once you live out your passions there are a lot of details you organize with the perspective and the vitality to be effective. You will be a much more effective kind of person with the lifestyle and passions once you apply these details.

It is possible to determine success any way that you would like to. Success is not only measured by income because anyone can generate large amounts of cash. The target is to make a lot of money by living out your enthusiasm. When you are working towards anything you are incredibly passionate about, you will usually be fortunate enough to make money. The important factor is that it is possible to glimpse back again on your existence and perceive you did every little thing you desired to do and you have no regrets.

The interest needs to make you whole. You need to concentrate not on just one factor, but each element of a pastime. Get pleasure from the occurrence in its entirety. Enjoy the approach of ordering the components and possessing them delayed over two weeks. Doing so may suggest a wonderful holiday for you while you are waiting around rather than a signal you weren't supposed to get going on the interest. Don't consider adverse things happening as an indicator. Be completely open with everything you do. Don't try to fake or win over another person with someone you are not.

When you are passionate regarding a thing you don't need to be an exhibit of enthusiasm so various individuals can see you. The enthusiasm comes from inside and if you actually really like that which you are accomplishing, afterwards this will come effortlessly for you. You should take pleasure in doing the job. If you design clay pots then you won't send a cracked pot to a consumer simply because you are passionate about the high quality. Doing so is because you will own it and your title should be on it. You can be proud of everything you do, because of the fact you are proud of doing so.

Leadership is an additional attribute that you do look at, because you want to display to people how living your dream can be done. You don't need to follow to be in the footsteps of everyone else. You wish to be passionate about leading–change in your life. You are making a significant change to keep the lifestyle how you want to. Produce the imaginative and prescient, and prospect the way by reaching the goals which you have set out.

As you are living your passion, you will not be putting out the best each and every single time. You need to uncover means to constantly increase procedures which are slowing you right down, creating poor quality, or frustrating you. When you start to enhance the procedure you should do much better as time goes by, and start to see how easy it is to do. Productivity is boosted with time as soon as you find approaches to make things better. Once you first start with passion, every little thing may appear as if it is in disarray and a mess. You can fix this but it will take time and trials. You may try a thing fifteen times before you hone a method down to the most effective and top quality procedure.

Action should be all-important to you when you are pursuing your passion. Because it has been so simple to procrastinate doing the job, you do not want to slide into a similar dilemma as before. It is important to contemplate action on your own, with people you include to help you and more.

Taking action is the important thing; keep away from procrastination. You need to work toward a big target which is the dream. Absolutely nothing is going to get in your way or slow you down. Put a sign up which says 'accomplishments' to remind yourself you are working towards your passion by frequent accomplishments.

You would like to have folks on the workforce that are action-focused also. Don't have folks working with you who are not action-focused. If you possess a genuinely supportive aunt that likes to sit nearby and talk, but not work hard afterwards, you cannot have her assist you with your passion. She may be the individual who will help you develop buzz for the company, but not to enact change. Find a position for her so she can assist simply because you need the support.

Often reward progress. By no means let progress and objective implementing go without any rewards. You want to reward every person assisting you and yourself. This doesn't suggest you do give out money you don't have. It is possible to reward another person by allowing them to know you respect what they are doing for you. Acknowledgement of hard work is often sufficient once individuals realize you actually respect it.

Choose at least 5 top heroes who you adore and you would want to be prosperous, choose and emulate them. Learn everything concerning your heroes and get to be an expert on them. Discover how they grew to become productive. Doing so means you should comprehend their complete autobiography.

ABOUT KAREN

Karen Leung (aka Karen K. Leung), also known as "The Best Wordpress Expert", is a best-selling author and marketing expert that is regularly sought out by local small business owners for her opinion on marketing campaigns that really work.

Karen is known for constantly asking the question, "How can she help local small business owners to get more visitors, how to turn visitors into customers and eventually how to increase sales?" She is "The Best Wordpress Expert", built business owners the "DoneformeWordpressWebsite", and recently founded the "DigiSpace Rental Marketing" Company, which provides advertising space and marketing for local business owners. It also provides advertising tracking and campaigns for clients nationwide. Her goal is to help millions of people become successful in life.

To learn more about Karen Leung, the Best Wordpress Expert, and how you can receive the Free Marketing Library to Kick Start Your Online Business, visit: KarenKLeung.com. Visit http://buildinstantwebbusiness.com to receive Free Online Business Building videos.

www.KarenKLeung.com
www.theBestWordpressExpert.com
www.hirewordpressexpert.com
www.wordpressexpertforhire.com
www.KarenKLeung-OneChickMillions.com
www.instantbuildwebbusiness.com
www.persuasiveonlinecopywriting.com
www.newautomationnet.com
www.howtomasterfacebookadvertising.com/freetraining/
www.ecoachingsecretsrevealed.com/freetraining/
www.gurublueprintforhighticketsellingsuccess.com/freetraining/

CHAPTER 28

FINANCIAL FREEDOM THROUGH INVESTING IN REAL ESTATE

BY MARK KUNCE

What is financial wealth? It is the unearned income to finance your life mission without having to work. It is creating investment vehicles that will create passive income—income that you generate that is not from your job. Financial wealth gives you the opportunity to live out what you truly want to do without having to worry about income or cash flow.

~ Gary Keller, founder of Keller Williams Realty
The Millionaire Real Estate Investor

ANYONE CAN DO IT...WILL YOU?

That's right, anyone can achieve financial freedom through building financial wealth but the fact is few will. The gap between the haves and the have not's in our country and throughout the world is widening. The financial crisis of the past few years has made many realize that their financial wealth and security really was not what they had believed it was at all. In this chapter we will look at how having goals, powered by proven models, leads to success in achieving financial wealth and freedom through investing in Real Estate. Specifically, how you can invest in Real Estate without ever being a landlord, finding a tenant, fixing a broken toilet or any of the negative possibilities associated with property ownership.

YOUR BIG WHY

In order to accomplish anything you must have goals. This is especially true of creating financial wealth. All of your goals should be to achieve a definite purpose. In *Think and Grow Rich*, Napoleon Hill wrote, "What a different story men would have to tell if only they would adopt a definite purpose, and stand by that purpose until it had time to become an all-consuming obsession." At Keller Williams this is referred to as your "Big Why". It should be big, it should be important, it should be why you get up out of bed and do whatever you are going to do each and every day. Your Big Why is your motivation to do everything else you do. All other goals should be to help you to achieve your Big Why.

You should begin looking at success as something you have to do rather than something you want to do. Think for a moment about the things in your life that motivate you the most. Try to look at this as your long term, or for lifetime Big Why. Material things are usually short lived and good only for short term motivation. Think of your Big Why as something more along the lines of being all you can be and for all the reasons that come to your mind. For me to become as financially wealthy as possible is the way to achieve my Biggest Why. In order to achieve big success financially you have to know your Big Why. Your Big Why brings focus, energy, and power to all your goals and to your financial success.

Setting goals and making a plan to achieve those goals are how we reach our full potential. Our Big Why should be our lifetime pursuit. Your financial wealth and freedom should be the goal to help you accomplish all other pursuits.

Once you set your goals you can set a plan for action to achieve those goals. I am sure you have all heard this over and over – set goals and make a plan. We all know this is easier said than done. Making a plan to achieve your financial goals can prove to be a daunting task.

USING PROVEN MODELS TO ACHIEVE YOUR GOALS

As a teacher and coach I stressed to my students the importance of having role models and following how they achieved success. From *Unlimited Power* by Anthony Robbins I learned you can often repeat or exceed the success of others by studying what the very best in a certain field does and copy it. The key is to learn how they achieved their goals and then to understand why they did it that way. Anthony Robbins calls this modeling. Using proven models can help you to raise our level of achievement dramatically in a much shorter period of time. You can also avoid many known stumbling blocks and reach your objectives much faster than you could on your own. Successful investors use proven models for selecting, buying, and owning real estate.

I shared the idea of proven models with a friend of mine who was looking for something to do with a 401K he needed to roll over quickly. He liked the idea of putting it into real estate. I spoke to him for awhile and gave him all the reasons I feel real estate is the best place to invest now and the best market it has been for investing in more than a generation. He said he completely agreed based not only on what I had said but also from other experts he had read and seen. All of them agreed this was the time to have a substantial amount of your investment portfolio in real estate. My friend went on to say he also knew the value of proven models to achieve his goals but that frustrated him because it would take him years of study and practice to really understand and to be successful as a real estate investor. He needed to get in the game now. I smiled and said there are many ways to become a successful investor. What he needed was a team. He had a key component that every investment needs which is capital. What he did not have was knowledge and experience. My advice was he could either build a team or join one.

Anyone can become a real estate investor and for some starting with the purchase of one single family investment property or even their own home is the first step in their journey to becoming a successful real estate investor. My friend needed to turn his capital (401K) over to someone who was already a successful investor and base his investment decisions on their advice. You may be somewhere in between. Wherever you are on your investment journey you need to surround yourself with the best team possible. If you want financial freedom, financial wealth and a lot of it you must bring together a powerful group of people, a dream team.

The most important part of your team or network will be your inner circle. Your inner circle consists of partners, consultants, and mentors. These people should truly and absolutely care about your success. They should all have more investment experience, knowledge and success than you. They should be willing and committed to mentor and guide you. You should think of this group as your personal Mastermind. Napoleon Hill in *Think and Grow Rich* described the Mastermind principle as:

> *"The coordination of knowledge and effort of two or more people, who work toward a definite purpose, in the spirit of harmony... No two minds ever come together without thereby creating a third, invisible, intangible force, which may be likened to a third mind."*

BECOMING FINANCIALLY WEALTHY THROUGH REAL ESTATE INVESTMENT

There are all kinds of strategies for investing in Real Estate but almost all investment strategies fall under one of two main categories: Buy & Sell and Buy & Hold.

- Buy & Sell: With this strategy, you are looking for one thing, cash, creating a fast net profit by quickly buying and selling. This strategy is often used to build capital for getting into the Buy & Hold option.

- Buy & Hold: This is the true financial wealth building real estate investment strategy. This is a long-term strategy that utilizes all of the power of appreciation and cash flow.

Buy & Sell is a strategy for short-term wealth building. Often it is necessary to start with the buy and sell model to build cash for investing in Buy & Hold strategies. Considering this chapter is dealing with Financial Freedom through Investing in Real Estate, I will focus on the Buy & Hold strategy for the remainder of this discussion.

Let's go back to the situation of my friend who was looking for a place to put his retirement money. He needed investments that would insure he could get steady long-term return that would enable him to maintain the lifestyle he and his family were accustomed to even after he was no longer working. Like many others over the past ten years or so he found himself disillusioned by stock market crashes, low interest rates of return, bursting bubbles of high tech, mortgage and real estate. He jokingly said maybe the safest thing would be to stuff what was left in his mattress. The problem with that is inflation and the dropping value of the dollar would soon eat that up!

I invited my friend to attend one of *The Millionaire Real Estate Investor* Seminars we hold at least monthly. These seminars are based on the bestselling book *The Millionaire Real Estate Investor* by Gary Keller. (Whether you are just curious about real estate investment or an old hand at investing, I highly recommend you read this book.) Following the seminar I asked my friend what he thought of the seminar and the information he received. He stated he thought it was a very good seminar but he still was not sure that investing in real estate was for him. His objections were the same as that of many of the people I consult with – which boils down to, "I do not want to be a landlord." They do not want to deal with: finding tenants, maintaining properties, fixing leaky roofs, collecting rents, evictions, floods, fires and any number of other possible problems. Of course, you can always hire a property management company but you still have to make all the decisions and make sure the property management company is doing their job as well as looking out for your best interest. For many people this is still too hands on. For those who want the benefits of real estate investment but want a less demanding or passive type investment the answer is in group investments also known as syndications.

A syndicate is the joining of two or more people for the purpose of making an investment. Syndicates are also sometimes referred to as group investments. For our purposes a syndicate implies one or more parties take an active part in the operation and management of an investment and one or more of the parties are passive. The investors bringing the capital are usually passive investors and provide the principal capital. The active investor or investors normally manage the syndicate and may bring capital as well.

By pooling their money, investors are able to purchase properties which would normally be out of their reach. Wealthy investors also use syndications to purchase large properties and limit liability and exposure. A syndicate can be as simple as two investors buying a single property or as complex as a group of domestic and foreign investors purchasing Rockefeller Center.

Syndicates offer economy of scale to an investor. Let's say you have $100,000 to invest and you have decided to put it into real estate. One option would be to find a property that costs $100,000 and purchase it for cash. This is all well and good. However, you are not taking advantage of one of the best features of investing in real estate, which is *leverage*. Okay, so you decide to buy an investment property using leverage. Most lenders now require 30 to 50% down payment on investment properties. If we use 30% for our example and you put $100,000 as a down payment you can purchase a property for $300,000. These examples are an over simplification but you get the idea. Now, if you find 9 friends who also have $100,000 to invest and you use leverage you would have $3,000,000 worth of purchasing power. If you are purchasing units which cost $100,000 per unit, you could buy one unit with your cash. You could buy 3 units with leverage on your own or the group of investors could buy 30 units.

In this scenario you own one tenth of 30 units, which is still 3. However, your expenses per unit decrease with the more units you have. The amount you pay for management, insurance, maintenance, and almost every expense associated with a property is reduced which in turn means a higher return on your investment dollar. The syndication is also one of the few ways to invest in real estate as a truly passive investment.

The most important thing for you to consider if you do decide to invest in a group real estate investment is who is the Syndicator. Some may disagree and say the offering (the property) is the most important; however, the offering is brought by the syndicator, so the knowledge, expertise and experience of the syndicator is essential to a successful syndication.

A great syndicator is an individual who strives to satisfy the investors desires while mitigating their fears concerning investing in real estate. He has the skills to find worthwhile projects and do in-depth analysis of the current and future potential of the property. The syndicator should never guarantee or overstate. He should present the facts both pro and con. The good, the bad and the ugly of the project. Then present his opinion of why this particular investment is a good one and how it can be made an even better one. He should demonstrate the ability to use proven models that can help you to raise your level of achievement dramatically while avoiding many known stumbling blocks. He should be someone you would want to include in your inner circle. Someone who you feel truly and absolutely cares about your success.

There are a lot of ways to make a lot of money investing in real estate. We have only been able to take a brief look at a few of the ways investing in real estate can help you achieve financial wealth. Focus on your "Big Why", put a plan into action using proven models, and get yourself on your path to financial freedom through investing in real estate.

ABOUT MARK

mark@sdmyhome.com

Mark Kunce grew up in a family involved in Real Estate Sales and Development and has over 30 years of Real Estate experience. He has been interviewed on the Michael Gerber Show and appeared on NBC, CBS, ABC and Fox affiliates. Mark conducts monthly *Millionaire Real Estate Investment Seminars*. He has assisted hundreds of investors to achieve their Real Estate Investment goals.

Mark is a Realtor and head of the REO Division at Keller Williams, San Diego Metro. He works closely with Financial Clients (banks, investment funds, and private investors) concerning the disposition of their distressed asset portfolios in order to minimize loss and maximize profitability. Currently his main focus is on group investments, syndications and creating investment opportunities for proactive as well as passive investors.

Having proudly served our Country as a United States Marine, he mastered discipline, leadership, organizational skills, and the mental toughness that is often required in Real Estate. Mark has a Masters of Education degree and has applied his teaching skills in the United States, Japan, and Mexico. He is dedicated to education and regularly conducts seminars, participates on panels, and speaks on numerous Real Estate related topics. He conveys outstanding knowledge, understanding, strength, and professionalism in representing your investment interests.

To learn more about Mark Kunce, and how to become a successful Real Estate Investor, visit www.markkunce.com or email mark@sdmyhome.com.

www.MarkKunce.com

CHAPTER 29

A NEW PARADIGM (OR TREND) IN REAL ESTATE: THE QUANTUM LEAP

BY RALPH CASE

I have been a Real Estate investor for over 30 years. In fact, I bought my first house a month after I graduated from college and landed my first job. Over the past 30 years I have been involved in Real Estate investment from just about every angle: Five years as a passive investor with a full time corporate job, a couple years passively investing while being an entrepreneur with a start-up computer company, 10 years as a residential and investment-oriented Realtor, and 3 years as a Sales Manager for a public company doing over $100 million per year in investment property sales. I have been a director of a property management company, a mortgage company, a Real Estate sales company and a Real Estate development and syndication company. Over the past 5 years, I have bought and sold over 1,500 residential properties either individually or with joint venture partners. What does this have to do with the concept of the Quantum Leap? I want you to know that I didn't just make this stuff up! I speak from experience. I've done the slow and steady route and I have done the fast track. Whether you are an experienced investor or just starting out I want to show you a few short cuts down the path to financial freedom. One of my favourite sayings is a Chinese Proverb: *"The wise man learns from his mistakes but the brilliant man learns from other people's mistakes."* Open your mind for the next few minutes and see if any of these ideas resonate within you.

FIRST THE FOUNDATION: WHAT IS A QUANTUM LEAP?

Quantum leap defined:

- In <u>physics,</u> an **atomic electron transition** or **quantum leap** is a change of an <u>electron</u> from one <u>quantum state</u> to another within an <u>atom</u>. It appears to be discontinuous – the electron "jumps" from one <u>energy level</u> to another very quickly. (I was a geophysicist in my corporate life way back when!)

- **It can also describe sudden or violent change**: Revolution, sudden, radical, sweeping organic change… a jump, leap, plunge, jerk, start, explosion, spasm, a storm. A clean, new model, a striking out with something new, a breaking with the past.

- **Quantum Leap**: going from first base to third. Getting into success fast – by skipping steps that others think they have to do.

So let me show you the steps to create "Quantum Leaps" in Real Estate. I want to show you real life examples of getting into success fast!

Before I get started, let me make it clear that there is nothing wrong with the slow and steady method of investing in Real Estate. In fact, many of my past clients have become multi-millionaires by practicing the adage: *"Don't wait to buy Real Estate, just buy Real Estate and wait."* I have co-authored a book on the topic of creating a Real Estate cash flow machine. There is nothing wrong with it, but let's look at the quantum leap as a way to get where we want to go faster. A good base-ball team needs steady players who hit singles consistently but it helps to have a few "long ball" hitters too!

Is this the year for you to take a Quantum Leap?

Let's face it: most people in the U.S.A. have been hammered in the Real Estate market over the past 3 or 4 years. So why, you might ask, would anyone want to invest in Real Estate now? There are two key reasons which I learned early in my investing career:

1. **Real Estate markets move in cycles** – In 1981 mortgage interest rates peaked over 20% and there was blood in the streets. I managed in my early 20's to make, lose, and make again my annual corporate salary by dusting myself off after being clobbered and having the guts to invest when everyone else was running for the hills. Warren Buffet said, *"Be fearful when people are greedy and be greedy when people are fearful."* Understanding and taking advantage of Real Estate cycles is a lesson I will never forget.

2. **Different Real Estate markets are not always in the same cycle** – some markets can be booming while others are tanking. Right now where I live in Vancouver, British Columbia the market is red hot, and I am buying in Phoenix where prices in some cases are less than half what they were 3 years ago! Take advantage of buying opportunities wherever they are.

In this much-touted high tech information age everybody actually has less time, more pressure and less certainty than ever before. To compete we need to look for change within – what we need is a breakthrough in our own thinking. **A breakthrough that gets us to do something different!**

Why Real Estate if the market is bad? You need to look beneath the surface and see what is going to make a change. In the United States today we are not building enough residential Real Estate to match the demand from population growth. Sooner or later demand will catch up with supply. In many cases prices are below replacement cost. The key is to invest when prices are down. Steel baron Andrew Carnegie once said that, *"90 percent of all millionaires become so through Real Estate."* MacDonald's founder Ray Kroc once told a group of MBA students that *"we aren't in the hamburger business; we are in the Real Estate business."*

Do you want to take the plunge into Real Estate? If so:

- **Quantum Leaping! – <u>You need to identify what you want and then go and deliberately create it!</u>**

We all know there are thousands of books and courses out there that teach the ins and outs of Real Estate investing. How do we take this information and create a Quantum Leap? We need to get ourselves out of the rut of "re-acting" to our circumstances and take charge. And taking charge by learning the secrets that the best investors know of identifying the right market area, the right type of properties and the right type of financing to build wealth. Identify what you want. Do you want to flip for fast profit or create long-term cash flow and appreciation?

- **Quantum Leaping! – <u>You need to go out and make things happen.</u>**

The biggest misconception people have in Real Estate investment: You need to have money to get into the game. WRONG! They key to success is to be able to quickly recognize a good deal and then get it under contract. If you truly have a good deal, trust me the money will find you.

My business partner and I lead a group of Real Estate investors who meet together monthly and then go "do their own deals." Last year we gave out four "deal of the year" awards to the best creative deals out of a group of 300. Here are the deals that won in 2010:

1. A 24 year old who bought a 5-unit property for $1.15 Million with a joint venture partner who put up the down payment and qualified for the mortgage. Their joint venture agreement is to split profits 50/50.
2. A 32 year old who bought a 36-unit apartment building and flipped it for a 6 figure profit in 60 days and no money invested.
3. A business owner who stands to make a 7-figure profit on a condo purchase with 95% financing.
4. A 30 year old who constructed a new home with two rental units and structured it:

(a) With no money down and (b) he can live in the house while his two rental units pay more than 100% of his mortgage.

All these investors found the deal and then the money found them!

- **Quantum Leaping! – <u>You need to develop a series of correct habits that will get you and keep you in ACTION!</u>**

EIGHT HABITS FOR QUANTUM LEAPING:

1. **Think Big.**

   You have to think Big! Read the book *"The Magic of Thinking Big"* by David Schwartz.

2. **Know the difference between Action Goals and Result Goals.**

   I call Action Goals "Yoda Goals." There is no try, there is "do or do not!" Result goals are the end result. "I want to own an apartment building." The Action goals are necessary to get to the Result goal. (i.e. You have to write an offer to own an apartment building. The offer is the Action goal!)

3. **Commit to Action Steps.**

   Once you have your Action Goals, list out the specific Action Steps you are going to take and commit to them!

4. **Be Accountable – Perform what you commit to!**

   Ralph Waldo Emerson said that *"Our chief want is someone who will inspire us to be what we know we could be."* Find someone to hold you accountable. It could be a spouse, friend, or business associate. Tell them what you are committed to and ask them to hold you accountable. It can be uncomfortable but you need to get out of your comfort zone!

5. **Measure results frequently.**

   Daily, weekly, monthly…it depends on the action plan you have set out to do. Be realistic.

6. **Adjust Course.**

   The definition of insanity is to continue doing the same thing while expecting different results. If your plan is working, great! If not, you have to either change what you are doing or do more of it – i.e., if you are talking to 5 Realtors a week for deals and not finding any deals, either talk to a different target or talk to 10 instead of 5!

7. **Use the Power of the Mastermind.**

You need the power of mentors. Read the chapter on masterminds in *"Think and Grow Rich"* by Napoleon Hill.

8. **Create Life Balance.**

This is important. Why do you want money if all you do is work and your relationships are all screwed up? The more time off I take, the more money I make. I know it sounds crazy but it's true. Try scheduling your vacation time before your work time. Try taking a week off every month. Try taking a month off a couple times a year. Best yet is get to your financial freedom point where you are only working because you want to! (Keeps the brain active!!)

IN SUMMARY:

Everyone talks about life balance; everyone wants the freedom of financial independence. We have the choice of either doing it quick or doing it slow and steady. Why not Quick? My purpose with this chapter is to open your minds. If you know how to do these types of deals, great. If not, start hanging out with people who do!

Let's face it, if you keep doing what you have always done, you will have the results you have always gotten. Now is the time to change your results. Get into new fresh thinking, start taking new empowered action and better yet – get there **fast**!

Take a **Quantum Leap of action** into real estate investment, into property ownership, into building an income-producing investment portfolio and do it in an environment where you have mentors to hold your hand and guide you while keeping you on track and accountable to your goals.

ABOUT RALPH

Ralph Case is President of **The Real Estate Action Group™**, an organization with monthly membership designed to help members take action in Real Estate investing. (www.reag.ca)

Ralph is also managing broker of a successful Real Estate company (www.worldwidereferrals.com) and owns a Real Estate development and syndication company.

Ralph doesn't just talk the talk, he practices what he teaches! In the last 5 years, he has bought and sold over 1,500 residential units either individually or with his joint venture partners. Clearly, he is a man of ACTION!

An investor since 1981, one of the key things he teaches is life balance. Work smart, not necessarily hard. Become financially free as fast as possible and use that freedom to enjoy life and make the world a better place. He has been an active Rotarian for 23 years and is a Paul Harris Fellow. He has also been married for 25 years and has three children who are budding Real Estate investors.

The Real Estate Action Group™
253 – 970 Burrard Street
Vancouver, B.C. V6Z 2R4
Phone: 604-683-1111
Website: www.reag.ca

CHAPTER 30

TRIPLE YOUR INCOME IN THE NEXT 12 MONTHS

BY RON LEGRAND

T o an employee working 50 hours a week to get by, that sounds far-fetched and totally out of reach. To a small business owner enslaved in a business and buried in minutia, it's a nice thing to think about, but about zero chance of becoming a reality.

To an entrepreneur who understands the law of leverage and automation and combines them with a business and plan to succeed, it's not only achievable, but for many a very conservative goal.

I know! I hang around, teach and consult with these entrepreneurs daily and have seen a lot of ordinary people achieve extraordinary things when shown the way. Many have become multimillionaires once they quit......

SWAPPING HOURS FOR DOLLARS

There's a lot of ways to make a million bucks but most involve some kind of business, and that business must have the potential to achieve a high income, or all one has is a low paying job he/she happens to own. We all have a choice. So why not choose a business that can make you rich?

I know a dentist who spent $400,000 on two sandwich shops which his family runs and can barely break even. There's no way to sell because there are hundreds on the market and a business making no money isn't worth much, especially when it has no upside potential. He's headed for a $400,000 seminar but hey, we all take them and look how much smarter he'll be the next time.

In 1982 I was bankrupt, broke, working as a mechanic, 35 years old and clueless. I got into a heated argument with my wife over a washing machine. She wanted a new one and I wanted to fix the old one because I didn't have the $150 to spend.

That night there was no sleep. All I could think about was how big of an 'a--hole' I was for arguing with a mother of four whom I'd already been married to for 17 years because she wanted to wash clothes for her family. The next day I started looking for a way out. I didn't want to live like this the rest of my life. There had to be something I could do to make a better living.

My way out was real estate. I started reading books and attended a seminar to get me started. Greed and hunger took over from there. Before I knew it I'd bought and sold several hundred houses without using my money or credit and still do it today, over 2,000 now.

I tripled my income easily the first year and it continued to climb for years thereafter until I started creating courses on what I know and selling them in 1987. Then my income tripled again.

Today my company continues to market information products to real estate investors and those who want to triple their income on the internet or learn how to start and grow any business. Since that has become my chosen field and hundreds of thousands have gone through our training, it puts me in a good position to see what people do right and what they do wrong.

One lesson I learned the hard way has become my credo:

The Less I Do, The More I Make

No, that doesn't mean you get paid for not working. But it does mean you must do only the things no one else can and let other people do what they do best and get out of their way. If your life is never-ending minutia and every day goes by with no activity to grow your business, it'll never be more than a job and soon be one you'll want to quit. The boss must stay focused on revenue and spend every day increasing it. No one else in the company cares about it more than the boss, the owner, the one receiving the major benefits of a business.

Most waste time the same way, day-in and day-out and not one productive thing gets done.

There are five steps to any business, regardless of its product or service. I buy and sell real estate, own a restaurant, have several online businesses, develop real estate, run an oil and gas reserve, own an information marketing company, a consulting business, speak at events and a few other odds and ends. These five steps apply to all of them. FYI, I don't have to be present for any of these businesses to operate and, in fact, I'm not present much.

HERE'S THE FIVE STEPS.

1. **Locate Prospects** – Without them there is no business and this is where many owners fail. They're great at doing the thing they sell but suck at marketing. I'd rather be great at marketing and suck at the thing I sell. It can and should be hired out anyway, not done by you. I'm a lousy cook so it's a good thing I'm not my own chef. I'm great at buying houses but not one thing I do can't be done by someone else. I love internet marketing, but the day you find me building my own website you have my permission to shoot me. My time is spent getting business until I replace myself, then I watch my replacements.

   Focus on Revenue Not Cost Control

2. **Prescreen Prospects** – There's a big difference between suspects and prospects. Until you receive money for a product or service you have a prospect, not a customer. Until a prospect shows serious interest and is predisposed to do business with you because they know what you can do for them, you have a suspect. Your objective is to get suspects to prospects to customers ASAP cost effectively. That means 20% of the budget should be spent on getting suspects and 80% on converting to customers, the exact opposite that most

businesses do. Usually 80-95% of any suspect pool will never buy so don't spend time trying to make chicken salad out of chicken manure.

3. **<u>Construct and Present Offers</u>** – With no offer there is no sale. In real estate it's the offer to purchase. In a restaurant it's the menu and a waiter upselling. Online it's the sales letter. In retail, it's the inventory proudly displayed or on sale. In all businesses there better be an offer and the owner must learn to present it in the form the consumer wants to receive it. That usually means multiple media. A business with only one way to get customers is a business on its way out.

One is a Bad Number in Business

4. **<u>Follow Up</u>** – 82% of the revenue in most businesses comes from the second to the seventh contact with a prospect. No doesn't mean no. It only means see me later when time and circumstance changes my mind. That means a business that doesn't follow up with a sequential campaign to capture customers will lose up to 82% of its potential revenue. Ask yourself, when's the last time a business, any business, followed up with you? The key is to work hard converting prospects and a little on suspects, but neither can be done without a database of both. I'm appalled at how few businesses even keep a list of their customers, which is their largest and most valuable asset. Have you seen a restaurant lately even ask your name, much less do any work to capture your contact info? I can assure you mine does. You ain't getting out the door until we give you a shameless bribe to get on our newsletter list.

5. **<u>Close Quickly</u>** – That means get the money. I'm shocked at how many businesses get the bride right to the altar and never ask for a 'call to action'. You must ask for money, fully expect to receive it and not quit until you do. There's no shame in swapping products and services for money. It's how businesses survive, and the better you get at it the faster you'll triple your income. Let the staff handle minutia while you focus on closing sales and training others to do the same, until

you're not needed anymore.

Let's recap! If you want to triple your income in a year you must:

- First, put yourself in a position to do so in a business where it can happen.
- Second, build a marketing system to attract suspects, convert to prospects and then to buyers.
- Third, repeat, repeat, repeat.

It's not rocket science. It's the Chunka Theory – the chunka comin in must be larger than the chunka going out.

Ron's Contact info:
For Real Estate: Recessionproofron.com
and
For Internet start ups: www.Dotcomsummit.com

ABOUT RON

Ron LeGrand has trained thousands of ordinary people to take their lives back and start their own home based business. If you'd like Ron's new book and a CD on how he makes money in real estate without banks, credit or money, go to: www.recessionproofron.com. If you'd like to start an internet business from home with no experience, product or even a website, check out his inexpensive three day training event at www.Dotcomsummit.com.

CHAPTER 31

REJUVENATION

BY KELLY COLBY

The hallways felt so cold and sterile. I had memorized every pattern on the floor and had inspected every painting that hung on the walls a thousand times. I was desperate to find something to keep my mind from wandering into the unthinkable.

My newborn was in surgery. The surgery was supposed to take two hours max, but four hours later, I was still pacing the now familiar halls waiting for the doctor to emerge. I closed my eyes tightly and pictured over and over that the doctor would come out with a smile on his face and tell me the surgery was a success.

Rewind a few days before and I found myself in labor, eagerly awaiting the baby I had waited 43 weeks to arrive. Although I felt something was wrong during my pregnancy, my doctor assured me I was only worrying and everything was fine. After a very long labor, my baby was born and I was about to extend my arms for him, when I suddenly realized the room was silent. Everyone appeared to move in slow motion as the surreal feeling took over. My husband told me there was something wrong with my new little guy and I had to let the doctors figure out what was going on. I was told that my baby had tumors in and around his mouth. After extensive testing, we were told that my son needed to have the tumors removed as soon as possible. The doctors told me that because he was so small, there was a great chance he would not even survive the surgery.

I wanted to know why he was sick in the first place. I was on a mission, but there wasn't one doctor that could tell me why my baby was sick. I knew that if I wanted answers, I was going to have to go a lot deeper than interviewing doctors.

Every hospital has a library. In the library I began my own research. Each clue led to the information that caused a mutation in his cells when he was forming. While I can never say for sure what caused the mutations, I do have my suspicions after years of research. I couldn't go back and erase the past, but I could figure out what I could do for him now; how I could repair this mutation. This is how stem cells entered my life.

Have you ever asked yourself what you want more of in life? Do you want better health? Do you want more youthful or radiant beauty? Do you want more energy? How about more happiness or the best relationships? Do we all agree that prosperity is not just the amount of money in our bank account? To have true prosperity, people need the greatest health, the greatest wealth, and the greatest love and spirituality.

Many people are familiar with Ponce de Leon's search for the Fountain of Youth. Myth states that drinking from the Fountain of Youth will bring back vitality, not only externally but internally as well. Aging is not bad, actually aging is quite an amazing and liberating event! What is not fun is losing quality of life. Once the cells that make up all organs and body processes lose the resonance with their original divine template, people begin to lose energy and feel bad. Our divine template is the blueprint for perfect health that most people start out life with. As long as our cells remain in-sync or in resonance with our divine template, we are vital and vibrant long into our elderly years.

In our current society, aging has been associated with a decline of quality, and a decrease in the spark of life. This is simply erroneous. Aging is not a decline of vitality, cellular mutations cause the cells to be out of resonance with our divine template and cause a decline in vitality.

Adults begin to feel less vital and energetic as cellular resonance decline in the body. We begin to look outside our own body, hoping to delay or reverse the symptoms of cellular aging. Men and women buy creams and potions, turn to cosmetic surgery or Botox to look more youthful. Some take hormone replacements, turn to supplements or herbs and work out like crazy to increase energy.

There are many products that help people look and feel more youthful, but nothing compares to the power of your Fountain of Youth. Like so many things in life, we have been conditioned to go searching for something extraordinary "out there". What if I told you that the very thing that many people throughout the ages have dedicated their lives, and many even lost their lives, for is not "out there". You do not have to raise money and gather a team to go on an expedition to some dangerous and mysterious, never before explored territory to find the Fountain of Youth. The Fountain of Youth is inside of YOU!

I was born with an intrinsic spirituality. When I became an adult, people asked me what guru I had studied under. When people found out I had not been the student of many great masters, I was told I couldn't possibly know anything or truly be spiritual. I was determined to learn to be spiritual.

I trekked around the world in pursuit of learning spirituality. Hundreds of thousands of dollars later, I came to the realization that my spirituality was not something I had to go seek out, I already had it inside me. I eventually learned that if given the right tools, I could unlock everything inside myself. I learned that I had internal access to everything from greater beauty to an overabundance of money. There are not some hidden keys to the Universe that only a few people had access to. I learned we all have these access keys inside of us and, with the proper tools, we can unlock great health, wealth, and happiness.

If I wanted a great relationship, I had to work on improving and falling in love with myself. If I wanted an overabundance of money, I had to change my beliefs, patterns, and actions. If I wanted radiant beauty, I had to change my diet and have extraordinary health so my skin would glow from the inside out. You see, there is nothing that is beyond your control that is outside of you. Exterior things happen, but we can counter these with our own internal power and influence. You are the perfect design. The perfect design has all the tools necessary for the job.

The Fountain of Youth is not outside somewhere, your Fountain of Youth is inside you. Your Fountain of Youth is your own adult stem cells. When people hear the term stem cells they often think about the controversial embryonic stem cell issue. The media has done a great job of highlighting only a tiny part of stem cell research while ignoring the rest of the stem cell world. What the media doesn't report is that the majority of stem cell successes actually come from our own blood. Stem cells with a simple blood draw.

The adult stem cells that we naturally produce are perfectly designed according to our bodily needs. Our adult stem cells are designed with the perfect amount of resonant essence for our developed body. There is an analogy that I love that perfectly describes why our own adult stem cells are all that we need.

Let's say I am building a brick house. For this project I need [x] amount of bricks. A truck comes and drops off the first load of bricks. As the house progresses more bricks are dropped off. Finally, my beautiful house is complete.

Five years later, a truck comes and drops off a load of bricks. But wait, my house is finished. I only need to maintain my house now. My original foundation has been laid and is structurally sound. I do not need more bricks. My building is done. I only need the materials to maintain and repair my house when necessary, not the original building bricks.

Our bodies are the same way. Before we are a fetus, when we are just a speck, the embryonic stem cells divide and form every aspect of us. Embryonic stem cells contain specific information to completely build a body from scratch. However, once our organs are built and we are grown, we need something else if that organ becomes sick or damaged. We do not need a build-from-scratch plan. Each adult stem cell is produced with the exact and unique chemical and energetic make-up our body needs to maintain and repair at every second. The body's needs are ever changing. The body has wisdom and is producing the exact renovation and repair materials we need. Our original design has already been built. We do not need more bricks.

Adult stem cells are really the superstars in the cellular world of our body. They are re-creator cells that can duplicate themselves consistently and develop to be any organ cell or process in the body; muscle, skin, heart, liver, brain, etc. These regenerative stem cells are constantly circulating through your body to repair and rebuild whatever is most in need. If part of your liver needs help, the sick cells within the liver will be replaced with the new healthy cells needed for rejuvenation.

Given the exciting discovery of our own Fountain of Youth, I wanted to figure out what would be depressing or interrupting the signals of our own stem cells that prevented total rejuvenation. There are too many people walking around sick, aging, and with low energy. If our bodies are capable of producing exactly what we need at every given second to rejuvenate naturally, there had to be something that was preventing the body from healing.

Everyone naturally assumes a stem cell is perfect and will heal everything instantly. This is not always the case. If there are mutations in the original cell, as the stem cell duplicates, the mutations will also duplicate and prevent full rejuvenation of the body. Most people are not aware that a person's stem cell production varies depending on many individual factors. A very healthy person has stem cells circulating throughout their body, like a fountain, every day seeking out what needs to be repaired or corrected. We often see a decline in a sick person's ability to produce adequate amounts of healthy stem cells. Without stem cells circulating in the fountain, the person becomes more sick and weak.

There are five things you can start doing today to turn on your own Fountain of Youth.

1. You can accept the helping hand of having your own adult stem cells produced in a natural, highly resonating way. www.resonantessence.com offers a pioneered approach to adult stem cells that is safe and simple to take every day.

2. Your daily diet is very important. Diet has a big influence on stem cell health and production. If you are eating unnatural foods laden with chemicals, your cells are being pulled away from their resonance. Opt for foods that are as fresh and as close to their natural state as possible.

3. Alkalinize your body. An acidic body will break down stem cells circulating in your body before they can do their miraculous work. Eat a diet high in alkaline foods and take mineral supplements. I also suggest adding additional amounts

of magnesium and potassium. Stem cells also love algae and seaweeds. Take a blue green algae supplement and sprinkle a good amount of seaweeds on your salads every day.

4. Your environment can cause defects in your cells. Electromagnetic fields, EMFs, are big contributors to harming your cells. Your cell phone, computer, and wifi are the biggest offenders of EMFs in your home and workplace. Luckily, there are several ways to harmonize this radiation so the effects on the body are not as great. Go to www.resonantessence.com for more information on how to harmonize EMF fields.

5. Your thought patterns are the soil in which your stem cells grow. If your soil is bad, your stem cells will not function at their best. Happiness is the key to vitality and a healthy body. Positive thoughts breed health, negative thoughts breed disease. Surround yourself only with positive people and situations. If the people around you do not support you, excuse them. They do not need to be around you and drag you down. Your life is too precious to waste. You've heard the phrase, "Misery loves company?" No, misery loves you. People will pull you down. Change your own thoughts about yourself and your world. Change your environment with people and situations. Small changes produce large results. Once you make small changes, your life will be one that dreams are made of.

While medical professionals discouraged, dissuaded, and denigrated my pursuit of alternative therapies regarding my newborn son's health, it was my quest for this knowledge that led me to the understanding of the keys that will turn on the Fountain of Youth in your own body. Go turn on your own Fountain of Youth. Find true prosperity in health, wealth, happiness, love and spirituality.

www.RejuvenationGirl.com

ABOUT KELLY

Kelly Colby, known best as "The Rejuvenation Girl" is a speaker, author, and a wellness expert that is regularly sought out by the media and people for her opinion on wellness and rejuvenation matters. Kelly has been seen speaking throughout the USA and her written work has appeared around the world. Kelly is known for constantly asking the question, "What is the core issue causing a problem in the body?"

Kelly is the spokesperson and champion for Liquid Stem Cells, a company that provides a person's own stem cells in a liquid form. Liquid Stem Cells gives continual support for the body for rejuvenation. Kelly turned to stem cells after her child became sick and realized the rejuvenation power held within the cells of each person's body. What sets Liquid Stem Cells apart is the company uses a (w)holistic approach to stem cell science, known as intuition-based science. This company and approach is the first of its kind.

Apart from Liquid Stem Cells, Kelly created a private, exclusive, members-only global association of individuals dedicated to achieving personal freedom, dynamic health, and emotional well-being. This is a unique and ground-breaking rejuvenation program that specifically targets a person's own natural stem cells within their own body to induce rejuvenation.

Critically acclaimed as the "Fountain of Youth in a Bottle", Liquid Stem Cells are just that because there is no other wellness system that puts the power and ease of real time results for rejuvenation on autopilot.

To learn more about Kelly Colby, The Rejuvenation Girl and how you can receive the free Special Report on "Your Fountain of Youth: 7 Powerful Reasons Why You Need Stem Cells for Rejuvenation," visit: www.ResonantEssence.com or email to: Kelly@ KellyColby.com.

CHAPTER 32

PROTECTING YOUR RETIREMENT PLAN FROM INFLATION & TAXES – AND THE WALL STREET BANKERS NOW PLANNING ANOTHER HEIST.

BY THOM GARLOCK

A goal without a plan is just a wish.
~ Antoine de Saint-Exupery

There is an entire generation of Americans now facing retirement who are at a loss on how they can afford to stop working and live the American dream.

We know the financial meltdown that started in 2008 has pushed out the retirement date for many Americans. While others have held on to a collection of employer-provided retirement plans, savings accounts and investment accounts, they hope these will provide not only the income they need for themselves, but possibly far more in case they are called upon to help their children and grand children. After all the destruction done to our savings and investment accounts in the last few years, it's no wonder the majority of Americans are afraid to calculate the amount they'll need to save for retirement.

Somewhere on just about every stock brokerage web site, you'll find a "Retirement Plan calculator" that will help you focus in on what you are going to need to save in order not to die broke. I encourage you to experiment with what the formula built into these calculators will project for you. However, there is an easier way to determine your retirement plan financial needs and I'll share that with you in a few minutes.

There is a far more important tool to share with you right now that 90% of Americans are not aware of. It's an investment approach that gives you full control of your financial performance and is not subject to the rollercoaster ride everyone on Wall Street wants you to experience.

THE SELF DIRECTED IRA - 401(K) PLAN

Since the creation of the Individual Retirement Arrangement (IRA) back in 1974, you have always had the ability to invest in many asset classes no one ever told you about, including Real Estate, Gold & Silver, Venture capital, Commodities, Private stock and income-producing hard assets. Wealthy investors have been using their Self Directed retirement plans to diversify away from Wall Street investments, local bank CD's and Insurance company annuities for several decades.

If you have been in the investing game for very long you may be asking yourself right now "Why haven't I heard of this" or "When I asked my broker about this years ago he said it was too complicated or illegal." You are not at all alone in asking that question. There has never been an incentive for your banker or broker to let you in on the secret, and I don't think there ever will be an incentive. Our financial system today is all based on fees and commissions for either selling you the investment product or for managing the investment as is the case with so many Wall Street products.

The key to opening the door to the world of Self Directed Retirement plans is to gain an education on how these accounts work and then finding a qualified Self Directed Custodian. As you begin to research the best Custodian for you (later I'll show you how to get a list), you'll see they all suggest the concept of "Invest in what you know" as the best way to gain control over your retirement plan and financial future.

For over 25 years, I've been investing my IRA into what Wall Street likes to call "Non-Standard assets," since these investments don't typically trade on an exchange like stocks, bonds and mutual funds. In today's global investment market, where an event no one has predicted can easily chop 10% or more of the value out a stock overnight, it's far too risky a game to play with your retirement funds.

Working with a few hundred investor clients each year has given me insight into how they have fared in the Wall Street game. The vast majority has reported neither a loss nor a gain over the last 10 years, which is of course a poor way to build a long-term retirement account you can live on. The money in their retirement plan can be tracked back to the deposits they put in the account. It has not grown and it has been subject to an ever-changing set of risks that will always be beyond their control. When you incorporate the effects of inflation over the last 10 years on their savings, most investors have been slowly sliding backwards in their effort to save for retirement.

The solution in my experience is to "Invest in what you Know," and keep as much control over the investment as you possibly can. For many investors who have chosen to own rental properties in their IRA, in the end, the only person they have had to put their trust in is the tenant, who they as the investor get to interview and select from potential candidates. If these investors elect to own an apartment building in the IRA and hire a property manager, their trust is placed in the hands of the manager, who again they get to select and can always change if the performance is not as advertised.

In a moment I'll introduce you to a few investors that have done their research into the Self Directed IRA method of building wealth, and are well on their way to never having to worry about whether they will out live their savings or be unable to help their children or grandchildren in a time of financial need. First, I feel an obligation to tell you that this approach to investing is not for everyone. There are a certain group of investors who have no desire to travel a path outside of the traditional Wall Street investing approach. I wouldn't say these investors are brainwashed into only owning Wall Street products, but they certainly have been influenced by the marketing and peer pressure that has been growing for generations -- to simply hand your savings over to a professional if you want to retire wealthy. No one is born with investing talent, it's an acquired skill that comes only after you believe in the *"If they can do it, I can do it"* mentality and then you take action to get some educational tools.

CHANGING THE GAME - THE SELF-MANAGED RETIREMENT PLAN

Bill and Donna are in their early 30's and the proud parents on two young, very energetic boys. They met while working at a Dotcom company which was generous when issuing company stock into their 401(k) plans prior to the IPO in the late 90's. Before the tech bubble burst, like many other young workers in their industry, they couldn't believe how quickly their net worth had grown. When their company had to merge with a competitor after the market crash, both still had good middle management jobs but had watched their account values drop by 70%. Fortunately for them, their new employer offered them the option to either rollover their old 401(k) into the new employer plan, or transfer their 401(k) account to an IRA. This is when they discovered the Self Directed IRA that would allow them to purchase real estate. In an effort to diversify their investments into assets they could better control, they began with buying a single family home in need of cosmetic repairs close to their home in Dallas, Texas.

Like most first time remodel investors they'll tell you they spent too much money making the home perfect again, but when they sold it for a $23,000 net profit, they knew this was something they'd want to do again and again.

By using their Self Directed IRA funds, they have avoided paying any tax on every dollar of profit earned on each of their property sales. Their retirement savings have grown much faster by doing their real estate investments in a tax deferred account vs. investing non-retirement plan capital. Bill and Donna had to make sure they didn't break any of the IRS rules that govern holding real estate in their IRA (I'll cover the common rookie mistakes in a minute), and have had a lot of fun turning ugly homes into beautiful homes that sell quickly at annual returns between 12% to 20% tax free in their IRA accounts.

In the last two years Bill and Donna have added a new approach to their real estate investment business. Since Donna has her hands full with the boys and they feel inflation is the next economic trend that threatens our economy, they have chosen to hold and rent the homes they buy for remodeling. The rental income now flows tax free back into their IRA accounts each month, and over time, the property values along with the monthly rents will increase. Eventually, their IRA's will own several homes free of any debt and generate a strong steady cash flow during retirement.

To free up more time to be with their sons, they now have a partner who does all the repairs when they buy another property. Bill & Donna make the decisions on what to buy and their contractor oversees the completion of the work. Their newest venture is the creation of a software company that has been funded with IRA accounts owned by local investors who believe in their ability to grow a successful company in an industry they have spent their careers in. All of their success is tied back to using their IRA funds in areas not directly connected to the traditional Wall Street investing approach.

THE "I DON'T WANT TENANTS" APPROACH

There are many ways you can approach owning real estate in the retirement plan. Some investors just don't want to be a Landlord. They are either too busy or realize that spending time trying to manage their own properties is just not a productive task.

That brings us to the story about Ed, a retired quality control manager that spent most of his career working at Boeing. Years ago he tried managing a rental property he had once lived in before his family outgrew the house he and his wife Liz bought after they were married. The people I've met that are quality control managers are good at their work because they are perfectionists. Ed just couldn't get along with his tenants, he tells me, because they didn't take the best of care of his property.

Before he retired, Ed came to me when researching the Self Directed IRA, because he had built up a sizeable 401(k) plan at work. He was very clear he didn't want to spend his retirement time managing tenants. However, he wanted to diversify his nest egg into real estate.

I'll never forget Ed's primary reason for wanting real estate investments. He said "I want my retirement plan invested in one or more of the three basic needs all consumers have; Food, Shelter or Clothing." He felt the Great Recession we were in at the time could only be resolved by returning the U.S. to a strong exporter nation again, and to accomplish that, the value of the US Dollar would have to be destroyed by those in Washington. In the years to come, inflation and taxes will destroy more retirement savings than any other financial event. Real estate is an income-producing hard asset and a good hedge against future inflation.

Ed now owns a 30-unit garden apartment complex purchased with funds in his IRA. The on-site apartment manager runs the property and Ed is free to enjoy his retirement as the rental income grows the value of his account each month. He has also learned how to lend his IRA funds to other apartment building buyers, since it's a business he understands. Ed clearly now only invests in what he knows.

THE 5 ROOKIE MISTAKES OF IRA REAL ESTATE

Owning real estate in your Retirement Plan is easy.... However, new investors make 5 common mistakes when they begin. Look to avoid these mistakes when buying real estate in your retirement plan.

1. **Finding the right property before finding the right IRA Custodian.** Too many investors begin shopping for a good investment property, before they have their Self Directed IRA account established. The best Custodians provide all the education you need and help you with your first transaction every step of the way. Just don't make offers to buy property before you have your Self Directed account established. Fortunately for us consumers, the IRA Custodian industry is very competitive and service fees are fairly consistent. Select your Custodian based upon the educational services they offer.

2. **Buying a property you plan to live in.** The IRS rules prohibit you from using the property while it's held in your Retirement Plan. You can always transfer the property out of your retirement plan as a distribution and then use it as

a vacation home or even a permanent residence. However, while the property is owned by the Retirement Plan, you can't use it.

3. **Renting to your children or parents.** You cannot rent properties owned by your Retirement Plan to your direct linear relatives. The IRS rules prohibit you from allowing any benefits from the property to be received by your children and grandchildren or your parents. Your IRA can however do business with Brothers and Sisters or their spouses.

4. **Paying yourself from the Retirement Plan for property management services.** You are allowed to manage the properties owned by your Retirement Plan, however you can't pay yourself a management fee and you shouldn't really want to collect a fee for management. Think about it? It's hard enough to get capital inside your Retirement Plan because of the restrictions on annual contributions; so depleting the account by charging fees for your services will only deplete your long-term purchasing power. Money you withdraw from the retirement plan is taxable unless it's a Roth IRA Plan. If you feel income tax rates in the future will be higher, you'll want to educate yourself on the benefits of a Roth IRA.

5. **Research all of your investment options before buying a property**. You don't have to become a landlord to own real estate in your Retirement Plan. There are over 9 ways we've discovered to hold real estate in your Retirement Plan that doesn't involve tenants. Experienced IRA investors have learned to use lease options, buy tax liens, make hard money loans, or invest in land. Many let professional property managers manage the properties to save their time, while they focus on building their tax-free wealth inside their retirement plans.

HOW MUCH WILL YOU NEED TO SAVE FOR A SUCCESSFUL RETIREMENT?

I mentioned earlier that there is an easy method to determine what monthly income you'll need coming in during retirement. After working with hundreds of clients and speaking with many financial planning professionals, the answer for most of us is that you'll need the same amount of monthly income that you are earning today, even when you do retire. Sure the house may be paid off and you won't have a mortgage payment, but as we age, the cost of medical care increases. Your travel costs to and from work may be gone in retirement, but they'll be replaced by vacation travel or family visits.

The largest future costs we all face are an increase in inflation and taxes of all types. By owning hard assets and self-directing your retirement-plan, you will be able to build retirement wealth much faster than sharing your profits with the tax man.

Now is a great time to begin your education on growing your retirement plan wealth. It's easy and we are here to make it fun to learn.

ABOUT THOM

Thom Garlock, Founder and CEO of IRAassets.com, is an author and educator in the Self-Directed Retirement planning industry. For over 25 years, Thom has guided investors to diversify their IRA and 401(k) Plans, away from Wall Street investments, and into tangible assets including Real Estate, precious metals and nationally franchised businesses.

Thom has presented at various wealth conferences and has appeared on America's PremierExperts® TV show on ABC, CBS, NBC and FOX.

Thom has been active as a real estate investor and developer in the Jackson Hole, Wyoming area and in Southern California since 1985. A Jackson Hole resident since 1995, Thom and his wife Karen appreciate the natural beauty of Wyoming along with its outdoor activities. They are members of: The Nature Conservancy, Trout Unlimited, Rocky Mt. Elk Foundation and the Yellowstone Association.

Thom is the Managing Partner of Teton Land & Development Group, LLC, a real estate development company, operating in the Jackson Hole, Wyoming market. The company develops master planned communities, designs and builds award winning homes, as well as commercial properties in Wyoming and Idaho.

In the 1980's, Thom was fortunate to be an early pioneer in the Cellular Telephone Industry Association and has been the principal in a variety of wireless communications license-based ventures that have held and developed 55 Metropolitan area cellular telephone licenses, and 9 Rural cellular telephone systems in the U.S.A.

To learn more about Self-Directed Retirement Plans and how you can easily diversify your investments into income-producing tangible assets, visit: www.IRAassets.com

Or call us toll free at: 800-914-2689

CHAPTER 33

FREEDOM OF TIME & FINANCIAL FREEDOM

BY LARRY D. GOECKEL, JR.

You went into business for freedom. That's right. Freedom. There are only two core reasons you go into business, Freedom of Time and Financial Freedom, that's it. But when I sit down across the desk or conference room of any CEO or Business Owner in today's economy they tell me how they are working ridiculous hours and the business owns them, they are not seeing their family or spouse enough and having to live with the day-to-day guilt. Then they proceed to open up and tell me their deeper pain of not having enough money, sometimes having to not take a paycheck themselves, just squeaking by to make payroll, or the reality of losing their home in today's economy.

So what is the magic bullet to fix this massive problem with small to medium-sized business owners in today's economy, aka "The Great Recession." I will share the magic bullet in just a bit. I owned my first real entrepreneurial venture/business at age 22. When I say real, I mean bank borrowed money, payroll, assets, liabilities, etc. That business was where I cut my teeth in business acumen. I didn't know anything about the 60 Government agencies that wanted to make sure I filled out every form and filing on time within their world of regulations. I truly did not understand how to read a P&L from my accountant, or how important filing and paying your employees payroll taxes on time are. I did not know how to make an employee handbook or hire or terminate an employee properly without any legal ramifications or lawsuits. What I am conveying here is that I learned from a lot of painful mistakes way back when. Because of that, I can help you avoid those mistakes altogether and grow your business faster, make more money and have free time to do the things you love with the people you care about – Freedom of Time & Financial Freedom. I went into business to do something I had a passion for, not to become an employer. But I soon learned I was in fact an employer first and my passion was a distant second.

Twenty years later, I now have the business acumen to teach and connect others to grow their business beyond their wildest dreams. First and foremost, you have to have a passion for your particular business, this will be your 'baby' and you have to love it. Next, write this down, seriously write what I'm about to tell you down. Change the little voice in your head to a positive one, believe in yourself and what you are doing. You will face challenges, and the moment you stop believing and go negative and allow that little voice to tell you otherwise you will be into a downward spiral in your business. Change the little voice in your head, no one else can do this for you, this is a must that only you can do.

Surround yourself with what I call your G7, go find 7 professionals, (Attorney, CPA, Technology/Social Media, HR Professional, Banker, Local Politician, Sales/Networker), to implement a checks and balances system for your business. Go ask these 7 professionals to be your Advisory Board of Directors non-fiduciary, allowing them the opportunity to put their name on your organic success, eventually becoming your paid Board of Directors for your business.

Successful professionals, aka Entrepreneurs, love helping other businesses. When those 7 understand what you're putting in place to grow your business, they will gladly jump onboard. Meet with your G7 monthly at first over coffee or breakfast, (breakfast is the cheapest meal of the day), then eventually quarterly. Do not include anyone in your G7 that you are currently friends with. If you do, it will turn into a club and not your Advisory Board of Directors for your business, very important. Order business cards for your G7, when professionals put their name on something they want to see it grow. Now when your G7 is talking to a client, prospect or friend those people will hear about your business from an Advisory Board of Director of your business. Do you know how powerful that is coming from them and not you? Very powerful.

Your G7 is twofold, an Advisory Board of Directors and a very powerful Sales Force for your business. Have your G7 be your industry expert in their particular field of expertise and hold you accountable to their insight and homework. When your business reaches the level to hire employees, sit down with your G7 and write a vision mission statement for your business. If you don't know your vision mission statement, how will your employees? Make your vision mission statement about your clients, not about you – core values your business is committed to, core purpose of the business and visionary goals of the business – that you will pursue to fulfill its mission.

So with success comes employees; these people will build your business or break it. Treat your employees as your greatest assets and they will build your business to your vision and more. I grew up with a 3rd generation IBM father (35 years with Big Blue, thank-you Dad), in the birth place of International Business Machines nicknamed Big Blue, Endicott, NY. The founder of IBM, Thomas J. Watson, Sr. personally spent time with each of his valued employees and treated them with respect and benefits. IBM was one of the first corporations to offer Group Life Insurance, Survivors Benefits and Paid Vacations. In the very early stages of IBM he introduced the Quarter Century Club to honor employees who would eventually reach their 25th year of service with the company. In addition, he launched the Hundred Percent Club to reward sales personnel who met their annual sales quota. He created the Suggestion Plan program where employees would receive cash rewards for suggestions that would improve IBM products or procedures. Thomas J. Watson, Sr. recognized at a very early stage of his business that his employees would be his greatest asset for his business, and created a corporate culture where as his employees wanted to see his vision grow faster and greater than any other business.

Today IBM has over 388,000 employees worldwide, and is one of the most profitable Information Technology employers in the world. It holds more patents than any other U.S. based Technology Company. They employ scientists, engineers, consultants, and sales professionals in over 170 countries. Employees have earned 5 Nobel Prizes, 4 Turing Awards, 5 National Medals of Technology, and 5 Medals of Science. Your employees are your greatest assets and the future of your business. Reward them as such and your business will grow beyond your vision and your G7's vision.

So what's the magic bullet you ask, your time is the magic bullet. That's right, your time, and time is money as they say. When I consult with a Business Owner, CEO, President or Partners, they all have one thing in common no matter what kind of business or practice, they all have time and what would or could they do with more time if shown how to get it. Could they make more money with their time and have a better quality of life with their family or spouse?

Let me give you a few examples of some clients and how I helped them find more time and money.

I consult with a three-year old business CEO who wants to grow his business to the next level for financial rewards and to have quality of life with his family. The Business Owner/CEO is working 16 hour days and is exhausted. His employees try to avoid him at all costs, and due to his exhaustion, you never know what you get with him, per his employees. He has employees who truly are "A" players, but are working at "B" and "C" level, due to his day-to-day personality and the feeling of being unengaged with any corporate culture or benefits. He has employees who were hired with very high skill sets for designated positions, but has them doing administrative duties for the business that they absolutely hate. My question to the Business Owner/CEO after I take all my observations and mental notes, questions, analysis of his business is, "Why are you intentionally losing money every month?" My recommendations were: Focus on what you do best and what your employees do best and what they were hired for their level of skill set. I immediately formed a G7 for his business then had him outsource his administrative, i.e., payroll, HR admin., implement a benefits plan, medical and a 401(k) retirement plan.

The employees were now freed up, some with half to whole days that had previously been tied down to administrative burdens, allowing them now to do the job that they were hired for originally. The employees were now working as "A" players and engaged with a Vision Mission Statement. Within three months, his bottom line grew 27% in profits and his employees love coming to work. With the new profits the CEO cut his work life to moderately comfortable work life, giving his family their loved one back. The CEO in his new work/life balance is a now a wonderful man to work for, and has refocused his job on growing the business. Instead of just running the business, he invested

20% of his new revenue into expanding the business with new equipment and employees, and is on track to more than triple his sales for the year – while working less and having a great quality of life.

Another example: I consult with an 8-year old company, the CEO is stuck on a plateau for growth. He is working hard, spinning his wheels trying to take his business to the next level. We agree to form a G7 for one year and take on their perspective of his company and where it is today, and what needs to happen to take it to the next level and double his growth. The first thing I discovered in my business analysis in speaking with his employees, is that they all dislike the CEO the first two plus hours of the day. They share with me that the CEO comes in first thing in the morning demanding and wanting answers to everything before they can even get their computers to boot up, setting a negative tone in the office for the day. They also shared that they love the company and believe in their products and services, but when the economy comes back they will most likely move on to another position at another firm/competitor. Within the first 30 days, the CEO and I reconvene and discuss what his G7-Advisory Board of Directors and I have analyzed in his business. The first thing we discuss is his employees dislike for him in the first few hours of the work day. He immediately wants to know which employee and wants to fire them. I politely and confidently told him I would not divulge specific employees and further emphasized this was a business issue with him and not the specific employees.

I went further into what this will cost him in bottom line dollars if he does not correct this issue with his business (employee turnover will cause your business to stall or even go backwards financially). I explained if you continue to run your business as such, when the economy turns around you are going to lose your top talent to your competitors and stall the growth in your company or possibly have to shrink. So with my recommendations, I got the CEO to agree to come into the office and the first hour was to be spent in his office with the door shut. The plan was for the CEO to get a grip on his day and his personality, and then, after that hour every morning, begin to interact with his employees. By the CEO doing this little thing every morning for just one hour, his corporate culture has become one where his employees love coming to work, they even joke with him now in the mornings and point to his office and he laughs. His employees are now engaged and operating as "A" players in his business, which in turn has increased his bottom line revenues 20%. His G7-Advisory Board of Directors are now pleased with the swift turnaround of the business, and are now making the right connections for him and his business. One recent connection has the potential to double his business revenue within the next 12 months. Your people are your greatest asset in your business. They can give you the Freedom of Time and Financial Freedom you went into Business to achieve.

ABOUT LARRY

Larry D. Goeckel, Jr. – **Larry The Connector** ™, saw what he wanted very early in life and filed a flight plan on how to obtain his goals and dreams. Tackled his education and paid his own way through University and Graduate School at "Harvard of The Skies"- Embry Riddle Aeronautical University, while garnering simultaneously Integrity, Character and Honor as a non-Commissioned Officer in the United States Navy Reserves, and honorably serving during the first Gulf War as a highly-decorated veteran.

Larry has been an Entrepreneur and Business Leader for the last 20 years, having built, bought, sold and directed businesses. Larry learned over the last twenty years in Business that it is truly all about the right connections and the right relationships, earning the title among his respected clients of **Larry The Connector** ™. He is a Business Performance Advisor to small and medium-sized businesses for turnaround and impactful sustainable growth.

Larry can be reached at:
Larry@LarryTheConnector.com
www.LarryTheConnector.com

"Simply put...Larry IS the CONNECTOR. If you want a sincere unconditional relationship with someone that will always be there for YOU and your successes, Larry is not only the guy, you will be remised if you don't have him as part of your arsenal. Period!"

~ Jim Hayden-CEO Jim Hayden & Associates

"With Larry's expertise in reaching out to the decision makers in industry he has proven invaluable to the growth of our company. The dynamic energy Larry brings to our firm, he is absolutely magical when it comes to continually expanding our network of contacts and focusing in on opportunities to collaborate with other businesses in the market place. Whether your an established company or a new start-up you can count on Larry to bring the passion and lead the way with a sense of purpose for infinite growth and expansion of your business and connections."

~ Brian Wimmer-President, Thompson-Wimmer, Inc.

"If you had one chance to seize an opportunity that could change your business-Larry is it!"

~ Wells Leger-President, Clean Sweep Property Services

CHAPTER 34

CLARITY, STRATEGY & VISION

THE FOUNDATION OF FINANCIAL FREEDOM IN REAL ESTATE

BY MICHAEL REESE

As I sit on a boat dock here at Lake Texoma, the largest inland marina in the United States, I'm thinking about how I ended up living in this oasis located in the middle of nowhere. It was only a few short years ago when I arrived here, and I'll never forget driving by and seeing the houses and boats of all the successful business people who live here, marveling at how nice everything looked.

The owners of these "dreams" come from all backgrounds – some are doctors, others are retired and former CEOs of banks. There's even one woman here who is the founder of a well-recognized women's cosmetic company that most of you would know.

And now, I live here, too, on a small, private property I own, where my perfect day is now shared with other successful, self-motivated entrepreneurs just like me.

These people truly are living their dreams and I feel very lucky to live here to share this beautiful, secluded place with such amazing individuals. Not surprisingly, the stories of success that come out of here are incredible.

For instance, one day while I was reading the newspaper I found out my neighbor actually sold his business to Amazon for more than $100 million.

Now, if you told me five years ago that I would be living here today at the age of 32, it would have been what I call a "stretch goal". I have completely taken over all the "W's" in my life and I feel like I have true freedom in all areas: I do what I want, where I want, when I want and most importantly, with whom I want. I have an extraordinary quality of life and I now understand why money is worthless without it.

I've had my share of luck in life, but luck has nothing to do with me ending up on a lake, where most of my working days start with a golf cart ride to the local resort – to jump on a conference call by the pool or to check on the progress of a project at the Island Bar & Grill's patio floating over the water.

You see, my current lifestyle was created as a result of my desire to relentlessly search for a better way of doing things. Not only a better way of living, but also of working, managing, marketing, and even learning. Through the process, I realized that there seemed to be major room for improvement in every area of my life. And because I so badly wanted the life I now live, I backed that desire with consistent, massive action. I honestly believe that I created what is now the present in my life.

As a real estate broker, coach, mentor and Internet marketer, I meet new people all the time, and more often than not, I can usually lead them to their own conclusion about what they want in life – when I ask them the right series of questions. Not surprisingly, a lot of people that I come across aren't clear about what they want when the exercise starts, and it seems as if they're making it up as they go along.

I've discovered that this is a result of their not having clear goals and a road map to get them where they wanted to go. I was a lot like that and I'd venture a guess that you may be in the same place yourself. For the most part, a great deal of people are reacting to what's coming at them in life trying to manage the present with no real plan for the future. Having experienced this myself, I now understand that I wouldn't have the fantastic life I now do if I continued going down that path.

I decided that I wanted more for myself, and honestly, I want a whole lot more for you too. And that's why I've written this chapter for you. Over the next several pages, I'm going to give you an introduction to my philosophy on business growth. I'll show you where you should start so you can create the business, and more importantly, the life, you deserve and want. By helping you get the start you need, I'm hoping to give you the springboard you need to achieve and get everything you've ever wanted in life.

As you read on, consider what a very smart man once told me: "The worst thing you can ever do in business and life is to climb to the top – only to realize your ladder was up against the wrong wall."

A. PRIORITIZATION

Our minds are like parachutes, they're most effective when open. In order to get the best results for yourself in anything you do, you have to be open to the possibility that there are different and better ways to get what you want.

For me, I had to be open to the fact that, while I thought I knew what it took to run a business, I was really just very good at sales. As a result, I made a lot of decisions based on fear rather than how a good business person makes them, based on what makes the best business sense and what has the highest priority.

Realizing this, the first thing I did to engineer exponential growth in my business was stop making decisions from a position of fear and start making them based on what I needed to do over all the other things I was doing. I prioritized my opportunities and how I needed to allocate my resources.

Your job (and your biggest challenge) as a business owner will always be how you allocate your resources – both human and financial. You will almost always be limited to the amount of resources at your disposal, so you'll need to learn when to sacrifice time or money and when to add more resources. As you build your business, your ability to do this efficiently will be elastic to having a clear vision, with a detailed strategic plan and well-organized priorities. More specifically, the clearer you are with where you are headed, the easier it will be to identify and allocate resources to let you be effective and efficient at the same time.

When I was running my real estate business full time, I knew that I had a limited budget and that I had to get everything I could out of what I had available. At the beginning of each year, the first thing I would ask myself when prioritizing my opportunities based on my resources was: "What is my objective?" Adopting this approach worked extremely well for me as I was able to experience exponential growth on a year-over-year basis without spending money I couldn't afford to spend. I simply reallocated my financial resources into more profitable business sources, which allowed me to be more effective and even more efficient in growing my business.

The good news is that you can do the same in your business.

Take a hard look at what you want for your business and life. From there, reverse engineer your process so that you know what to do and in what order you need to do it, to get the best results in the fastest possible time. Along the way, identify the resources you'll need to keep you on your path and decide when you need to spend money and when you need to put in some sweat equity. Done properly, you'll experience levels of success you've only dreamed of to this point. Remember, it's not about getting things done, it's about getting the right things done in the right order.

B. STRATEGIC PLAN

The late Peter Drucker, author and management consultant, said you cannot predict the future, but you can create the future. Every decision and choice you make or fail to make in your business has an effect on what ultimately becomes your past. Knowing that you can create the future, it makes sense to have a plan in order ensure you get the future you want.

Here are a few of things to consider when creating a strategic plan for yourself:

- When you engineer growth in any business, you should first focus on the things that will get you the best results while requiring the least amount of effort. Here's an example of what I mean: Imagine you're in a room with gold, silver, bronze, even lead coins. You first goal should be to first pick up all the gold coins. Then you move on to the silver coins, so on and so forth. The gold is worth the most and it weighs less than lead, so it makes sense to pick it up first.

- The two most important days in your business are: 1) the day you decide where you want to be in 5 years, and: 2) the day you figure out what you're going to be doing in the next 90 days to get there. After that, you take the middle out and focus on just those things.

- Implementing a strategic plan means not only that you want to know exactly what needs to be done but also what you need to stop doing in order to get you where you want to be. You have to take both sides into consideration when creating a true strategic plan to ensure that you get the most out of it. For example:

In my early twenties, I owned a lawn business and after things started to pick up, we had a decision to make about either increasing production by means of buying more trucks, equipment and hiring more employees or deciding not to grow and keep things as they were.

We decided that we wanted to grow, but not at the cost of leveraging ourselves to the hilt by owning a bunch of shiny new equipment. In order to be profitable, we had to hold our employees accountable and get them to more jobs in a shorter period of time. They had routes and start times that went with every job and missing a few minutes on one or more jobs meant breaking even, or worse, losing money.

To improve profitability, we implemented a strategic plan that was already being used successfully by other businesses like FedEx and UPS to accomplish our growth. It required us to start doing certain things we hadn't been doing and stop doing others.

The solution was simple, rather than routing the jobs as we had been and risk losing money due to traffic, longer travel times and other influences that were out of our control, we decided to route the jobs based on taking as many right hand turns as possible to get to them.

Why you ask? It's simple.

Let's say we serviced 30 accounts in one day and there is a possibility that in-between each account there could be 2-9 stop lights that take 2-5 minutes apiece. The fewer lights we ran into or the less time we needed to spend at each light could turn into some major profits by getting more jobs done in a shorter period of time.

The more efficient we were, the more effective and profitable we could be.

You don't need a PhD to become a good strategic planner. Focus on what's the most profitable with the least amount of effort, figure out your long term goals and what you need to do NOW to get there, and then determine what you need to do (or stop doing) to get the best results. Have good data in hand to make your decisions and you are all but assured success in implementing a solid strategic plan.

C. VISION

Prior to becoming an entrepreneur, the only time I thought about the word vision was when I went to the eye doctor. I had no idea what vision was and, honestly, didn't even have the desire to figure it out. As my business grew, and I grew, I came to realize that you must have a clear vision of what you want if you want to succeed and it must be pervasive in everything you do.

For instance, in the early days of the space program, NASA's vision was to put a man on the moon. They felt so strongly about it that it was even written above the door in the janitor's closet. For me, seeing how having a clear company vision lead to huge success for my real estate company is where it started to change for me.

What really cemented my vision, though, was a chance encounter with a small group of top Internet marketers who were at the top of their field – some making 7 and 8 figures a year in the industry.

As we stood on the roof of the Hard Rock Hotel in San Diego, my paradigm completely shifted and my vision took root after a very short conversation with one of them.

His name was Sam and although I don't really remember the question that sparked his particular answer, he shared something with me about his perspective on money. He said: "You know there is no such thing as money. Money is simply a bi-product of value. People trade money for value. Your goal should be to stop trying to make money and start trying to bring more value to people lives. It's really simple: try to bring as much value to one person's life, then try to do that to as many people as you possibly can."

Blown over by his comments, I decided at that moment that this would be the cornerstone to my philosophy on business. It would help craft the vision and mission of everything I was working on at the time. My vision for everything I did or decided not to do, was as a result of this new filter I called value.

Whether you work by yourself or part of a team, your vision must be clear and accepted as the focal point of your business. My belief is that offering the most value you can to your clients should be part of your business, but that's up to you to decide. Either way, be crystal clear in what your vision is as it will lead you in any direction you want to go.

What I've shared with you here is not rocket science. If it was, I wouldn't have been able to put it to use in my own business and achieve the level of success I have in such a short period of time. If you're strategic in your approach to business and you make your plans based on good data, a solid vision and the right priorities, you can have just about anything you want for yourself and your family. The right roadmap will get you wherever you want to go. It may not always be in the time frame you want, but it will get you there.

If you'd like a free copy of the same template I use for the strategic plans I create for my businesses, and more information on my philosophy on business growth send an email to: Michael@MichaelReese.Me or visit: www.MichaelReese.Me

ABOUT MICHAEL

Michael Reese, a Lawton, OK native, has risen to the rank of award winning realtor in just 7 years. However, if you knew his past, you would know he's been groomed for sales and excellence his entire life. The son of a Command Sergeant Major, his mother would say, "There is only one way of doing things, exactly and completely; there is no gray area." As a result of this adherence to following through, Mike has excelled in every sales job he's had. In fact, as a teenager Mike would sell candy his mother bought in bulk at his school. He was so successful that the school asked him to stop, because he was outselling the school and cutting into their profits!

In 2002, after a visit with his friend Jay Kinder, Michael decided that real estate was the career for him. In his first two years in the business, he sold over 100 homes. In his third year alone, he exceeded that two-year total by more than 24 homes. By the end of his 5th year, at only the age of 27, he achieved what most real agents dream of, earning over $1,000,000 GCI in a twelve-month period. By the end of his 6th year, he had sold over 500 homes in his short real estate career and he's on pace to sell almost 250 homes this year.

In 2006, he and his team at Keller Williams were voted "Best of Business" for Frisco, TX. In addition, he was voted in as a member of the prestigious "30 under 30" group for Realtors across the United States. In 2007, Michael ranked within the Top 5 for Keller Williams in the Southwest Region, and currently holds the ranking of 19th worldwide.

Understanding that you get more when you give, Michael regularly instructs new agents at the Champions Real Estate School in the Dallas area. He values what he learned there and wants everyone to be successful in his or her real estate career. He has also created systems and programs within his real estate business that allow his agents to be successful and still have balance in their lives. These same programs have created a great real estate enterprise that delivers amazing results to his clients.

His philosophy is very simple. He believes that you don't have to be the best Realtor, just the best marketer. The one with the most clients makes the most money. The more people you can get in front of, the better chance you have to sell more homes and the more people you can help.

Michael currently coaches real estate agents across the country alongside Jay Kinder. He is also in talks with several real estate organizations, who would like Michael's expertise in training their employees. His goal is to help others meet and exceed their wildest dreams and expectations.

CHAPTER 35

A TRENDSETTER TO PURPOSEFUL LIVING

BY PHILIP BRULEY

L ife can change so quickly. We've all read about or heard stories of others who lives have been dramatically altered through an accident, the birth of a child, a divorce or winning the lottery.

My life-changing moment was a little less dramatic. There I sat, almost 40 years old, alone and in my car at the local convenience store. I stopped here every single evening on the way home from work. Now all I had to do was start the car and head to my apartment.

In a little less than 10 minutes I would be comfortably relaxed on my couch, the sandwich and the newspaper I had just bought by my side, flipping through the channels to find something on.

Instead I just sat there, unable to start my car and with the same exact thought going over and over in my mind. "Cut the strings, Man, cut the strings." I couldn't even tell you exactly what it meant but I do know in that moment I felt miserable.

Really, wasn't my life pretty good? I had recently been hired as Fitness Director at a 240,000 square foot health club. Just a little over 3 years after deciding I wanted to be in the fitness business full-time and here I was near the top of the profession in the Pittsburgh area.

Then again, I thought, this was my 7th job in the last 10 years since I had left the Army. I had held my first one, an absolutely wonderful position as an International Public Safety Consultant for 6 years. So that's what, I thought, 6 or so jobs in just 4 years.

I had been a car salesman, recruiting manager for a telemarketing company, youth counselor for a couple of organizations and a Real Estate salesman. I had left each and every one because I was not happy. What had seemed like it would be an exciting new venture never quite left me feeling fulfilled.

I thought how lucky I was not to have been married. Any woman would be beside herself with all of those job changes I went through and our relationship would probably die a quick and ugly death.

But then again, that's the way my relationships were all going anyway. I dated a lot. But as soon as things got rough, or even a little bumpy, I was gone and never looked back. I'd wait a week, start dating again and the cycle would continue on.

I thought back to when I had left the Military. I was a highly decorated Staff Sergeant with combat experience who was already on the list for E-7. I remember how much I loved the military. But something inside of me had wanted to get out and start living an adventurous, challenging and fun-filled life on my terms. The day I left the Army was actually one of the happiest days of my life filled with a lot of hope and promise for the future.

Now I thought again of all those job and relationship changes. I had left each one telling others – and myself – that I was too adventurous; that life was too short for me to be stuck in something I didn't really want. Nope, not for me. I would not settle. Life was all about living.

And then it hit me. Hit me hard. I wasn't adventurous. I was scared. I was not living. I was a puppet. I was letting life direct me with pretty much no control on my part thinking every time I made a change that, maybe then, I would finally be happy.

I started to cry for the first time since I was a little kid. I'm not talking about getting a little misty here; I mean sobbing hard with big old salty tears running down both cheeks and completely oblivious to Life that was happening all around me.

I cried for an hour, maybe closer to two with the same thought getting louder and louder in my head. "Cut the strings, don't be that puppet."

I looked in the rear view mirror, wiped my eyes off on my shirtsleeve and started the car to head home. It was time to determine what I truly wanted in life and start getting after it. It was time to start really living.

Maybe on some level you can relate. I regularly talk to, coach and just plain observe lots of folks who seem to be going through the motions in life without much of a plan.

Whether it's your career, family, finances or health you absolutely have the control to make changes. It's been almost 8 years since I made the decision to get real and start living a purposeful, satisfying life. Man, are things ever different now!

After all those years of relationship hell I am now happily married to my dream girl. I wouldn't have it any other way but it hasn't been easy. I had to take the time – and of course I am still working on it – to learn the skills I was lacking. Anything you want in life requires skill and luckily for all, us skills are learnable.

I spend my days doing what I really want to do – coaching and writing – to help other folks live more powerful and successful lives. I get to work mostly from home and on my own schedule. Since we split our time between homes in Greensburg, PA and Myrtle Beach, SC when we are not traveling, this is perfect for me.

I am in the best shape of my life. My wife and I own a fitness club in Pennsylvania but we are rarely there. Instead we stand-up paddle surf, run, hike, snowboard, cycle and engage in a couple of whole body, functional fitness training workouts each week, usually outdoors.

My life is absolutely better than ever. I'd love to tell you how I drove home after that fateful evening all those years ago, went to bed and when I woke up the next morning everything started going right.

The truth is that it has taken time. I've made some huge successes and made some big mistakes. But each and every day I can honestly say I am working on living the life I really want. I am no longer a puppet.

How can you start living a more real and authentic life where you are in control? Here are a couple of simple but powerful ideas you can use.

1) ASK THE TOUGH QUESTIONS

I'll admit it. I tried affirmations for years. Sometimes even for hours each day until I was exhausted. Pretty pathetic approach to try to change my life but I was determined.

Instead I put my subconscious to work by spending a few minutes in the morning and a few in the evening asking myself the questions to which I really want the answers.

Try it. Ask yourself how you can get what you want out of life, who are you meant to be, how to get in the best shape of your life, how to be a better mate or whatever else is important to you at this time.

Don't worry about the answers coming to you right then and there, as I find usually they don't. But be prepared for some big changes that will be coming in your life if you do this a few times daily.

It's simple. Ask a question. Your subconscious gets to work finding the answers. Usually these answers came to me without my even realizing it. I just started to naturally adopt new habits until suddenly my goal was reached. Or sometimes I would wake up in the middle of the night with "Bam!"… the idea that I needed.

2) DO A DAILY STARE DOWN WITH YOURSELF

Take it a step further. Don't just ask yourself the questions you really want answered but do it in front of a mirror with a complete, dead-on stare with the one who matters most: you.

Making this daily eye contact with you is weird at first. Most of us only look in the mirror to see what we like and what we don't like. But our eyes are powerful and scheduling some face time with a mirror can be a radical life-changing daily event.

Spend a few minutes a couple of times each day getting to really know yourself. It's powerful.

3) PUT YOURSELF FIRST

I graduated from a small high school up in Vermont and was awarded a

4-year college scholarship to attend a local university.

But me, what I wanted to do was join the military. I didn't know what I wanted to do for a living, was tired of school and really wanted to have a few adventurous years before I settled down.

So what did I do? Exactly what 99% of people told me to do – I went to college. I spent 4 miserable years there and switched majors so many times that I never even ended up with a degree.

I couldn't bring myself to start a 5th year and finally enlisted to become a US Army Ranger. The next few years were great. I learned tons of stuff, I traveled, I matured and I really enjoyed that phase of my life.

It's okay, and downright necessary, to be a little selfish. You can't make others happy if you are not happy. So if you have spent the time getting to know yourself and determined what it is you really want in life then I say go after it with all you've got.

4) TURN OFF THE TV

I used to watch 5 or 6 hours of TV every single night. What an absolute waste of time. My whole evening would be planned around what was on for that night and many times it would be re-runs.

Most people don't even realize how much television they watch. Spend a week or two and track your hours in front of your set. Then think of all the other things you could be doing. Want to write a book but don't have the time? Learn a new hobby? Play some games with your family? The list goes on and on. Break this addiction!

The funny thing I was worried I wouldn't have anything to talk to people about the next day. It turns out that when someone asks you "Hey, did you see that crazy singer on American Idol last night?" and you tell them you were too busy learning to play the guitar, the conversation takes a whole new direction.

5) USE YOUR COMPUTER JUDICIOUSLY

Facebook, Twitter, Google. Yeah I get it. Your computer is pretty cool. The trouble is that it is way too easy to get on there and get lost – I mean several hours of being gone – before you realize what happened.

I check and reply to e-mail twice a day. I get on Facebook and Twitter for about five minutes each morning and again in the evening. When I need to do some research or want to check out a couple of interesting websites I do. I absolutely love computer time but I don't let it take over my life.

Control your electronics. Don't let them control you!

5) BE GRATEFUL FOR EVERYTHING

Establish the habit now of being grateful now for everything you have in your life. Be thankful for your clothes, your home, your car, your friends and everything you can think of. Say "thank you" to yourself hundreds of times each day. Say it to your friends. Say it to your acquaintances. Say it to strangers.

I honestly believe that when you are grateful for everything you have in your life – no matter how small – the Universe wants to reward you and give you so much more to be thankful over. Plus life is just much better when you are grateful and can see beyond yourself.

Most of all be thankful you are still drawing breath and have the chance to experience all that life has to offer. There's no better time to cut the strings and really start living than right now.

ABOUT PHILIP

Philip Bruley is a former US Army Ranger and International Business Consultant who now works full-time as a Certified Life Coach and CrossFit Trainer. He is the founder of Better Dude LLC, through which he is committed to helping other guys live more purposeful and adventurous lives.

Philip and his wife Beth split their time between their homes in Myrtle Beach, SC and Greensburg, PA where Beth owns the local Snap 24-Hour Fitness. They also travel frequently both nationally and internationally, where they volunteer their time helping others create better lives.

When not coaching or traveling, Philip spends his time stand-up paddle surfing, trail running, hiking and conducting group CrossFit workouts. He also enjoys writing and he has been published in numerous magazines.

To contact Philip directly, or to learn more about Better Dude Coaching, please visit him online at: http://BetterDude.com where he publishes regular free information. You can also find him on Facebook at: http://www.Facebook.com/BetterDude.

CHAPTER 36

THE NEW SCIENCE OF SALES

BY MICHAEL SALETTA

LINKING THE SALES PROCESS TO YOUR CUSTOMER'S BRAIN

INTRODUCTION

Driving sales is at the heart of every business, and whether you're a company of one or 10,000, the game is won when you learn to consistently sell your product and service. Over the past 20 years, my work with thousands of clients from nearly every industry, I have learned the downfalls, barriers and challenges that individuals experience in the selling process. My greatest sales experience has not come solely from teaching sales courses; rather it's been through my need to sell training and consulting before I had the opportunity to be the Trainer and Consultant. I started selling on the phone, as so many sales professionals do, and later initiated jumping on planes and selling to top executives of Fortune 500 companies. What began with trial and error, and lots of dumb mistakes, ultimately created a proven system that I have repeated with near-perfect success. My sales have ranged from individual classes priced at $2,000, to large consulting contracts that have exceeded the million-dollar mark.

Achieving near-perfect, sustainable selling success comes from duplicating the sales process. My quest for duplication began with the pursuit of dissecting each sale and later turning it into a predictable science through my study of Psychology and my work in the field of Neuroscience. In 2005, my training and consulting work brought me to CIMBA University in Asolo, Italy. This led me to Dr. Al Ringleb and Dr. David Rock, co-founders of the NeuroLeadership Institute. Together through their research and brilliant network, the pieces of the sales process began to solidify in theory and application. I will share the selling steps and brain science that will allow you to create your own consistent sales trend!

UNDERSTANDING THE CUSTOMER'S BUYING BRAIN

The human brain is the driver of our thinking, emotions, and behavior, which include the thoughts, feelings, and actions that drive our selling and buying practices. To create consistent sales performance, it makes sense to understand how the brain functions to positively influence the sales process. At its core, the brain is emotional and therefore must be engaged emotionally to compel the customer to buy. To avoid going into an in-depth lesson on neuroscience, I will focus on what I consider (and many neuroscientists would agree) two of the most important parts of the brain when it comes to the sales process – the Limbic System and Mirror Neurons.

THE LIMBIC SYSTEM

If we had to choose one part of the brain that plays the most important role in the sales process, it would be the Limbic System. The brain's limbic system is largely responsible for our emotions, motivations, survival mechanisms, and memory functions. The limbic system is profoundly intuitive and makes decisions faster than our conscious comprehension. This function of our brain will make unconscious decisions in mere milliseconds. For this reason alone, it's essential to learn what triggers the buying brain to create sales consistency. The brain's limbic system has been developing for millions of years to preserve our survival. The survival function known as 'fight or flight' has more recently evolved to 'threat or reward' and is key to the sales process. In fact, remember this core theme in the sales process:

"Threat or Reward = Away or Toward"

In other words, if the customer's brain feels threat, it will move away from the sale. If the customer's brain feels reward it will move toward the sale. This concept is critical to selling to your customer's brain and I will link its application to each step of the sales process.

MIRROR NEURONS

One of the most exciting new findings in the field of neuroscience is the discovery of Mirror Neurons. These amazing neurons in our brains were discovered accidentally in 1992 by an Italian neuroscientist, Dr. Rizzolatti. Ongoing research has found the human brain has multiple mirror neuron systems that specialize in understanding the actions of others, their intentions, the social meaning of their behavior, and their emotions. These special neurons fire in the brain to mimic or mirror an action or emotion that is being observed; therefore, we feel and experience others just by watching and observing. When we see someone yawn, then we yawn. When a woman runs her nails down a chalkboard, then we grimace. When you see a person smile, then your "smile neurons" also fire. The understanding of mirror neurons will bring immense power when selling to your customer's brain. I will guide you in learning to use this knowledge and again link it directly to the sales process.

THE SALES PROCESS

CREATING RAPPORT

Every person has an innate connection with other human beings – it's the degree of the connection that determines the success of the sales process. The limbic system of our brain is both social and emotional and this is why creating rapport is such an important aspect to selling to your customer's brain. Creating rapport is the brain's way of saying, "I like you," "I connect with you," and "I trust you." Building rapport is an active process that involves consciously working towards a "feeling" of comfort between the salesperson and the customer. When rapport is built, there is a level of trust that is established, and this trust closes sales. If the customer experiences a lack of trust, the limbic system experiences a threat feeling and moves away from the sale. Remember, *"threat = away" and "reward = toward"*.

Building rapport happens naturally as we all gravitate toward people that are like ourselves. To consciously and proactively create rapport, look for ways to develop a common interest with your customer. The smallest association can create an immediate bond and may include things like hobbies, hometowns, sport teams, family, restaurants, occupations, and recreation. Beyond finding things in common, it's important that your customer feels you sincerely 'like them.' Show that you really care and like your customer and you will begin to build a trusting relationship.

The process of creating rapport simultaneously activates the customer's mirror neurons. Start by matching the customer's body language; when a customer looks you in the eye and offers a firm handshake, return the eye contact and match the handshake ...when a customer leans back, casually do the same ... and when a customer is observing a product, get side-by-side and discuss the product together.

Salespeople often make the grave mistake of moving too quickly through the step of creating rapport. Their thought of "let's skip the small talk and get right to the product" may prove to be very detrimental when it comes to closing the sale. One of the greatest pieces of advice originates from Theodore Roosevelt: "No one cares how much you know, until they know how much you care." Creating rapport moves the customer's buying brain toward the sale, and this becomes the essential first step that allows you to move on to the next step.

CLARIFYING NEEDS

The process of clarifying needs with your customer builds naturally on the first step of creating rapport. Clarifying needs fulfills the brain's desire to feel listened to and understood. To understand the customer's needs, the salesperson asks questions to progressively uncover their personal and practical needs. Asking questions at the personal level reveals the customer's feelings and buying motivations. Clarifying the practical needs of the customer exposes the fundamental problem they want solved, the useful aspects of the product or service, and the matter-of-fact details. When we take the time to sincerely understand our customer's needs, the customer again feels safe thereby moving toward the sale. When we rush through process of clarifying needs, the customer instinctively reacts with a threat response and moves away from the sale.

When tapping into a customer's personal needs, it's essential to discover the underlying motivations to a customer's buying decision. Ask questions such as: What is important to you about this? How will this product help you? How do you feel about this service? How will the benefits positively impact you? These questions need to be customized based on your actual product and service, yet when asked correctly, the answers will provide valuable insights into your customer's mind.

To activate your customer's mirror neurons during the process of clarifying needs, ask questions that emotionally engage and instinctively interest them. Being an effective sales person is less about doing all the talking, and more about listening. In fact, a good ratio is 70% listening to 30% talking. As you listen carefully and respond by summarizing the customer's answers, their empathic mirror neurons will fire. Through the careful summarization of your customer's responses, they will hear the sincerity of your voice inflection and unconsciously their brain responds positively creating a social-emotional connection. As you continue this process, your listening skills build trust with your customer, again moving them toward the sale.

CONNECTING VALUE

After taking the time to create rapport and clarify needs, the next step involves making clear and specific connections between your product or service and the customer's needs. Connecting value fulfills the brain's motivation to get what it wants. The 'real value' of the product is driven from the degree the salesperson's product and service matches the needs of the customer. The cardinal sin created in this step often occurs because the salesperson gets overly excited about what they have to offer, that they begin to 'verbally throw-up' on their customer, thereby disregarding all of the pertinent information they just received. The other fatal mistake made by salespeople involves rushing through the process of clarifying needs with only a few surface-level questions. When this occurs, there is nothing tangible to connect the customer's needs to, thus resulting in a huge disconnect in the buying brain.

The process of connecting value strategically links each of the customer's personal and practical needs to the product or service being sold. This step of connecting value is important to the brain because millions of neurons are firing to process information by making neural connections. Neuroscientists have a common saying, "neurons that fire together, wire together." Help the customer's brain make the 'need-value' connection, to move them toward a buying decision. When there is little-to-no-value, the customer experiences a threat response and they instinctively move away from the interaction. This threat response is precisely the problem when a salesperson operates with high-pressure sales. By taking the time to connect value, the customer feels they are getting exactly what they want, and their brain's reward system fires letting them know it's okay to buy.

Connecting value influences the brain's mirror neurons by giving us a feeling that we are seeing and getting what we desire. Use effective visuals, colorful graphics, pleasing images, and product demonstrations to connect value. When a customer sees something they want and desire, their mirror neurons are activated. Explicitly show the customer what it would be like to own the product, use the product, and benefit from the value of the product. This is reason why the salesperson has you sit in the new car, and it's also the reason the good-looking model is shown in the display ad. Our mirror neurons say, "Hey, I want to look cool in that car," and "I want to be sexy like he or she is."

CONFIRMING COMMITMENT AND CLOSING THE SALE

Closing the sale is a natural progression of the previous three steps along with guiding your customer through the process of confirming commitment. Confirming commitment is the brain's intention to move forward with a plan of action. This step is about getting your customer to commit to the value that your product or service brings to their life. Throughout the sales process, the salesperson must continually ask questions that will consciously make the customer aware of their buying decision. As the customer says "yes" and agrees that the value of the product meets their needs, then the customer finds it difficult to argue with him or herself; i.e., the brain does not wish to counter its own data and commitments. As you specify the actions you will take and confirm these actions with the customer, the customer comes to an agreement that places both of you on the same side of the sale. When you and the customer are working together, the limbic system experiences a sense of partnership that moves them toward a buying decision.

To trigger the customer's mirror neurons when confirming commitment, actively use your body language to gain their commitment. Nodding your head, visually showing the next step, and shaking the customer's hand will assist you in gaining their commitment.

As you recap the sales process, work to achieve multiple yeses to strengthen the brain's commitment into buying your product or service. When you expect the customer to move forward with the sale, they will instinctively feel the need to follow along. Closing the sale is the emotional brain's way of saying yes to the reward of what is being sold.

OVERCOMING OBJECTIONS

Objections can show up during any stage of the sales process. Objections are normal for the brain, as they represent our desire to protect ourselves and remain safe. Sales people typically dread objections and many go to the painstaking effort to rehearse objection-countering scripts. This approach is ineffective because the customer's intuitive sense and emotional brain recognize the rehearsed scripts, thereby moving away from sale. Instead move toward the objection to understand it, which will make the customer feel secure in the sales process.

A salesperson must begin by reframing the meaning of an objection by recognizing that the customer still has needs that have not been met. In fact, I have a saying, "An objection identified is a need to be clarified." When this becomes your objection mindset, you look forward to digging deeper into understanding your customer's needs. The best approach for overcoming objections involves summarizing the objection, which activates mirror neurons, and makes the customer feel understood. Then proceed by asking additional questions to once again clarify the customer's needs. As needs are clarified, connect the need to your product's value. When you reconfirm your value meets the customer's need, then the objection is eliminated. It's important to remember that the customer may not even be consciously aware of why they are objecting; they just 'feel' like something is wrong. Take the time to further engage the customer's brain to help them move past the threat and toward the reward.

CONCLUSION

Corporate executives often turn to outside consultants and training organizations in search of guidance and expert sales advice. More times than not, tangible changes in sales performance fall short of expectations due to the lack of knowledge about how the customer's brain reacts to the salesperson and their selling process. Learning the 'New Science of Sales' will greatly improve your ability to achieve consistent sales success. When it comes to selling to your customer's brain, each step has the ability to positively influence the limbic system and mirror neurons, and then both you and your customer will 'feel good' about closing the sale.

ABOUT MICHAEL

Michael Saletta is known as the "Master Facilitator" in guiding companies to define and drive their business strategy. He is the founder and CEO of Saletta Leadership, LLC and Leadership Partners, LLC, consulting companies dedicated to driving sales, aligning team performance, and producing a guaranteed return on investment. The diversity of Michael's consulting services is based on his ability to analyze, design, develop, and facilitate every step of a client's business strategy needs.

As the past CEO and Co-Owner of an international training and development organization, his team worked with more than 10,000 companies, directly impacting over 250,000 individuals. For more than 20 years, Michael's specialized knowledge comes from his direct involvement in the field with thousands of clients including La-Z-Boy, Electrolux, U.S. Army, Department of Energy, U.S. Forest Service, Wells Fargo, Revlon, Michael Kors, Whole Foods, Associated Builders & Contractors, Oldcastle, Marriott, MGM, Royal Bank of Canada, and CIMBA University in Italy.

Michael may be reached at: Michael@SalettaLeadership.com

And: www.SalettaLeadership.com

CHAPTER 37

ANOTHER THING

BY REBECCA BARCY

Is your life made up of another thing, then another thing, and then another other thing? It describes almost everyone, I know. There is always a push and pull with time. Just when you think it's handled, another thing always comes up. We can be cute and call it Murphy's Law. Pretty much the immediate solution is: suck it up cry baby, and manage it. So I did that, a lot. I managed myself right into being a zombie. Once I was giving my credit card number to a phone rep and read 9LS9 LS0h 868E 9L0h. I didn't even realize a credit card upside down looked like letters, did you? The rep keeps saying she doesn't understand, but I am thinking, what is wrong with *her*. I am sure she was thinking what is wrong with *me*. I was surviving on auto pilot and didn't even realize it. I was absolutely working harder to achieve less success. It had affected everything in my life. I started to withdraw from anything that was unnecessary and guess what happened? When I slowed down I was more productive. I was adding more value to my relationships and I was happier.

When I was trying to do everything I didn't even look at what everything was. I didn't even pay attention if I even wanted or needed to be doing that. Get drastic! What is it you want to accomplish at the end of the week, month, and year? What is your story going to be at the end of your life? What is going on in your daily life that needs to stop, so you can accomplish what you really want? Time is flying by.

You were going to … You meant too… You wanted to… You should have… If your relationships are chaotic, you will feel overwhelmed, overworked, and be less successful in anything and maybe everything you are doing. If you FOCUS ENERGY on your INTENTION, then your energy goes in the desired direction you always wanted, in the first place, and away from chaos! Chaos does not have to be your default!

Does this sound familiar? You work so hard. So much is going on around us. Even if another thing didn't come up (with your child, your aging parents, repairs for something, people who don't do what they said they would) everything on your plate is a *priority*. Even taking a break or trying to enjoy yourself for a minute makes you feel guilty, right? You have been going and going and doing and doing. And then guess what? Your client goes with someone else, you lose your job, your finances aren't great, your friends are disconnected or your marriage and family is falling apart.

Why don't they see value in all of the things you do? Why? Because they are going and going and doing and doing, too. When you think you are being taken for granted they might be thinking the same of you. You might be resenting them and they might be resenting you. Disconnected relationships create more work, worry and exhaustion so everything is harder and overwhelming.

How do you mesh INTENTION with value in your relationships? You ask good questions! We are all motivated differently. Therefore, we don't always recognize what demonstrates value, for other people. We do things that we think show value, because they are important to us. We get so caught up in the daily "to do" list that we don't even notice our fan club dwindling.

I started here first; everyone is on this fast paced rollercoaster and many of us spend A LOT OF TIME complaining about the ups and downs in any given day. Even if you complain only 5% of the day you lose 72 minutes complaining in just one day! We all probably complain *or listen to complaints*, more than that! You'd lose 504 minutes, a week, complaining! (That's a whopping 8 hours and 40 minutes.) In one year, you will lose 26,280 minutes or 438 hours that you will never get back, complaining! If you complain, or listen to complaints a lot less than 5% of the day, you will have a lot more time!

However, its human nature to like to complain, so don't completely deny it. In complaining you can often find a solution, if that is your INTENTION. However, set a time limit *before* you start complaining. You can listen to someone else complain but learn how to say graciously, but in essence, "Time's up". This will help you find more time for relationships with value.

HOW: when you are trying to figure out something, mad about something, can't believe something... try these suggestions:

SUGGESTION 1

ASK YOURSELF, "WHAT IS THE INTENTION OF REPEATING THIS INJUSTICE TO ANYONE?"

IS IT...

a) I just want to vent – there is no solution.
b) I am sick of this happening over and again; I want a solution.
c) I want someone to hug me and tell me they are sorry this is happening to me, not make me feel bad.
d) I want someone else's point of view and I will listen even when it is hard to hear and may or may not be correct advice, for me, at this time. I will not repeat what they said and start a new complaining and gossip session about them, to someone else.
e) I am bored and like to get riled up, and complaining is really fun for me.
f) If you tend to ramble and go into ten other subjects write down the word INTENTION, and keep looking at it. (Remember the less than 5% rule and stay focused)
g) Pick the right person to complain to, about this issue. Don't pick every person you know.
h) Tell your complaining partner what you need from them so they don't have to guess, and get it wrong.
i) Remember *your true* INTENTION is…. you fill in the blank.

SUGGESTION 2

HOW MUCH TIME ARE YOU GIVING THIS?

3 minutes, 10 minutes, 1 hour? Set the time. Stick to the time set.

SUGGESTION 3

IF SOMEONE IS COMPLAINING TO YOU:

a) If someone just starts complaining, use this as a quick response. "I am very sensitive to anything difficult." Then ask them "Is there anything good that might come from this bad thing happening?" or "Tell me about something else in your life that's working pretty well."

b) Ask them, "Do you just need someone to listen to you or are you looking for an opinion?" (by the way- no one is ever looking for your judgment)

c) Say, "I'd like to be able to give you my full attention, I can block out this amount of time." When that agreed amount of time is *almost* up, refer to 3a

d) Don't be afraid to say, "I only have/had this amount of time." Add words like, "I hope listening has helped." "You are going to be so proud of yourself when you solve this challenge or get through this." or "I am so proud of you for concentrating on the positive instead." If you begrudgingly listen you are devaluing your relationship and creating resentment. That is *probably not* your INTENTION.

e) If this is a relationship that is challenging for you, remember INTENTION, be kind but be honest.

SUGGESTION 4

STICK WITH YOUR INTENTION.

Sometimes we don't think about INTENTION because we just want to be right. This often results in a silent contract for disharmony and maybe even destruction. Begin by setting the opposite INTENTION of how you feel. If you feel disappointed or angry you have to set the opposite INTENTION for anything to change. Be quiet for a minute.

Remove yourself from whatever the situation is and be quiet.

    a) WHAT IS YOUR TRUE INTENTION? The solution flows from there.

SUGGESTION 5

ASK PEOPLE WHAT THEY WANT.

a) What is the most important part of this (business, friendship, family, co-worker) relationship TO YOU?
b) What does this (companies, family) reputation say TO YOU?
c) What is the best thing you like about this company, your job or this friendship/family?
d) What do you least like about this company/your job as co-workers or this friendship/family?
• How can we change that? (Don't automatically take on more work. Get your family to help you or set up a forum at your company, of people who want to see the same change.)
Good managers care about their employees. When employees know you care about them, they will be loyal employees who protect the company's reputation.
e) Ask your child, spouse, family, friends; "What memory do you want to have of us when you grow up, or we are old together, etc?" It might surprise you that it is usually simple and doesn't require another line on your project "to do" list. Listen and repeat and repeat and repeat. It is how you make someone feel *consistently*, that builds a relationship, with value.

SUGGESTION 6

TAKE 5 SECONDS TO GREET PEOPLE.

(The receptionist, the janitor, your co-worker, the grocery store clerk, a neighbor, your husband, your child.)

Do you dismiss people? Do you take people who are always there for granted? Small things break down your relationships. Every person around us makes up our team. Always look at people and acknowledge them. What if you lost this person, this job, this store, this community?

When you don't have strength and value in your relationships you start to lose confidence in yourself too.

SUGGESTION 7

BE GRACEFUL AND ASK QUESTIONS.

If you aren't communicating well with your aging parent/child/spouse/co-worker talk to them. Ask them questions. "What is the worse part of your day?" "What is the best part of your day?" "What can we change, together?" Tell them they are important to you. Share that you realize this is frustrating to them. Let them know you want to be in their corner. Tell them you are, "for them." Even a smile says, "I am for you!"

SUGGESTION 8

ASK FOR PERMISSION BEFORE YOU START TALKING TO SOMEONE.

Just a simple two second question, "Is this a good time to ask you…?" This simple tool will make a relationship better instantly. If you acknowledge someone else's needs they will listen to you better now, if they have the time, or better later when you set another time to meet/talk.

a) If they always set the time for a later date, remember your INTENTION. Realize they are showing you how they work best. If you keep this in mind, you will have a better relationship.
b) Tell them what you want to talk about.
c) Tell them how much time you need and then be sure to get to the point and wrap it up in that amount of time.
d) If you need more time say, "I realize now I need more time. I want to acknowledge your time limits; should we finish this up now or would you be more comfortable making another appointment?"

SUGGESTION 9

APPRECIATION WITH INTENTION

When a relationship feels like you are hitting a brick wall, take the time to write down what you appreciate about the person first. Then write down what you wish would change. Remember your INTENTION. You must put thought into your INTENTION. You should not respond based on your feelings alone. INTENTION is powerful. Even if your words aren't perfect, people will get what you mean if your INTENTION is pure. Think more about how you can solve this issue from their point of view. Put forth your best INTENTION for a solution. How can you get there from here?

a) Stop telling everyone else about it and take the time to tell the person directly.

SUGGESTION 10

INTENTION CARD & TEA LIGHT CANDLE

At our company, new interviewees, employees, clients, and vendors are given a 3x5 card and a tea light candle. We tell them to take the card and candle home and write their personal INTENTION on the card. Then, with the written INTENTION in mind, we all try to light our candles at 8pm. It is our company goal to be part of the community. We care about people. We are sending good thoughts out to each other. We don't know how many people are burning the candle at 8pm, but you can definitely feel a connection when you do it. People have called and said that their hearts desire and their true INTENTION came true. It's about being part of something and someplace and someone who cares about you. It is beautiful and simple.

SUGGESTION 11

SAY....

Say I Love You a lot, but get their attention and say it differently. Say I value YOU. I appreciate YOU. YOU make it easy for me. I enjoy YOU. I look forward to seeing YOUR face. Everything is Right in the World, Now. YOU are a good person. YOU are the stars and the sun and the moon to me. 'Corny' makes people laugh, and a smile on two faces is a beautiful INTENTION.

The busy "to do" list will still exist. There is still only 24 hours in a day. But, I promise if you strengthen and add value to your relationships you don't have to give up sleeping, healthy eating, exercise or having fun. Your TRUE INTENTION will create the life you wanted. Chaos will be manageable, your recovery time will be faster and your life will be a lot better.

ABOUT REBECCA

Rebecca Barcy is the Executive Director for *I Need An Angel, Inc.*, its division *I Need An Angel Too* and *High Fives Charity Network, Inc.* *I Need An Angel's* principle products and services include Home Care that helps seniors and others (recovering from surgery or suffering from chronic illness) stay at home. *I Need An Angel Too* guides and supports clients, without bias, through options for Home Care, Assisted Living Housing, and Skilled Nursing, when health or injury has turned their life upside down overnight or overtime, and they don't know what to do. Rebecca Barcy also partnered with the non-profit, *High Fives Charity Network* 501(c) 3, as an advocate for caregivers, who are always helping others, and seniors who don't have enough help. Mrs. Barcy was inducted as "VIP Woman of the Year 2011/2012" in recognition of the strides she has made in the Home Care industry demonstrating professional leadership, creative management and outstanding support of NAPW's commitment to networking and community involvement. Rebecca certification as a CSA – Certified Senior Adviser – supports her desire to be an educated and positive influence in the community. Her true expertise is Creative Management and Intuitive Solutions.

Rebecca also believes that as a businesswoman, balancing work and family life can be challenging, but has the utmost importance. Mrs. Barcy has built numerous businesses with her family members working alongside her, even as young as three weeks old! Her daughter, Amanda, son-in-law Jeremiah, and son Nathan, help run the above corporate entities, with the help of 50 staff members. Her husband of 22 years, Dan, helps with the companies as needed, and all four grandchildren often spend time in their offices. Rebecca's Queensland Heeler, Jax and kitty Nolan, and even her 21-year old kitty Littlefoot, who passed away this year, have accompanied her to the office where she works from an old 1900's roll top desk. She feels her clients, employees, and vendors are an extension of her family and she loves her family!

To receive a free "10 Questions You Must Ask When Choosing a Home Care Company", visit: www.ineedanangel.com

To learn more about I Need An Angel and its division I Need An Angel, Too Inc. visit: www.thegreatestcompanyever.com or www.ineedanangel.org -- Or call: (480) 951-4083

To learn more about High Fives Charity Network, Inc [a 501(c) (3) non-profit], buy a Change Can Be A Scary Thing T-shirt or make a donation, visit: www.highfivescharitynetwork.org or call (480) 529-9798 – Or email Rebecca at: yesway@ix.netcom.com

CHAPTER 38

TRENDSETTER MINDSET

BY WAYNE JUSTIN

T rendsetters are those committed to thriving in today's world – regardless of economic or personal circumstances. The reason you are learning the mindset of a trendsetter is for financial and emotional freedom. What that means to you is that you or your family no longer worry about health or financial difficulty, no matter the economy. You become one driven by actions. It takes a strong mental structure to make that happen today. You can make it happen.

It took an extreme amount of pain and dissatisfaction to get me to a point of realization that something could make my life better. Although I had been working two jobs and I was burnt out from sleeping only three hours a day, that did not push me over the edge. All my spare time was spent helping friends with various issues. All I ever thought about was sleep. Life was a little tough, but I knew it would get better. Oh. I forgot to mention that I had a wife who was demanding my attention too. Then suddenly, one day I woke up and everything I knew was somehow different, somehow better. I got rid of the stressful work habits, got some much-needed rest and time – which helped smooth things over with my wife.

Well, let's try this again. The truth is that I got fired from work and got a divorce. I then had an epiphany. I was going to have to change. I also went crazy. I lost my mind. I got so mad and crazy I planned revenge. I sat down in the heat of the moment and I vowed I will never get fired again and, furthermore, I won't put up with women who just don't care. And no more long worthless hours at work. That began my career as an entrepreneur.

Yes, change happened. Not at all for the right reasons, but it happened. The main thing that changed was my mind. The more I changed my thoughts, the more my actions changed. I see others every day carrying around those old beliefs about life, about work, about family that I used to have, but I know that they're gonna have to grow. That was the beginning of waking up. I can't tell them, but by showing you, maybe you can. Waking up will make you a trendsetter, but you must first realize that you are asleep. Today is your first call to live the life and dream the dreams that thousands have found. They all were trendsetters to be remembered forever.

What's important in that story was that change happened. This was the first realized stage in my evolution, but I can assure you that I have grown. I am happy and proud that I can see great reasons to grow even today. I understand that difficulty brings those greatest rewards. Today I can honestly say that I am different for all the right reasons, and thank goodness for the wrong reasons. This is your call to action. When trendsetters get that call, they answer.

As you are able to think as a trendsetter, you easily become a master within your niche or field by always having a good grasp on the foundation of life. There are cowards and then there are trendsetters. As a trendsetter, you will walk where cowards stumble. Trendsetters know that challenges are the only way to grow, … and with growth the mind expands and they welcome it. The trendsetter mindset will allow you to easily make decisions correctly, which otherwise would seem counterintuitive. In other words you won't be judging any book by its cover. You will actually be achieving the success you are aiming for. You will understand clearly how to avoid taking any action steps that will not benefit you. Becoming a trendsetter allows you to have a clear strong grasp of your market or field of experts. If you do not have those essential skills of a trendsetter, you will not survive in a constantly-evolving economy. Growth is never easy, but that's the only way your new better life will come.

New research shows that 31% of new employee businesses will fail within the first two years, 49% will fail within the first five years, and 74% will fail within the first fifteen years. The surviving few are trend-setters. That is, they possess the secret that allows them to maintain value through the 'ups and downs' of economic growth and decline.

THE TRENDSETTER MINDSET FOLLOWS FIVE SIMPLE CONCEPTS THAT ANYONE CAN FOLLOW.

The first of these concepts is your ability to be driven by love of passion. The second trendsetter mindset is that you must be willing to overcome fears and take unbelievable risks. Third comes the ability to welcome change. Fourth mindset of a trendsetter is your ability to tell the absolute truth. Fifth is believing in yourself.

First. Trendsetters have a passion so strong that it compels you to stay up at night, travel halfway across the world just to watch a sunset, or venture deep into space among the stars just to look back and watch the earth spin. Everyone has passions so strong that they may not always be logical or rational. The fact that they exist is all that is important.

Second. The second trendsetter mindset is the ability to push forward in the face of fear. They are the brave souls of the world. Some call them wild and crazy, but they pave the way of success for us all. Trendsetters are ones who face the greatest fear in each generation and survive, despite the odds. They risk the greatest amount for the simple promise of a dream. In them we find equal rights, freedom, love, legacies and much more. They give us the strength to believe in the dream again and to own the greatest things in the world. You may lose friends, money, time, energy, sanity, husbands or wives, but your courage must be that strong.

Trendsetters know that their gold is at the summit and not at the foot of the mountains, and the ends hold a much greater promise. So aim high, as high as you can think. You can do this and you deserve it.

Third. Third comes the ability to welcome change. Trendsetters will go through various stages of change acceptance within their lives. Acceptance does not mean settling for less than you deserve. What is the difference between the fire that boils water in the wild and fire that warms a T.V dinner in your microwave? I say that they are the same thing. They are just the result of a stretched-thought process. If you took a microwave oven back in time, and attempted to show our ancestors that this oven will cook food, it may quickly be called witchcraft – and someone may have to pay the price for the ignorance of a culture. On the other hand, if we decided that the microwave oven was too high tech and that we needed to get back to basics and learn to build fires like we do in the wild, some may starve. I challenge you to see the evolution in that statement. The fire in the wild and the microwave are the same thing. An expression of the same thought. There is the evolution of thought.

While that example was a bit of a stretch, I just want you to see that you're gonna' have to grow if you want something different. It's ok to look at things from a different perspective – that doesn't make it different, but you have to be able to think of it differently to see the fire inside the microwave. Change is just allowing thought to evolve. Embrace it! That's the beginning of the magic of being a trendsetter. For trendsetters, change happens so often it is almost welcomed with every breath. What you gonna' have to do is live with the question… how else can I look at this? … or who else is seeing a better picture? Yes, you can change your point of view and take theirs. Yes, things are still the same, they just have a better view. With the change of just a few thoughts you can do that too. Changes are always happening. Embracing them – that is the only way to grow.

<u>Fourth</u>. Fourth mindset of a trendsetter is your ability to tell the absolute truth. The reason honesty matters is because that's where your clues are when you should be changing your point of view. Is your life boring? Are you burnt out at your current job? Are you making the amount of money you think you deserve? Would you rather be just anywhere else right now? If you answer truthfully to any of these questions that you are not satisfied, then you've got a call to action. What is the truth about your life or business? What really needs to change for growth to happen around you? I challenge you to see it's your mindset.

You don't have to lose your job first, like I did, to know that if you don't change willfully someone else will do it for you. That is the worst type of change. On the day you get fired and you are trying to understand, how they could fire me, their best worker? And you are justifying it in your mind saying, "Well, I was tired of their B.S. anyways." Your wife will be home planning the change to your best friend and you'll be thinking, "Man! She moves quickly." You ask yourself later, "Was I the only one who didn't know?"

Find out the truth about your life or business and it will save your life. As a trendsetter, I believe we should face the truth about it all.

Questions you should ask to find out essential truths about your business. What is my business costing me now? Who is running my business? Most struggling businesses are operating over budget. What are the numerical vital signs of your business? Operating cost, income cost, payroll cost. Trendsetters need to do the same thing for home and personal life. Get help, let's make it happen. Honesty saves lives; change happens too early or late without it.

<u>Fifth</u>. Fifth is believing in yourself. The reason you have got to believe in yourself is that nobody else can instill a trendsetter mindset within you. Only you can do that. Without the essential belief in oneself, growth fades with every breath. When a seed is planted, it is not wise to uproot it often to check on growth. Here's how I found faith and luck. I woke up one day complaining, "I don't have enough time at home with my family." "The pay was not enough for those hours I put in." I thought my coworkers' aim seems to be to make my life uncomfortable. By this time, weeks had gone by since I had been feeling that way.

I woke up one morning knowing that this was it; I had had enough. I felt that if I did not change something, then soon someone would do that for me. I felt that I had lived with that fear for long enough and I was going to do something about it. I had decided to quit that job, it had made me unhappy for long enough. That day I walked in and offered to take a leave of absence for as long as I could get. Yes, that was my easy escape, not exactly heroic, but it would work. Well, not exactly, I was informed that in order to get a leave of absence from work I was going to have to put in a two-week notice. I wanted out right there and then. I knew that I was not going to work at that place one more day and a leave of absence was now out of the question. I quickly rationalized and walked out jobless.

I was now going to start my own business doing something I loved. I knew my love and a few of the things I that I had a natural talent for. I followed them, and as unbelievable as this sounds, fate seemed to line up people and circumstances to get me to where I am today, a complete success. This process would be repeated time and time again in my life, never to fail. I now say that belief in oneself is a wonderful thing. Most of the actions in this story are counterintuitive, but they work, I don't know why. They just do. You must simply be able to go on faith that you will have a tree in time, and it will produce your intended fruit. Trendsetters believe in themselves because they know that the answers to the toughest questions are hidden in their beliefs. With a strong belief in yourself, rather than give up on your project or passion, you will seek friends, resources, money, and information to keep the fire of your investments going when things get tough. The stronger your belief in yourself , the more you will notice family and friends flock to you for help or advice, and you can feel confident that you are steering them the right way. ...The Trendsetter way.

ABOUT WAYNE

Wayne Justin: Born May 14th 1983 to Cynthia Dosithee and Joseph Justin. Arrived in the US at the age of ten as a US immigrant from St. Lucia. Napoleon Hill, Tony Robbins, Jim Rohn, Michael Gerber, Henry Ford and other great minds have influenced Wayne's accomplishments. Two of Wayne's dominant passions are travel business so you will find him mixing the two as often as possible. Today Wayne has found successes as an accomplished internet marketer, network marker, traditional business owner, personal coach and author. As a father of four Wayne loves to Spend time being dad most of all. He is a huge soccer fan. His favorite quote is "Every morning in Africa, a gazelle wakes up. It knows it must run faster than the fastest lion or it will be killed...every morning a lion wakes up. It knows it must outrun the slowest gazelle or it will starve to death. It doesn't matter whether you are a lion or a gazelle...when the sun comes up, you'd better be running."

CHAPTER 39

ADRENAL RECHARGE STRATEGIES FOR HIGH ACHIEVERS

BY DR. RITAMARIE LOSCALZO, D.C.

Jackie sat at the edge of her chair, tears streaming down her face as she shared her story with me. How had it come to this? She'd been a successful account executive, hard-driving and climbing in her firm at record pace. She'd started to put on a few extra pounds around her midsection and attributed it to lack of time to exercise. She was working long hours and just didn't seem to have the energy to get up at the crack of dawn to spend time at the gym before work. She ate a lot of her meals on the run, and figured all that fat in the fast food was contributing to her growing waistline. No worries. As soon as she got this promotion, she'd take a vacation, get started back on her exercise program and cut out some of the fast food.

Next came the periods of mental fogginess so severe she'd stop mid-sentence, unable to finish her thought. She'd managed to squirm her way out of it the first couple of times it happened during an important meeting, but it had gotten to the point where her mental lapses and inability to focus were being noticed.

By three o'clock in the afternoon, her fatigue was so severe that if she could have curled under her desk in a fetal position and taken a nap she would have. The only thing that kept her from falling asleep at her keyboard was the extra-strength iced tea and diet cola she usually drank continuously, starting at lunchtime.

Jackie, like many of my patients and clients with similar stories is suffering from adrenal burnout.

The world is one of constant activity and pressing deadlines. You're fed fear by the barrelful on news broadcasts and in the daily papers. Fast food is the rule rather than the exception. As a result of a continuous stream of stressful events, your adrenal glands get a work-out practically 24/7.

These little glands that sit nestled atop your kidneys are tiny powerhouses with a big mission…to keep you alive in the face of danger. In the olden days, your adrenals would have only had a workout in the face of a saber tooth tiger or similar threat. The cascade of activity in your body set off by the sight of a tiger is exactly what you need to escape or to fight. Your adrenals give you that burst of energy that allows you to run faster than you ever thought you could, because fear mobilizes every ounce of your strength at just the right moment.

The events that can save your life in the face of a tiger can cost you your life, or at the very least your quality of life, when your "tiger" does not pose any physical danger at all. When your "tiger" is the day-to-day fear and worry generated by thoughts about stressful life events, those same internal reactions can hurt you rather than help you.

If you're suffering from more than three of the following symptoms, you, like Jackie, may be on the verge of an adrenal meltdown.

- It's hard to get started in the morning. You don't really seem to wake up until 10 a.m., even if you've been awake since the crack of dawn.
- You regularly experience an afternoon lull, consisting of "brain fog", inability to focus and the desire for a nap between 2 and 4 p.m.
- A burst of energy hits later in the evening, often resulting in the inability to fall asleep until 1AM or later.
- You crave foods high in salt and fat.
- You have low blood pressure, or have noticed that you often get dizzy or lightheaded when you stand up too quickly.

- You find yourself sensitive to cold and feel chilled even when others around you are warm.
- You've recently noticed an increase in PMS or menopausal symptoms.
- You experience mild depression, decreased motivation or mood swings.
- Your memory seems to be failing you. Sometimes when you walk into a room to get something, you forget why you're there once you arrive.
- Your sex drive seems to have taken a sabbatical.
- You regularly experience lack of energy, muscular weakness and feeling rundown.
- You seem to have developed intolerance to foods you used to handle well.
- Constipation, diarrhea or other digestive upsets have become frequent complaints.
- You frequently crave something sweet to eat, especially at the end of a meal.
- You notice an increased sensitivity to bright lights, especially bright sunlight.

These are just some of the major symptoms of adrenal fatigue. Like the gas tank in your car, your energy tank needs to be refilled with high-octane fuel on a regular basis.

Workplace and family stress, processed food devoid of the nutrients your body needs, and living with fear and worry deplete your energy tank.

In my experience with over two decades of coaching and counseling people like Jackie back to vibrant health, I've learned specific steps that protect your adrenals and get them working again as your ally. I'm going to share those with you here. First let's look at some of the behaviors that can result in adrenal stress:

- Skipping meals and yo-yo dieting, especially severe calorie restriction
- Eating processed foods
- Not exercising or over-exercising
- Shallow breathing
- Lack of relaxation as part of your day-to-day routine

- Ignoring fatigue to finish working
- Using sugar, caffeine or nicotine to push yourself further when you're already tired
- Insufficient or erratic sleep
- Exposure to toxins in the environment and in food
- Worrying about things over which you have little or no control
- Living in fear
- Taking care of others first and putting yourself last

THE STAGES OF ADRENAL BURNOUT

Over the last several decades, there's been quite a bit of research on adrenal fatigue and the effects it has on overall health. Dr. Hans Selye first introduced the concept back in the 1930's and reported on what he called the General Adaptation Syndrome (G.A.S.).

Selye proposed that the stress response occurs in three phases: the alarm phase, where your body responds to the initial stress, the resistance phase, during which you adapt and your resources become depleted if the stress is persistent or recurring, and the exhaustion phase, during which your body's resources become depleted and you are unable to maintain normal function.

The alarm stage occurs when a danger or threat is perceived. Your adrenal glands respond by producing hormones and neurotransmitters, the most important ones being adrenaline and cortisol. As a result, your heart rate, blood pressure and respiration rise in order to supply your muscles and brain with more oxygen. More blood is sent to your skeletal muscles and brain, and less to your stomach, kidneys, skin and liver. Sexual and immune functions are suppressed. Hormones acting as natural opiates are released, so you feel good during the alarm phase.

Cortisol stimulates the breakdown of muscle protein to amino acids which are used by the liver to produce glucose. Fatty acids from fat cells are released and converted to glucose too, because in a true danger situation, you need the extra blood sugar to convert to energy and escape or fight. This causes a rise in insulin. Cortisol also inhibits the higher level thinking functions of your brain and sharpens the survival centers. It turns off your "wizard brain" and turns on your "lizard brain." You become keenly focused on survival and pretty inept at making high level strategic business decisions!

The stress response causes your thyroid to secrete more and your gonads to produce less. Thus, chronic stress leads to loss of sex drive, increased blood pressure, digestive problems, diabetes and immune disorders.

When you're in a hyperadrenal state and you're nervous and worried or scared, or running away from a tiger, efficient digestion won't keep you alive. The valves in your digestive tract close and enzyme production slows down. As a result, when you eat under stress you can get a heavy feeling in your stomach and experience constipation.

Your adrenals influence your heart rate and blood pressure. If you're running from a tiger, this is good. When you're sitting at your desk stewing over world events or your demanding boss, the high blood pressure and increased heart rate strain your cardiovascular system.

The adrenals also have the highest content of vitamin C per gram of any tissue in the body. One of the things that happens when you're under stress is that you deplete your vitamin C stores, because the adrenals rely so heavily on this important vitamin. You may have heard that vitamin C is good for stress and for fighting a cold. Part of the reason is because vitamin C is so important for adrenal health.

To mobilize your resources to run away from a tiger, you need to have plenty of sugar in your blood ready for action. Cortisol mobilizes blood sugar to provide the energy either to fight or take flight. Chronic stress leads to chronic blood sugar elevation, which leads to the overproduction of insulin, insulin resistance and excess belly fat, potentially leading to diabetes.

Adrenal dysfunction can also lead to thyroid problems. In fact, most people with thyroid issues have underlying adrenal dysfunction.

Perhaps the most unpleasant side effect of adrenal distress is loss of sex drive. What most people don't realize is that adrenal hormones and sex hormones share a common precursor -- cholesterol. Cholesterol gets converted to pregnenalone, which is the precursor to what are known as the steroid hormones – estrogen, progesterone, testosterone, DHEA and cortisol. Chronic stress causes excess cortisol production, which leaves less pregnenalone available to make your sex hormones. Thus adrenal exhaustion leads to less fun in bed!

5 POWERFUL STRATEGIES TO REFUEL YOUR ADRENALS SO YOU FEEL ENERGETIC AND FOCUSED AGAIN

Many health practitioners address adrenal dysfunction with lots of supplements. I've found that diet and lifestyle changes are at the core of a successful adrenal restoration protocol. When you combine a powerful, whole foods, nutrient dense diet with balanced movement and rest, stress management and supplements targeted to the individual, the results can be outstanding.

The rate of recovery depends on the duration of the problem, the stage of adrenal dysfunction and how dedicated you are to diet and lifestyle modification. Here are the top strategies that can move your adrenals from exhausted to energized efficiently and effectively

1. **Start your day with a power breakfast.** Toast and juice don't cut it when it comes to supporting your adrenals. You need an abundance of nutrients, a moderate amount of protein and foods that will keep your blood sugar stable for several hours. The two breakfast foods I've seen produce results the quickest are green smoothies and chia seeds. Loaded with mineral rich greens and antioxidant and vitamin C rich fruits, green smoothies supply a substantial dose of protein as well. Adding a heaping spoonful of chia seed to the smoothie gives it more staying power and regenerates energy faster than any food I know. Chia is the secret food of Tarahumara Indians in South America, the world's best runners. A free green smoothie recipe guide is available at www.GreenSmoothieCleanse.com

2. **Give yourself an oil change!** It's unfortunate but true…most of the fat consumed by the average American is highly processed, dominant in inflammatory omega 6 fats, and destructive to your overall immune and hormone function. To produce energy, you need sufficient omega 3 fats. These are obtained dietarily from plant foods like chia seed, hemp seed, flax seed, walnuts and

algae. They are abundant in deep ocean fish as well.

3. **Replenish the nutrients that stress destroys** and nourish your adrenals with rebalancing herbs. These include Vitamin C, the B vitamins, especially vitamins B5 and B6, zinc, manganese, Vitamin E and omega 3 fats and can be obtained by eating whole fresh foods and avoiding processed and refined foods. Herbs that balance and nourish your adrenals include licorice (avoid if you have high blood pressure), ashwagandaa, siberian ginseng, rhodiola and schisandra berry. An experienced practitioner can guide you to choosing the ones that are best suited to you.

4. **Balance your blood sugar.** If you eat foods high in sugar or refined carbohydrates, your body will produce insulin to remove the sugar from your blood and transport it into your cells. The more carbs you eat, the more insulin your cells produce, resulting in a more rapid clearance of sugar from your blood. Low blood sugar, also known as hypoglycemia, sends an alarm signal to your adrenals and they produce cortisol, to mobilize fat stores and raise your blood sugar. This further stresses your already overburdened adrenals, leading to worsening of your symptoms. If you eat whole fresh foods, a higher proportion of vegetables, nuts and seeds, and supplement with Chromium and Magnesium, your blood sugar will normalize and reduce the adrenal burden.

5. **Balance between movement and rest.** Too little exercise is a stress on your adrenals as is too much. Running a marathon is not recommended for those attempting to recover from adrenal fatigue. Light exercise, like walking, swimming and cycling are fine. Short intense 30 second bursts can be very helpful for rebalancing hormones. Heavy weight training is usually contraindicated during the recovery from adrenal fatigue. It can leave you feeling exhausted for days. Relaxation and rejuvenation breaks throughout the day are extremely beneficial. Since the main cause of adrenal burnout is the over secretion of cortisol due to chronic stress, mini vacations throughout the day during which you breathe deeply and mentally visit a place where you feel at peace,

can shift your internal chemistry and assist your adrenals in rebuilding. One of my favorite practices is called Heart Math™. It combines deep breathing with sincere appreciation and has been clinically proven to have the ability to shift you from the stressful state where cortisol is dominant to the calmer state that favors DHEA, the anti-aging hormone. Finally, sleep is a vital component of recovery from adrenal fatigue. Plan periodic sleep-athons, where you stay in bed most of the weekend and you'll find yourself finally feeling refreshed and alert.

Recovery from adrenal burnout can be a slow process, depending on the duration and extent of damage your adrenals have suffered. It's best to recognize the early warning symptoms. Get off the spinning hamster wheel while you can. Take time to refuel and recharge before you reach burnout. In the case of adrenal overdrive, take time to replenish your reserves before they are depleted. This will keep your mind alert, your body lean and trim and your pleasure centers working just as they should.

ABOUT RITAMARIE

Ritamarie Loscalzo MS, DC, CCN, DACBN also known as the Women's Fatigue Expert and the Energy Recharge Doc, is an internationally-recognized nutrition and women's health authority. She's an author, speaker and health practitioner with over two decades experience empowering health through education, inspiration and loving care. Her online health programs guide high achievers worldwide to recharge their adrenals, balance their hormones, flatten their bellies and refuel their energy tank – so they can experience more juice in their relationships, success in their careers and joy in their lives.

As a doctor of chiropractic with certification in acupuncture, a certified clinical nutritionist, a diplomat of the American Clinical Board of Nutrition and a medical herbalist, Dr. Ritamarie marries ancient healing wisdom with modern scientific research to create an Energy Recharge Roadmap customized to the individual. She's a master at unraveling the mystery of your unique biochemistry and designing diet, lifestyle and nutrition programs that address your unique needs. She specializes in hormone balancing, detoxification and women's fatigue issues, and her primary tools are a fresh whole foods diet, abundant in green plant foods, supportive lifestyle habits, food-based supplementation and herbs.

Because most people bite off more than they can chew when they embark on a new health regimen, Dr. Ritamarie focuses on simple, effective ways to optimize your diet and lifestyle to achieve vibrant health. She dishes out simple steps with a dash of fun to motivate you to achieve your health goals.

Dr. Ritamarie's passion for creating delicious foods that support optimum health has led her to develop recipes that not only taste great, they energize and heal as well. She's been teaching the power of whole, fresh, green plant foods for over two decades and she lives the vibrant life that eating this creates.

Dr. Ritamarie resides in Austin, Texas with her husband and two teenage sons.

To learn more about Dr. Ritamarie and get her free e-book and e-course "7 Simple strategies to Jumpstart Your Energy Practically Overnight" visit: www.JumpstartYourEnergy.com . Call 877-727-5992 or visit: www.DrRitamarie.com to find out how to hire Dr. Ritamarie as a speaker or adrenal recharge coach.

CHAPTER 40

STAGING YOUR HOME

BY MEGAN MORRIS

Your house is probably your largest asset. Selling it can be one of the most important decisions in your life, so you want to ensure your house sells fast and for top dollar. Home staging is your best investment. Not only do you need your home to stand out amongst the competition, you want it to evoke an emotion so that potential buyers like what they see and feel compelled to buy it! Most home sales are a result of that overwhelming feeling of "I want it now." Your goal as a seller is to generate that feeling of "home" that will facilitate a quick and lucrative sale.

The greatest benefit of a staged home is that it will sell for more money in a hot market and sell faster in a down market. The real beauty of staging always works to a seller's advantage. If the housing market is sluggish, staging will give your home an attractive edge over the competition. If the market is strong and the home will likely sell regardless, you can use staging to increase the selling price.

Let's take a deeper look at this. As in any market, the potential for selling your house will be governed by the laws of supply and demand. When demand is high and supply is constricted, it will be quite easy. However, when homes are in plentiful supply and demand is low, it becomes a real challenge.

Demand is influenced by many factors, but fundamentally, it comes down to the number of people who want to buy. And this in turn is influenced by whether mortgages are freely available, the interest rate that defines the cost of the mortgage, and whether buyers are confident about their future. On the other hand, supply is influenced by the number of homes for sale in a given geographic area, and whether there is a healthy supply of new homes. When builders have unsold stock and banks are trying to sell homes that are the result of mortgage defaults, there is a plentiful supply.

When the market is slow-moving, the laws of supply and demand make the sale of homes very difficult. Buyers gain the upper hand. Supply becomes plentiful as a result of short sales and foreclosures. Demand then becomes constrained by the economic downturn, with rising levels of unemployment and constraints on mortgage availability. When this happens, home staging comes to the rescue. This unique system has proven to help sell homes faster and/or for more money in every market.

Another important reason to stage is because what people look for in a home is drastically different today than yesteryear. In year's bygone, a home was simply a shelter. Maybe everything and everyone was in one room. But as time went on, more and more rooms were added to a home to serve specific functions. Individual bedrooms came on to the scene. In the 1960's more than one bathroom became the standard. In the last decade, we've seen the emerging demand for home offices and theaters. And "mud-rooms" have made a come-back.

Even the purpose of many rooms has evolved over the years. For example, some of us remember growing up when entertaining was done in the formal living room. The kitchen was small and served mainly for the preparation of the food. But today, the kitchen is the heart of the home – it's used for entertaining, and the formal "living" room has almost become "extinct." When you walk into a house that has this "relic of a room," you find it now serving as an office, a recreation room, or maybe even closed off "to save on electricity."

In essence, our homes are now an extension of how we live and of our personality. Because the way you live in your home is different than the way you sell it, staging becomes essential. And every home is different, so staging is a way of preparing it to stand out from the competition by making it impressive and memorable. "Whether it encompasses little more than adding fresh flowers and removing clutter, or involves hauling away and replacing major pieces of furniture, the goal of staging is putting a house's best foot forward and give it the gloss of a marketable commodity," advises Barb Schwarz, a California-based real estate practitioner who first coined the word "staging" back in the 1970's. Schwarz goes on to say, "The home should be staged, whether it is an $80,000 house or a $4,000,000 one. Homes that are staged sell faster in slow markets and at higher prices in stronger markets."

Today's buyers are busy, usually a dual-income family, needing to quickly get on with their lives. Most buyers look for a house that is "move-in ready" – they aren't interested in moving into a home that requires "move-in repairs." If staged, real estate agents will have great confidence in showing your home to potential buyers, because they know it is ready to be sold. In fact, when a house is staged, the realtor has the option to put a "Staged Home" sign under the FOR SALE sign. Some savvy buyers will even ask to see a "staged home" first, knowing it will show best and will save them time and effort.

Staged homes attract the widest audience of viewers, targeting the potential homebuyer because they are more appealing and are quickly earning a reputation of "the best properties to see." Buyers generally do not buy for potential. They want "move–in" condition property.

Ambience is what sets staging apart from just decorating. It is the art of making elements of the home simply irresistible. With hard work, you have created a sense of spaciousness, cleanliness, good repair, and low maintenance. Ambience is a secret weapon to creating a memorable feel that lasts beyond the tour and makes the buyer want to come back to your house…to live. It is selling a lifestyle, a new life, a new beginning. Preparing homes to sell helps the client show their home at it's best to get the maximum return on their sale. It is fast and effective. Sellers may already have made repairs, such as painting and carpet cleaning, but they do not always realize the power of small details. First impressions count and you may not get a second chance. The real secret is "Dynamizing," staging rooms to generate feelings – every area and around every corner – that make buyers feel a visceral connection to your home. With methodical and imaginative dynamizing you create impressionable moments when a buyer looks at the house. These are seen through a door in your house, upon entering a room, or even a closet, and there it is that something extraordinary occurs.

Keep in mind that buyers are looking for a house that meets their physical and psychological needs, and most of the sale is emotionally based. They want to feel comfortable and to enjoy a place of beauty and harmony; a haven from the hustle of daily living; a space to be proud to show family and friends. To succeed at selling your house quickly and profitably, you will need to evoke those very feelings. Keep in mind that the more senses (sight, sound, smell and touch) you reach with your message, the more successful your communication. Ambience appeals to all the senses: not only vision, but touch, smell, hearing, even taste. Ambience throughout the house ensures that buyers are constantly surprised and delighted at what they find, such as a glass vase filled with elegant roses greeting them in the entry-way, or the good smells of baking in the kitchen, or a playfully arranged stuffed-animal tea party in a child's room.

Every space inside and outside of your house is a communication opportunity. Staging a kitchen area with an open cookbook, simmering spices, and a beautiful display of vegetables, invites buyers to imagine the good times and warm feelings that lay in store. When your house is the one that buyers lose their hearts to, the competition does not stand a chance. Dymanizing is neither hard nor expensive if you tackle it using these simple techniques. As you work though your house, you will find numerous dynamizing opportunities to deliver subtle messages of home and build an atmosphere of excitement. Here are dynamizing ideas that can work in any house:

- A bowl of candy in a movie room
- Marshmallows on sticks in an outdoor patio area
- A bucket of champagne with 2 glasses, fancy towels and luxurious soap – next to the master bath
- A dining room set with the best you have to offer in entertaining
- A tea set outside on an open terrace
- Patio furniture and topiaries in a patio area to make it look even more inviting
- A dining room with fresh fragrant flowers

Potential buyers make the decision within the first few minutes if they like the house. Some people do not go any further than the foyer. "Consider the foyer a prologue to the story each house has to tell – a teasing trailer for the feature attraction. It is a place to greet guests, to check the mirror one last time before leaving, to enter grandly from a staircase above. It is the first and last part of the house you see, and as such unifies the decor of the house, leaving an impression of the owner's taste to whoever passes through. A home's entryway can also affect the mood of the home as well as its dwellers. According to Feng Shui specialists, the foyer sets the tone for the lives of those in the house. This manifests itself in various ways; often the first thing one sees when they enter the house can either positively or negatively impact the person passing through." In a recent article titled *Hello and Goodbye: It's all said in a Foyer,* by Sara Liss, she is quoted as saying, "Space is also another consideration when designing a foyer. An open and spacious front entrance for greater flow and transition between the outside world and the home."

Ambience is also important in other areas of the home. In the master bedroom, try to make it look romantic. A bottle of champagne, fruit, serving platter, etc. As for children's rooms, we try to keep them simple and cute. If we have more than one, we will usually do a boy theme and a girl theme. In a bigger room we might use twin beds. The beds are always made perfectly with only a couple items in the room. If there are a few rooms, we will also decorate gender neutral and make it look like an inviting guest room. In the dining room we like to set a dramatic table setting. We use china to complement the décor of the house. If the tone is neutral, this might be a place to splash some color.

Staged homes maximize the best features of a house and minimize its faults. What you are striving for is a "love at first sight" response. It is interesting how many people start house-hunting in a very logical state of mind, but ultimately end up buying for emotional reasons. A chief reason to stage a home for sale is to arouse the powerful feeling: *I belong here!*

ABOUT MEGAN

Megan Morris is the founder of MHM Professional Staging Inc., a successful Home Staging, Décor and Events company in Orlando, and has worked in home staging and design for the past 10 years. In this capacity, she has been responsible for promoting business, managing a team of employees, monitoring projects and customizing client needs on an ongoing basis. Her expertise in visual displays and space planning has been recognized and honored in several design competitions, and she has been hired as the lead set decorator for several commercials, including Nike, Werthers, New York Life and ESPN. She has also been featured on FOX News, CNN, MSNBC, HGTV, Bravo and CNBC as an expert in her field.

Her exclusive event company specializes in providing top quality, unique event experiences for her clients. Past clients include The Orlando Convention Center, celebrities, professional athletes, Fortune 500 companies and even international royalty. She was a partner in the launch of the Christian Audigier golf line, and was responsible for the kickoff event. Her background also includes marketing and merchandizing when she worked for several department store chains including Nordstrom, Macys and Polo.

In addition to the staging company, she has been involved in several real estate projects where she has been an integral part in their profitability. Her responsibilities included ensuring the highest profit margins, meeting deadlines, working closely with vendors to reduce costs, monitoring shipments while promoting environmentalism, and overseeing quality control.

Megan holds a bachelor's degree from the University of Southern California. She is a member of NAWIC, National Association of Women in Business and National Association of Women Business Owners. She is a member of Junior League and is involved in several other philanthropies.

CHAPTER 41

IF YOU'VE "TRIED THEM ALL BEFORE," GIVE THIS CONTROVERSIAL WEIGHT LOSS PROTOCOL ONE CHANCE. IT WILL CHANGE YOUR LIFE.

BY TIFFANY PRINSTER AND LINDA PRINSTER

Have you been on every diet under the sun with no progress to show for it? Do you have that knack for losing 5-10 pounds, but then you gain that back and then some? Have you given up on weight loss all together?

These feelings are ones that many of our clients express. Many are skeptical before trying the revolutionary HCG Diet Protocol because it sounds too good to be true. What are the promises of the HCG Diet Protocol? Lose 20-30 pounds in about a month, completely reshape your body (in all the right places), effortlessly reset your appetite and taste buds to enjoy more healthy foods, and (here's the best part), keep it off! Plus, it is only done for about a month at a time with **little to no hunger** and there is **no exercise required**.

We know it sounds too good to be true. Please don't let that scare you away. In this chapter, we are going to give you a short origin of the HCG Diet Protocol along with a quick summary of this amazing weight loss system. Then, we'll tell you where to "get the goods" to change your life (and your waistline) forever.

ORIGIN OF THE HCG DIET

Let's review a bit of history of the HCG Diet Protocol to set your mind at ease. In Italy during the 1950's, Dr. A.T.W Simeons developed the HCG Diet Protocol. Simeons studied obesity for 40 years and worked specifically on developing the HCG Diet Protocol for over 20 years. He worked with the rich and famous 'under the radar' to avoid conflict and controversy within the medical community.

The HCG Diet Protocol remained largely under wraps in the United States until about 2006, when Kevin Trudeau released his revolutionary book, *The Weight Loss Cure 'They' Don't Want You to Know About*. Since then, it has been gaining popularity as more people see their neighbor, friend, wife, colleague, etc. *literally* SHRINK and reshape in only about one month.

WHAT IS HCG?

HCG (Human Chorionic Gonadotropin) is a hormone naturally produced in large quantities during pregnancy. Dr. Simeons found that small regular doses of HCG caused the body to release abnormal fat only when used in conjunction with a specific Very Low Calorie Diet for about 30 days. (Details in Dr. Simeons' manuscript *Pounds and Inches: A New Approach to Obesity* available for download on HCGDietBooks.com.)

Important Note: This Very Low Calorie Diet is only comfortable and advisable when using HCG. People on the HCG Diet Protocol are generally not hungry and have plenty of energy. However, if you are not using effective HCG and are trying to just do a low calorie diet, you will feel tired, weak, and, most likely miserable, because you are so hungry.

The diet works great for women and even better for men, as usual. That's right guys, don't let the fact that it's the 'pregnancy hormone' worry you. We promise you're not going to get pregnant, start growing breasts, or start crying when Hallmark commercials come on. In fact, HCG is frequently used for infertility treatments for both men and women and is considered safe and effective in the U.S. and around the world.

HOW HCG WORKS FOR WEIGHT LOSS IN YOUR BODY

According to Dr. Simeons, when taking HCG and following the Very Low Calorie Diet (see manuscript for details), the HCG allows your body to tap into your abnormal fat reserves, which are typically inaccessible. These abnormal fat reserves include your belly, upper arms, and buttocks. Unlike most weight loss programs, the HCG Diet Protocol addresses those areas that are usually the hardest to minimize.

We know this whole concept sounds a little too magical. And, when we explain how it works in purely scientific terminology, most people's eyes simply glaze over and they lose the chance for an utterly life-transforming experience. On the other hand, if I just say 'Hey trust me…it works", there are a lot of people out there that say, "No, I don't know you and I'm not going to just trust you. I want more information." So, what we are going to do is explain the protocol in plain English, without letting it sound so magical that the believability goes out the window.

Here goes. Back in the 1950's, Dr. Simeons discovered there are three main kinds of fat in your body. Let's talk about each of them. One is structural fat. This is one of the good fats that your body needs. Life would be painful and ugly without it. For example, structural fat around your joints keep them comfortable, and there is a layer of structural fat in your face that helps maintain its softness and look. If structural fat is lost, your joints would hurt and your face would be harsh and bony. You would look like a skeleton. Ladies, we all want thin, but not quite that thin. Am I right? So that's the first kind of fat – structural. Let's leave that fat securely in place, shall we?

The next type of fat is normal reserve, which is your energy reserve and is also a type of good fat. Simeons compared this fat to the money you keep in your regular bill-paying checking account. You know… fat goes in…fat comes out on an as-needed basis. If your body needs a little extra energy, this is where it will go for the extra burn. Or, if you eat a little too much and your body thinks, 'Well, I am good for now, but I might need a little extra energy tomorrow', this is where the extra energy or fat goes for temporary holding. Normal reserve fat is easily available for your body when you need a burst of energy or extra endurance, e.g. a marathon run. On most diets, this is the type of fat that is lost first.

We've all done diets where you lose a few pounds really fast. Those pounds are this normal reserve fat. However, this loss usually comes to a screeching halt as you hit the dreaded plateau and it seems like you can't lose anymore. Sadly, women usually quickly lose inches from the chest instead of in their saddle bags, belly, upper arms, butt, etc. and men lose it in their legs and butt instead of in their beer gut, love handles, etc.

That's because most of the fat in the belly, the butt, and those lovely waving flaps on the upper arms is what Simeons described as the (sometimes present) third type of fat in your body: inaccessible or abnormal fat, which is not considered good or healthy fat. And, it practically takes an act of Congress for your body to even recognize it, let alone start burning this abnormal fat. Until you find a way to get your body to release and burn it, you will suffer needlessly and have little hope of successful or comfortable weight loss.

Enter the HCG Diet Protocol. Dr. Simeons discovered that abnormal fat is not simply the result of eating too much and/or not exercising enough. Surprised? We weren't! According to Simeons, the problem with abnormal fat starts with a little center in your brain called the hypothalamus. Now don't worry. There is not a test at the end of this, but the short explanation is as follows.

According to Simeons, the hypothalamus influences your base metabolism and acts as a gatekeeper for fat usage/storage, but sometimes, or often, things get a bit out of whack. If your hypothalamus is out of whack, it may send improper signals regarding when you are full, when to burn fat, and when to lock fat away into your inaccessible fat reserves.

To sum it all up, according to Dr. Simeons, the HCG and Very Low Calorie Diet combination allows your body to burn your abnormal fat (along with all the nutrients, calories, etc. the fat contains) and release it into the bloodstream, which in turn satisfies your hunger. Dr. Simeons also noted that following the plan with the healthy, specified foods for the minimum 21 days potentially allows your hypothalamus to rest and reset, creating a lasting change in the way your body handles incoming fat and nutrients, i.e. improving your base metabolism in some cases and resetting the base metabolism in others. This is the good stuff that no other diet proposes.

A SNEAK PEEK INTO A "ROUND" OF THE HCG DIET PROTOCOL

DAY 1 AND 2: THE GORGE (FIRST 2 DAYS ON HCG)

Take HCG and gorge. Eat as much fatty food as you can without making yourself sick. Simeons emphasized that these days should be spent eating as much fattening food as possible to restore structural fat and avoid hunger at start up.

DAY 3 TO 26-43: VERY LOW CALORIE DIET (VLCD) PHASE AND THEN "HCG EXIT DAYS"

Take HCG and follow the Very Low Calorie Diet (VLCD) for at least 21 days, but no more than 38 days. During this phase, you will eat from a very specific list of foods, but don't let that scare you. The foods and drinks allowed are foods you can find at your regular grocery store: coffee, tea, chicken, white fish, steak, tomatoes, lettuce, cucumbers, apples, grapefruit, strawberries, and more!

HCG Exit Days: Once you have done at least 21 days, but no more than 38 days, of HCG with the VLCD, you will stop taking HCG, BUT you will continue to follow the VLCD for 72 hours while the HCG is exiting your system. If you do not follow the VLCD for three days after you stop taking HCG, you will gain weight during these days.

MAINTENANCE:

Here's where so many diet plans ultimately fail: Maintenance. Once you are done with your three days of the VLCD with no HCG, then you move into Maintenance, which consists of a minimum of two 3 week periods.

1ˢᵗ 3 Weeks After Stopping HCG and Completing the HCG Exit Days: Eat anything you like, except sugars and starches, and do a Steak Day* on any day that your morning weight is 2.1 pounds or more over your last HCG date weight.

2ⁿᵈ 3 Weeks After Stopping HCG: SLOWLY start adding back healthy sugars and starches and do a Steak Day* on any day that your morning weight is 2.1 pounds or more over your last HCG date weight.

*Steak Day: eat nothing for breakfast or lunch, but drink plenty of water throughout the day. Then, in the evening, have one large steak followed by an apple OR a raw tomato. This should put you back in range of your last HCG date weight.

MOVING ON WITH LIFE AS THE NEW, SLIMMER YOU

This is when you move on with your new, healthy lifestyle in a smaller size. You get to eat like a normal, healthy person. After all, you are actually craving healthier foods and feeling quite energized. To control weight for the rest of your life, you just weigh daily. And, if you are up more than 2.1 lbs over your last HCG date weight, you guessed it: do a Steak Day.

HOW TO FIND EFFECTIVE HCG AND GET STARTED TODAY

If you go out looking for HCG, you will most likely be overwhelmed. There are different types and hundreds of sources for HCG. Not to be scary, but all HCG and all HCG plans are not created equal. We have tested several brands of HCG and some simply do not work.

There are providers with plans that have been adapted to slow the rate of loss. Obviously this will require participants to pay (and diet) longer. These providers play on the fear factor that the originally prescribed Very Low Calorie Diet (about 500 calories) sounds dangerously low. And 500 calories IS too low UNLESS you understand what Dr. Simeons says the HCG is actually doing: releasing between 1500 and 4000 calories into the bloodstream per day from abnormal fat reserves. This means your body is actually getting the benefit of the 500 calories taken by mouth, PLUS the 1500 to 4000 calories released into your body by losing your abnormal fat, which brings the daily total to between 2000 and 4500 calories.

Another common 'mistake' that providers make is to edit to the HCG Diet rules after working with the protocol for only a few weeks or months. This leads to slower weight loss and lower maintenance success rates due to lack of long-term experience.

Our companies, on the other hand, stick with Dr. Simeons original HCG Protocol explicitly and provide only the most reputable sources for HCG and related products to save you hours of research and provide the best possible probability for success on this tricky HCG Diet.

WHICH HCG DIET COMPANY IS BEST FOR YOU?

We thoroughly understand Dr. Simeons' protocol and have helped thousands to complete it correctly and successfully. We are also authors of several HCG books that are leaders in the HCG community. Our companies have knowledgeable HCG experts supporting our clients and we only offer 100% tested HCG Drops and HCG-safe products to ensure maximum results for each participant. You can choose HCG diet products and services with confidence if you decide to give your business to any of our companies.

If you prefer someone to take you by the hand and lead you quickly and painlessly through this process with support, accountability, and a 20 Lbs Loss in 40 Days Guarantee, your best bet is Pounds and Inches Away (www.PoundsandInchesAway.com). Many people benefit from the personal support and accountability that the full-service packages at Pounds and Inches Away provide, saving you tons of time and offering the confidence of the 20 Lbs Loss in 40 Days Guarantee.

However, if you are a Do-It-Yourselfer who takes pride in doing your own research, likes the challenge of doing something on your own, or simply doesn't want to spend as much money, then you are perfectly suited for DIY HCG (Do-It-Yourself HCG) at DIYHCG.com. Our site is the #1 most trusted website for the HCG Diet on the web. And unlike most HCG companies, we have real people behind our site who are ready to interact with our customers. We provide only 100% HCG-safe information and our HCG drops and HCG-safe products are the best on the market, allowing you to have the opportunity to be as successful as possible as you do the HCG Diet Protocol on your own.

THANKS AND GOOD LUCK

"When the world says, 'Give up,' hope whispers, 'Try it one more time.'"
~Author Unknown

Weight loss, self-confidence, and body image are some of the biggest struggles in our lives. Whether or not you decide to proceed with the HCG Diet Protocol to help with these issues, we wish you the best in your pursuit of health and happiness.

ABOUT TIFFANY

After graduating university in 2008, Tiffany Prinster moved into entrepreneurship. At 22, she started <u>DIY HCG, Inc.</u> and has since grown the company into a multi-million dollar business and helped tens of thousands of people to finally lose their excess weight using the <u>HCG Diet</u>. She is also author of *<u>My HCG Tracker</u>* and co-author of *<u>Pocket Guide to the HCG Protocol</u>*. Plus, she is the creator of the <u>Tiffalina's</u> HCG-safe personal care products, which can be used by clients on the HCG diet.

Tiffany loves spending time with her family (she is the oldest of eight children) and her friends. Her passions are self-growth, creativity, entrepreneurship, and all things funny.

ABOUT LINDA

Linda Prinster is a 47-year old mother of eight whose doctor once described her as "extremely metabolically resistant." She tried many popular weight loss programs before she found the HCG Protocol. Prior to founding Pounds and Inches Away, she even owned an exercise studio. Like most lifetime dieters, she gained and lost the same 20 pounds many times over the years. After participating in the HCG Protocol, she lost 25 pounds, but more importantly has kept the weight off for more than 4 years--now wearing size 8 jeans for the first time in her life.

Prinster is the author of the *HCG Weight Loss Cure Guide* and co-author of *101 Worry Free HCG Diet Recipes*, Over 201 Worry-Free HCG Maintenance Recipes, and the *Pocket Guide to the HCG Protocol*. She holds a PMP certification, and has significant consulting experience in management, research/documentation, and weight loss.

She is the founder of Pounds and Inches Away Inc., which offers franchises, and co-founder of other HCG related companies. Her companies have assisted thousands in successfully completing the HCG Diet Protocol.

Linda and her husband of 25 years and the father of all the children, Gary, reside in O'Fallon, Missouri.

CHAPTER 42

PROFIT PIGS ARE GREEN

EMBRACE YOUR INNER PIG

FROM THE PAGES OF PROFIT PIGS ARE GREEN

BY RUTH ANN REESE & HEATHER HUDDLESTON

In our book *Profit Pigs Are Green,* we provide business owners and upper management of every size and type of business a fun-filled and motivating journey through the process of restructuring business operations with a specific focus on profit. Loaded with insights and ideas to increase profit, it will inspire you to take immediate action. Statistics on business failures have always been daunting, even more so in recent years. These statistics should compel business management to continually question expenditures, and aggressively pursue every opportunity for additional profit. *Profit Pigs Are Green* with Profits all the way to the bank!

Suggesting you consider the Profit Pig Approach to business is new, and we hope it becomes the iconic and renowned methodology for the future of measuring and increasing business profits. Oh to become famous for such an imagining! To have our Profit Pig join the ranks of other famous pigs: Miss Piggy, Babe, Porky the Pig, Arnold of Green Acres, Charlotte's Web's Wilbur, and the Three Little Pigs. A nationwide Profit Pig movement is more reasonable than you might think. There is much we can gain in business by emulating... well... pigs.

Pigs have many characteristics that are invaluable to successful business management. Pigs are highly intelligent, very resourceful, form close bonds, are clean and tidy, and have very powerful senses. Great reasons to Embrace Your Inner Pig! Join the *Profit Pigs Are Green* movement today.

PROFIT PIGS ARE INTELLIGENT

Pigs are very intelligent and learn quickly, picking up tricks faster than dogs! Pigs rank fourth in animal intelligence behind chimpanzees, dolphins, and elephants. Baby piglets learn their names, responding when called by two to three weeks of age. Profit Pigs are quick to use their intelligence learning to understand business financial reports; they know that this is key to increasing profitability. OK, we get it! Learning why some items are posted to the Balance Sheet verses the Profit and Loss report can feel like speaking Pig Latin! Gaining this knowledge is powerful as you strive to create a prosperous and thriving business. Consistent review of key business reports will help you have a clear understanding of the health of your business; easily recognize trends so you can make timely adjustments in your business operations; identify opportunities to cut costs and increase revenue. Get started creating a big fat Profit Piggy bank.

We understand you started your business because you were passionate and skilled about your product or service, not because you had an overwhelming desire to become a quasi-accountant in your spare time. Regardless of the size or condition of your business, implementing this process will result in increased profitability. Start by putting a 30 minute recurring appointment for financial analysis in your calendar every week. Pour yourself a fresh cup of coffee, turn off your phone and emails, and focus on the review of your most recent financial reports. Make notes on the report as you have questions or ideas. Review these notes with your bookkeeper/accountant each week. No question is a bad one, and every idea is worth investigating. You will learn a great deal about your operations in the process. For those of you who already routinely review financial reports monthly, step it up to weekly, and complete the review with a specific goal of increasing profit. Be a Profit Pig, sniffing around for profit potential!

Throughout years of business management work with clients, we always start with the accounting department, making sure the records are both accurate and up to date. Then we schedule review meetings with the client on a weekly basis. Without fail, by the end of the fourth review meeting, the client is asking for additional reporting. This is a very exciting transition, as we know our clients are on their way to discovering Profit Pig potential in their business. Whether this results in immediate savings from a contract negotiation or incremental cost cuts on other expenses, we know they are beginning to move thousands of dollars into profit. Their Profit Pig is alive and becoming more Green!

PROFIT PIGS ARE RESOURCEFUL

Pigs are resourceful animals, rolling around in the mud to cool their skin, and the layer of dried mud protects them from the sun. Doesn't sound profound unless you stop and wonder how they first determined that dried mud protects them from the elements and began to mud cake on purpose when needed for protection. In business management we need to continually stretch and seek solutions that are outside our current understanding of our business operations. The utilization of technology applications in business sales and operations has rapidly changed over the past decade and we are just starting to recognize the dynamic impact technology can provide. It concerns us that we still encounter many businesses that are not embracing and capitalizing on the profitability that can be gained by taking advantage of current and upcoming technological advances. Profit Pigs are extremely resourceful and would tell you to stay current on using every aspect of technology in the development of your business, right now!

If you find yourself thinking it is not yet the right time for the utilization or expansion of technology in your business for sales, operation, or both, you are wrong. This is the time. We worked with one company in 2010 to implement a CRM technology for programs involving customer information flow, which provided more consistent customer communications, improved customer satisfaction, and generated an increase in annual profits of $32,000. Profit Pig strikes again.

PROFIT PIGS FORM CLOSE BONDS

Pigs are extremely social animals, forming close bonds with each other and even with other species. They enjoy close contact and lie close together when resting.

Forming close bonds with those we work with is another move towards more profit, especially as our companies grow in size and diversity of products and services. We've all experienced the difference in efficient results of a team of people who are all genuinely committed to project success, as opposed to a fractured team laden with politics and poor communication. As leaders we need to create a foundation of cohesion and communication. Far too often, we fail to confront a situation with an employee that is counter-productive, resulting in turmoil amongst what would otherwise be a powerful team. Working to transform that employee or ultimately to remove that employee may be the last thing we want to undertake, so we often allow it to continue with hopes it will work itself out. Did a name or situation in your company just come to mind? Stop right now, schedule 30 minutes in your calendar within the next three business days and solve that situation. It is our job as a leader to provide our team their best opportunity for success, which ultimately improves profitability.

PROFIT PIGS ARE CLEAN AND TIDY

From the time piglets are only a few hours old, they begin to leave the living area to relieve themselves. How many times do we find out we have a project or department that has morphed into a mess? We knew it needed attention, we knew that something was not going smooth, but we didn't make it the priority. A crises strikes because issues that should have been cleaned up were not. This eats away at profit.

The story you are about to read is true, the names have been omitted to protect, well, the egos of the business owners involved. We have provided business services to two entrepreneurs who started businesses within a couple years of each other. They provide very similar services and products, but in two completely different industries. They truly desire to help the customers they serve with similar levels of quality in their products and services. One owner does everything top cabin; the

Cadillac version, loaded with high maintenance extras and much attention to appearances, while the other chooses a less expensive path. Fast forward approximately ten years. The Cadillac version has grown larger at about one and a half million in annual revenues, while the other business is grossing about half that. There are a couple of very notable differences. The Cadillac version requires more labor to maintain all of the extras, which also requires more management time from the owner, and results in a low profit margin of about 5%, while the other owner is working a lot less and bringing home the bacon at a margin of about 40%, a true Profit Pig!

PROFIT PIGS HAVE POWERFUL SNOUTS (OINK, OINK) AND EXCEPTIONAL VISION

A pig's two most powerful senses are their highly developed and sensitive snout, and a great field of vision because their eyes are on the sides of their heads. In my career in corporate management and turn-around projects, it is imperative that I constantly keep my eye on the horizon, using every intuition to successfully transform struggling companies into profitable ventures.

In the 90's, I worked on corporate turnaround for a company in the Infomercial Industry. Do you remember those days where every night right during dinner your phone would ring with an offer for the latest and greatest product? This company was pre-bankruptcy when the corporate accountant and attorney asked me to complete an analysis. Long story short, I determined it could be salvaged and got busy creating and implementing plans that transformed it from a $3.5M nearly bankrupt company into a $5M company with a 38% profit margin, all in under 3 years. I am not writing this to brag, there is a point to my storytelling, so stick with me.

Always keeping an eye on opportunities for growth, I scoured the horizon seeking additional ways to expand profitability. The World Wide Web captured my attention with its ability to reach a very large audience based on specific types of products, presenting an incredible opportunity to sell infomercial products with higher profit margins. I developed a proposal including projections and statistics on this "World Wide Web" concept, and scheduled a meeting with the Board of Directors. On the flight to Washington, DC, I spent additional hours poring over the concept notes, enhancing the Powerpoint presentation, and fine-tuning the proposal. I had already primed the two board members that I knew believed in technology, and they were supportive. Certain this would be immediately approved, I envisioned all of the cheers and champagne dinner that would ensue. Not to mention my very fat bonus checks in the years to come! They rejected it. After much debate and weeks of phone conferences, they determined this new proposal was not timely. Not timely! Ask again in a few years, they said! I resigned over this and other conflicting points of view, and that company was dissolved a few years later when telemarketing laws devastated performance. Had they embraced the WWW concept in the 90's with its budding potential, where would they be now?

As leader of your organization you must keep your eye on the horizon of your company, your industry, and your competition. Study and research to gain a better understanding of the customers you serve and the changing trends in their wants and needs. Stay curious about the future of your industry. Become involved in industry organizations. Like a pig uses that powerful snout, sniff around! If you provide a product or service that is also provided by other companies but to a different industry than you currently serve, attend one of the education events in that industry. You will be surprised what you learn when you utilize your senses and stretch your field of vision.

EMBRACE YOUR INNER PIG!

In recent years, lists have been published in news articles about businesses that were predicted to either fail or were scheduling substantial location closures... how shocking it was to see serious businesses that have been icons for decades being brought to their knees during these recent years of economic downturn. These businesses with many years of opportunity to create and stash profits to support them through this downturn were failing. *Profit Pigs Are Green* was born from our hearing and experiencing many heart wrenching stories of business struggle and failure, which in many cases could have been prevented had there been an ongoing focus on creation of profit.

We desire to compel you to become laser focused on profit, to start taking immediate actions that will create more profit. Right now! Today! That is the sole purpose of *Profit Pigs Are Green*. You see, we expect over the years you have: read great books on business management, attended top-notch business seminars and trainings, completed hours of web research, and listened to the best business educators. We understand you have learned a great deal about many business solutions, have been inspired, have been motivated, and you implemented some of these changes. Have you transformed your business operations? Has your business profitability dramatically improved? Or do you still have serious questions about your business strategies?

Don't be a Boar! Pig Out on each chapter of *Profit Pigs Are Green* and you will decide to join the Profit Pig movement! You'll Squeal with Delight as you identify your company's strengths and weaknesses in Welcome to the Pig Pen; be compelled to strive for service excellence in Ham It Up; gain keen understanding on how to evaluate your competition in Who's Afraid of the Big Bad Wolf; and utilize tips for travel savings in When Pigs Fly. These are just a few of the chapters that will change how you do business.

Profit Pigs Are Green has one sole purpose; to encourage, motivate, and educate you into becoming a very fat… Profit Pig. And in the words of one very famous Pig… ***"Th-th-th-That's All Folks!"***

ABOUT RUTH ANN

Ruth Ann Reese, co-founder of Business Infusion, is a seasoned, multi-dimensional, C Level executive with a breadth of experience spanning a wide array of industries. Her passion for leadership of a company's most valuable asset, its people, has resulted in superior organizational achievements throughout her career. Her successes are a culmination of her creativity, innovation, operational excellence and collaborative management techniques.

This diverse background creates an uncommon vantage point when considering business strategies for profit growth. Her career spans industries including Aviation, Infomercial Marketing, Spa Salon Industry, Jewelry manufacturing, and Chamber of Commerce management. "Through my wide-ranging background, I have learned innovative and dynamic sales and marketing techniques, cutting-edge technology applications in operations and marketing, diverse organizational management approaches, and superior methods of team and consensus building processes," she shares.

Ruth Ann's *work hard, work smart, but have fun doing it* approach to business is apparent, as you talk with those she has worked with throughout her career. "I believe quality teamwork is the fuel that allows common people to attain uncommon results." Through many years of corporate management and consulting, Ruth Ann has found she "falls in love with companies and views them as living, breathing entities that need the same nurturing, education, and support she provides as a mom to her children!"

"My partner Heather and I joined forces from our common desire to provide small business with high quality reasonably-priced products and services," Reese states. One example is they both experienced over the years that most business consultants and coaches will teach their clients to have ongoing marketing campaigns to drive sales and new client development, but missing is the "with what?" Many small business owners are spending countless hours and hundreds to thousands of dollars to create the various marketing pieces needed to support a successful marketing campaign. So Reese & Huddleston got busy and launched www.MarketingInfusion.co, offering a Marketing Kit that is ready to customize with your company logo and contact info, get it printed, and get started growing! Each Marketing Kit includes eight unique Marketing Campaigns, and each Campaign includes a poster, flyer, email template, postcard, referral card, stand-up shelf talker, stationery, and gift certificate. All designed by professional graphic artists, and custom to specific industries. Enough marketing campaigns to complete a full year for $395.00.

In their book *Profit Pigs Are Green,* www.ProfitPigsAreGreen.co , these two corporate power houses provide business owners and upper management of every size and type of business a fun-filled and motivating journey through the process of restructuring business operations with a specific focus on profit. Loaded with insights and ideas to increase profit, it will inspire you to take immediate action. Statistics on business failures have always been daunting, even more so in recent years. These statistics should compel business management to continually question expenditures, and aggressively pursue every opportunity for additional profit. *Profit Pigs Are Green* with Profits all the way to the bank!

"When I am not at work "geeking-out" with my business partner, look for me playing on or near the closest body of water, enjoying my two daughters, cooking up a great meal to entertain family and friends, or digging in the dirt in my garden," states Reese as she shares this glimpse of her personal life.

ABOUT HEATHER

Heather Huddleston is co-founder of Business Infusion, Inc. and her biggest cravings in life have always been to continually learn and to teach and support others with her attained knowledge and skillsets to assist in bettering their "current" situation, whatever that may be. After obtaining her BS Degree in Resort and Lodging Management and Tourism from CSU Chico she worked the next 20 years as an Executive Sales Manager, Assistant Director of Sales and Marketing, and Director of Marketing within the hospitality and tourism and education and coaching arenas. She decided to embrace the technologically-changing environments around her and obtain a secondary degree in Media Arts, plunging her head first without fear into all things web, graphic design and CRM.

Layering this enhanced technological skill set over her existing sales and marketing background, Heather has been able to help individual businesses understand the profit potential of their business through the use of an enhanced web presence, proper lead capture system and CRM implementation.

Collaboration with her business partner Ruth Ann in all things technology, profit, and marketing has cultivated some amazing projects and ideas. With the launch of: www. marketinginfusion.co Heather and Ruth Ann brought to multiple industries a much needed piece in any small businesses marketing tool belt; a "kit" that contains an entire year's worth of promotional collateral and ideas to "Get Noticed" and to "Get the Word Out" without a weighty price tag, only $395 for the entire kit. Simply download, edit and print and your promotion is on its way to bringing you bottom line profit.

Another sacred cow, or should I say "PIG," that Heather and Ruth Ann are passionate about is helping companies understand the true power of operating with a focus on profit. Hence was born the book "Profit Pigs Are Green" www.profitpigsaregreen.co , a one-stop-shop book for understanding all things profit related. The book includes quick tips on things to start today to help every business owner understand and improve their bottom line and 'bring home the bacon.'

Heather's zany sense of humor keeps things "real" and down to earth in her world. When she is not "geeking-out" researching and understanding new technologies, she is enjoying time with her husband, trying out a new recipe (or devising one of her own), taking a yoga class, researching a new place to travel and explore and reading, of course.

CHAPTER 43

PASSION, PURSUIT, PERFORMANCE, PAYOFF

BY TOM TOMBLIN

It was in the cold, dark winter of 2005 that I faced a decision: a) sell the business, b) close the business and put my tail between my legs, c) "get a job" as an employee, d) shrink the business, or e) do something very different in running this business. I chose the latter – to really change the business to survive and fight another day. This is a story about finding your passion, re-igniting it, growing your knowledge, and infusing everyone around in your belief. Passion begets performance, productivity and ultimately profit. It was all done with our business and website: www.modeltrains.com.

BACKDROP

We were the typical small business, operating with a variety of stand-alone business solutions, just like most small businesses. We had Outlook for our e-mail system, QuickBooks for our accounting system, yellow sticky notes all over the place for reminders, phone messages on papers, tasks that needed to be done in the future. Our website used Microsoft FrontPage. For any sort of management analysis, we exported data from QuickBooks into spreadsheets. If anybody phoned us or e-mail us, we had no customer contact system. We had a DOS-based email system to pump out emails, it just took 12 hours to send a batch!

In 2002, I had purchased ownership of CMT. From a dozen years of business operation, CMT had about 3,800 valid names and email addresses in our accounting system.

IGNITE YOUR PASSION

The business had to change enormously. In order to do so, I had to change. Rather than follow the same path, I chose to pursue something radically different. I had a vision of a very different business, a model train dealer (and more) unlike anyone else. Why?

Each day presents opportunities for you to be a follower or to take charge and be a leader. For our world to function we need both leaders and followers, in business and in our society. Leaders are not born, you grow into it. The skills of leadership are learned. You gain wisdom and insight only after many years of trial and error, successes, failures, and false starts. As entrepreneurs, we are optimists. The glass is ¼ full; to everyone else it is ¾ empty. It is our belief, our passion, which sets us apart. We think, no, <u>we know</u>, that we can change our part of the world in some fashion. It requires visualization of a future that is very different than the present.

Now, I thought I was smart, but that is not enough. You don't have to be the brightest, have the best athletic skills or the fastest reflexes to survive in business. What you do need is the knowledge of what to do. Without that, you will not survive. I started to re-educate myself to gain that missing knowledge.

PURSUIT OF KNOWLEDGE

I started devouring books (see Appendix). Now my background was accounting and finance and my hobby was model trains. Like most small business owners, I believed if you have a good business and good people, customers would come running to your door. Not quite.

I was determined to get it right. Not with some grand master plan, but all the little things that are so important to success. Getting every phone call and subject logged into the system, capturing every email "touch" with the customer, truly listening to the customers, finding out what their interests were. Then build the best communication system to inform customers about future products, updates, sales, etc.

I had the bigger task of figuring out a way to build a system around communicating with modelers about their interests. "I had a dream!" – but not the one that Martin Luther King stated. My dream was just like the movie quote, "If you build it they will come."

In NLP (Neural Linguistic Programming), they call it the "As if Frame." You see the world as if your problem is solved, and what you need to do afterwards. You now view the world as if the problem, the hurdle, was overcome. It changes the mindset, it gives you confidence.

PURSUIT OF SOLUTIONS

I went searching for an integrated solution, which would combine a CRM (the customer database using Customer Relationship Management software), the back office functionality of inventory, invoicing, purchasing, etc., and an e-commerce website. In January 2006, we had imported 3800 names with or without e-mail addresses. We started to learn how to use the CRM.

We began to capture the points where we had contact with a customer: incoming phone calls, outgoing phone calls, emails both ways, at trade shows, etc.

It was in 2006 that I began attending many of the events hosted by our local Chamber of Commerce in Oakville. I attended Small Business Week in October 2006. There were eight seminars covering a broad range of topics. One of the seminars was hosted by Core Marketing Strategies, and I was hooked.

Over the course of the next year, we developed our marketing strategy and mapped out a plan. We began to execute that marketing strategy. We took our customer database in our CRM and we segmented the database by the customer's interests. In addition, we surveyed our customers in June 2007. Instead of the usual 1-2% response rate, it was closer to 20%, an unheard of response rate! People wrote extensive responses as no one had ever asked them what they wanted! The results were a gold mine. By asking the right questions, we learned what was important to them. Many modelers had never been surveyed by any dealer before. They appreciated that someone valued them and they had the opportunity to tell us their thoughts.

IMPLEMENTATION AND PERFORMANCE

We switched from treating customers as an "It" to "You." You know you are being treated as an "It" when you receive a "Dear Customer" or "Dear Member" or even better, "Dear Valued Customer." Over the course of time, we switched from generic announcements to a whole new approach. We were now communicating with each individual, with their first name, for their specific interests. We had changed from treating customers as an "it" to "you" – a huge change.

Segmentation of our CRM opened a whole new world. We moved from generic newsletters sent once a month to specifically-targeted newsletters to customers. They were targeted based on their interests: modeling scale, railroads of interest, the era they were interested in, and type of material (expensive brass vs. mass market plastic/diecast models). Nowadays we can send out 6 or 7 newsletters in a day, what a difference!

We opened up more channels of communicating with customers, not just a retail storefront and ads in magazines. I looked at different industries, went to different tradeshows in other fields. I studied how they showed their products, how they set up their tradeshow booths, their signage, their people and how they reacted with their customers.

Armed with this knowledge, we began the process of configuring a mobile trade show display. After several iterations of different sizes, we created an incredibly efficient trade show display. We can set up or take down a 10' x 40' booth, with carpets down, goods on display, in under an hour. It used to take us 5-6 hours before. What a pleasure! I look forward to going to trade shows and meeting our customers or future customers. With a Dodge diesel truck and a 7'x 20' trailer, we bring our trade show all over North America.

PAYOFF

With our communication system, we have grown over 500% in 5 years. Our pipeline sales, based on future reservations are up 400% – in the millions of dollars. We have grown from being a small dealer, to a big dealer, to a distributor, to manufacturing our first train product.

We have plans to create a whole new market, with branded products.

With the growth in leads, prospects and customers, we are now able to solicit our database of customers. We can ask them their desire for specific products and approach manufacturers to produce exclusive products. By doing so, we are helping our customer base obtain models that do not exist, we make a profit on it, and the manufacturer produces a larger run-size, making more profit. It is a joint venture where everyone wins.

SOCIAL MEDIA

More recently, I spent time attending seminars, webinars, reading articles or books about social media. We had created accounts in LinkedIn, Twitter, Facebook and YouTube, but they were dormant. We developed and began executing our social media strategy.

We wanted to increase the awareness of who CMT was, build trust, and ultimately help people choose us as their supplier. We began to develop a number of videos to post on YouTube and our website. These would be educational and humorous.

We also started working on our Facebook page. Facebook is a conversation with your customers. It is not social if you are shouting at them to buy, buy, buy. Facebook is a platform, it is one that engages you with your customers, bringing you closer together.

In early March we invited our customers to join us on Facebook. Then a truly shocking event occurred.

On Friday, March 11th 2011, the earthquake/tsunami struck Japan. When I saw the news, I had the same feeling in the pit of my stomach as I had watched the twin towers in NY come down. We were all powerless then. That was then, this was now.

I thought about it and within 30 minutes, I used our CRM system to send a fast message to our customers in Japan, telling them I had just seen the news, asking if they were OK, and offering our assistance in any way. Surprisingly we had quite a few responses over the next 12 hours.

Here was an opportunity to use the power of Facebook in a way I had never thought about. I posted my original email message to Japan on Facebook, and then starting posting the email responses from Japanese modelers on Facebook. (Some responses could not be posted, due to their personal nature.) The following morning and afternoon, I sent out close to 12,000 emails around the world, telling modelers what we were doing.

Transparency was critical, this was not about selling a 'box', this was about people connecting to each other, in a worldwide manner. We could build the platform that brought the world together and help people connect.

Within 10 minutes of my morning email blast, the 1st response came in, and then the flood of responses began. I took the email responses and posted them up on Facebook, without the full names. I encouraged everyone to go to the Facebook page and "talk" there. We then saw people posting comments directly on Facebook, which is what I wanted to see happen. Japanese customers and the worldwide modeling community were communicating through us.

From zero people on Facebook, we grew tremendously. After two weeks, I could not believe what had happened. I wrote an open letter, posting it on our website, on Facebook, and in an emailed communication that went out to 120,000 people. I wrote with conviction and passion about the world uniting and how much I had learned from the experience. I am truly awed with the response from around the world and how we helped people connect.

There is a long list of people who phoned or wrote, thanking CMT and me personally for what we did. For me, it was very gratifying. I was only using the tools we had developed, in a way that I had never envisioned. Through purely philanthropic reasons, we created an incredible loyalty from people to CMT for what we did. That was never my intent when I started, but it became an unexpected result.

Just remember a great quote, *"Givers get!"*

As a business owner, you have a grasp of situations, unique knowledge, pertinent skills that reside in you. These can be put to work helping others in business or in non-profit volunteer ways. Just open your mind to the possibilities.

INTANGIBLES – THE HIGHEST AWARD
YOU CAN RECEIVE

One of the worst experiences in life showed me the positive side of entrepreneurship:

A number of years ago, I joined our local high school parents council and was Co-Chair for several years. Based on the knowledge I had learned from our business, I implemented a CRM system for the school to communicate with parents.

At a high school ruby game several years ago, one of our students was severely injured with a head trauma. This event became a national story. It was a circus everyday, with TV and radio trucks from national networks and cable systems. I was closely involved over this time period, visiting the school once or twice a day, talking with the Principal, staying updated, and sending out multiple messages a day to parents, keeping them informed. With my staff keeping things running in the business, I offered my help in other ways.

Unfortunately, the parents had to decide whether to keep or turn off the life support for their 15 year old son, Manny. They decided to let him slip away.

After the funeral, a memorial event was held at the school. Over 1,000 people attended. Amazingly, Manny's parents attended, and were escorted by his uncle, who lived directly across from the school. At the memorial, I was introduced to family, as I had never met Manny, his parents, or his uncle before. What can you possibly say to a parent in those circumstances? When they were told my name, they exchanged glances and his uncle asked me to stay, he wanted to say something after he finished escorting them. Later he found me.

I was asked about all the things I had done, as he knew all about it. Then the question, "Did you know Manny?" I replied, "No." Disbelief showed on the uncle's face, then he asked "But if you didn't know him, why did you did this?" My reply was simple, I told him that could have been my son on that field. You see, our son, Spencer, played football for the junior football team, as quarterback. He nodded in understanding.

Before I turned to go he said, "Wait, I have something to ask you. We are having a family gathering back at my house, the relatives are here from Spain, from Mexico." "We would like you to attend." "No," I replied. "I would just be intruding." "No," he said, "For everything you have done in the past few weeks, you are like family." I was floored, I accepted.

I stood there dumbfounded, went out to my car, closed the door and tears rolled down my face. I visited the house and was introduced to all the family members as Tom, the guy who did all the stuff for Manny. I was the only non-family member there.

To be asked to come into someone's home, in the tragic circumstances of a teenaged son's death, in such a gracious way, "you are like family," what can you say?

That is the highest compliment that anyone has paid me in my working life. I made a difference in someone else's life.

All of this was possible because I helped use my business skills in volunteering for our local high school. Again, I never expected such an outcome.

LESSONS LEARNED

What did I learn from being an entrepreneur?

Look inside yourself. You have passion for something. Let it out, show the world that you care. It will help your business, your community and yourself.

Remember, "Givers get!" Each of us has knowledge and skills that can help others, whether locally, regionally, nationally or worldwide.

Then, implement technology to help enable you to run your business. Automate many areas, the possibilities are huge. Then dream about what you can do if you had no "baggage" in your head, and you could "fly."

Redefine possible.

Best regards,

Tom Tomblin, President,
Canadian Model Trains Inc.
www.modeltrains.com

Appendix:

The E-Myth Revisited by Michael E. Gerber
Differentiate or Die by Jock Trout.
Good to Great by Jim Collins
Marketing to the Social Web by Larry Weber.
Predictably Irrational, by Dan Arielly
Leading Change by John P. Cotter
What Would Google Do? by Jeff Jarvis
Duct Tape Marketing by John Jantsch
The Speed of Trust by Stephen M. R. Covey
Social Media isn't Social if you're Shouting by James Burchill

ABOUT TOM

Tom Tomblin, also known as "The Train Guy" is the owner of Canadian Model Train Inc. (CMT), a highly successful model train business. From university, Tom went into a CA firm, then into the banking industry, where he left at a level of Assistant Vice President, to follow his passion for model trains.

CMT has been a leader in innovative marketing in the model train industry. It was one of only 30 companies out of 60,000 that was selected for the Growing Ontario Firms pilot program. CMT has implemented new technology, using a segmented database, to create the best communication systems in the industry. CMT keeps modelers informed of items of interest specifically to them. CMT produces multiple newsletters a day and sends them out, informing customers about new products, updates and trends in the industry. As well, CMT uses this system to ask modelers what they want produced, and is able to bring new products to the marketplace as a result.

With this technology, CMT has grown over 500% in the last five years into a global business, with over 20,000 customers worldwide. CMT sells to retail customers, distributes to hobby shops, and has started manufacturing their first model train product. Using the social media of Facebook and Twitter, Tom writes entertaining and informed notes on a daily basis. Their YouTube channel is being loaded with content to help educate and entertain modelers.

Their current project is the first ever model train product survey, where modelers rate the products. Participants receive the summarized results, to compare their opinions with others. The results are used by manufacturers to help improve their businesses.

Contact Information:

www.modeltrains.com
www.facebook.com/railroadmodeler
www.twitter.com/railroadmodeler
www.youtube.com/canadianmodeltrains